Know it All,
Find it Fast
for Youth
Librarians
and Teachers

More Know it All, Find it Fast titles
from Facet Publishing

Bob Duckett, Peter Walker and Christinea Donnelly
Know it All, Find it Fast: An A-Z source guide for the enquiry desk
ISBN 978-1-85604-652-7

Heather Dawson
Know It All, Find it Fast for Academic Libraries
ISBN 978-1-85604-759-3

Know it All, Find it Fast for Youth Librarians and Teachers

Christinea Donnelly

facet publishing

© Christinea Donnelly 2012

Published by Facet Publishing
7 Ridgmount Street, London WC1E 7AE
www.facetpublishing.co.uk

Facet Publishing is wholly owned by CILIP: the Chartered Institute of
Library and Information Professionals.

Christinea Donnelly has asserted her right under the Copyright, Designs and
Patents Act 1988 to be identified as author of this work.

Except as otherwise permitted under the Copyright, Designs and Patents
Act 1988 this publication may only be reproduced, stored or transmitted in
any form or by any means, with the prior permission of the publisher, or, in
the case of reprographic reproduction, in accordance with the terms of a
licence issued by The Copyright Licensing Agency. Enquiries concerning
reproduction outside those terms should be sent to Facet Publishing,
7 Ridgmount Street, London WC1E 7AE.

British Library Cataloguing in Publication Data
A catalogue record for this book is available from the British Library.

ISBN 978-1-85604-761-6

First published 2012
Reprinted digitally thereafter.

Mixed Sources
Product group from well-managed
forests and other controlled sources
www.fsc.org Cert no. SA-COC-1565
© 1996 Forest Stewardship Council
FSC

Text printed on FSC accredited material.

Typeset from author's files in 10/13 pt Aldine 721 and Nimbus Sans by
Flagholme Publishing Services.
Printed and made in Great Britain by MPG Books Group, UK.

Contents

PART 3 SCHOOL AND HOME LIFE: ISSUES AND CONCERNS 153

PART 4 HOBBIES, LEISURE AND SPORT 207

Section 1 Hobbies and Leisure 209

Introduction

The main focus of this version of KIAFIF is as a guide and reference resource for front-line library workers, teachers and parents, who are faced every day with enquiries from or about children.

The scope for such enquiries is huge and can be related to school work, homework, social and personal life and children's free time.

As a result, it is often daunting for even the most ardent searcher. The scope of the guide covers from Pre-school (age 3–4) to the end of Year 11 at secondary school (age 16). It covers the school curriculum from Foundation/KS1 to KS4. The curriculum is explained for England, Wales, Scotland and Northern Ireland. However, bear in mind that this is an area of change, and, as I mention throughout, it is best to check the relevant websites for the latest information. Some of the sources may be of use to teachers, especially those in training or starting their careers as newly qualified teachers, and while it is not intended to teach or preach, they may find themselves tempted to look at a few of the suggested sources that may have passed them by. After all, none of us can really 'Know It All'.

It is hoped that this guide will point library workers, schools and parents to sources of information that can answer their questions. It is amazing how much information is available related to children as their lives in the 21st century get busier and busier. Their school life is filled with an array of subjects, targets, exams and assessments, while their home lives can be hectic, with a host of activities and experiences to divide their attention. Children are busier people than they have ever been, and the proliferation of enquiries relating to their lives reflects this. All of us, educators, parents and information providers, find it increasingly difficult to keep up with them. This book may contribute in a small way towards amalgamating the various aspects of information related to children into one source, and provide a starting-point for those who find that they are faced with any number of queries.

The book has two secondary functions. Firstly, as a librarian I realized that it is often helpful to know which sources are useful to invest in, in order to provide a good collection for enquiry work. In the current climate, with finance and resources stretched, this is even more pertinent. To this end I have highlighted sources that I believe are worth considering. This may prove beneficial for those in the happy position of being able to buy new stock, if only as a guide as to the type of resources to consider. These are marked with an asterisk (*).

Secondly, as a parent of four children aged from 5 to 16, I have been there, tearing my hair out and trying to find information for school projects – always at the last minute and practically always from the internet 'because we have to'. I spotted an opportunity to help with this, and at the same time to create a resource that could be used for entertainment. I have recommended websites that may give you something to suggest when you hear the complaint 'I'm bored'. Not that I advocate children sitting in front of computers playing games, but sometimes it's wet, it's day 29 of the school holidays and you've run out of options. These highlighted sites offer something different, such as walking through a Van Gogh picture (www.eduweb.com/insideart/index.html) or setting up weather experiments (www.metoffice.gov.uk/education/kids), and of course they have a subtle educational value. I have tested them with my own children, who I believe are typical of their species. They enjoyed the novelty and indeed have kept some bookmarked. It may be worth a try: by the time they've been rejected the sun may have reappeared! These are marked with a dollar sign ($).

Finally, this guide is not intended to be comprehensive, although it is substantial. I have included resources on the basis of their usefulness and clarity to children, either to help them directly or to help those providing information for or to them. I have not included resources simply because they exist, and therefore you may find some well known titles absent, and others in their place. Likewise, it does not list school textbooks, although there are a few exceptions. I have avoided subscription services, favouring the freely available websites offering clear and high-quality information. The reason for this is that this guide is about children having access to information, and for many, subscriptions are not an option. An exception in this area is the online libraries now available in most UK public libraries, such as Oxford Reference Online. The difference here is that the subscription is paid by the library and children have free access via their library ticket. Such excellent online resources complement the many websites that have been created by galleries, museums and organizations to make their information accessible and relevant to children and young people. It is hoped that this guide will encourage children to use a range of resources and enable them to develop enthusiasm for research and strong information skills. Equally, I hope that it will prove a useful starting-point for all those who help children to find information – front-line library staff, teachers and parents.

PART 1

General Sources

Section 1 Schools and Education

Typical questions

- Have you got the latest school league tables?
- Where can I get advice on choosing a primary school?
- Are there any schools especially for children with specials needs?
- Who can I talk to about educating my child at home?
- I'd like to look at the Ofsted report for . . .

Considerations

This section looks specifically at the sorts of questions asked by parents and carers concerned about starting education either via schools or at home. Despite the decline in popularity of school league tables, such queries are still asked on a regular basis, as well as others concerned with the choice of schools in certain areas or for certain criteria. Ofsted reports provide useful information to parents, to teachers going for jobs and to others who need to know about the school. The main consideration is to keep sources up to date; in the current climate, there are many changes in education, so this is even more important. Also bear in mind that church-aided schools may be listed elsewhere. Both the *Catholic Directory of England and Wales* (**Gabriel Communications**) and the *Church of England Directory* give details of their church-aided schools. Other religious denominations also have schools and it is best to check relevant directories for details or to use the sources listed below. For more detailed enquiries, such as those concerned with legal requirements, it is advisable to direct the enquirer to recommended specialist resources which your library may have, or to organizations that offer specialist advice. The sources listed below are excellent and should answer or provide guidance on many of the regular and recurring enquiries. It would be useful to bookmark websites that you find particularly helpful.

Where to look

Schoolswebdirectory

www.schoolswebdirectory.co.uk

This contains 33,000 UK schools and colleges with 20,000 websites and allows searching by county, local education authority, name of school or postcode. It also includes independent schools. Excellent.

3

Sunday Times School Guide
www.thesundaytimes.co.uk/sto/public/goodschools
A subscription service to a searchable interactive guide to the UK's top 2000 primary and secondary schools.

Try also www.schoolsearch.co.uk.

Choosing a school

For advice and guidance on choosing a school use www.direct.gov.uk. Select Parents, then Schools, learning and development. Select as appropriate.

Good Schools Guide 2011, **Lucas Publications**
www.goodschoolsguide.co.uk
A guide to over 1000 of the UK's top schools, based on reviews from parents and publisher's visits.

Ofsted (Office for Standards in Education) Reports
www.ofsted.gov.uk
Some parents find it helpful to look at Ofsted inspection reports on schools they are interested in sending their child to. Ofsted inspection reports provide detailed information on schools, covering primary, secondary, independent, community and independent special schools. The reports cover the school's effectiveness, it's achievements and standards, the quality of provision and the school's leadership and management. However, do check the date of the report; a lot can happen in three or four years. My advice would be to use the report as a tool to guide you when formulating questions that you would like to ask the school when you visit (if you get to that stage). This will enable points to be clarified, or weaknesses that have been addressed since the Ofsted inspection to be highlighted for you.

Special educational needs

Good Schools Guide – Special Educational Needs, **Lucas Publications**
This provides comprehensive information and advice on special educational needs (SENs) and UK schools. It includes the range of SEN conditions and the implications; the kinds of schools available; help inside and outside the classroom; the law; sources of help, and, importantly detailed reviews of 350 good schools for a range of SENs.

Which School? For special needs, **John Catt Educational, Annual**
A guide to independent and non-maintained schools and colleges of further education in Britain for pupils with sensory, physical, learning, social, emotional and behavioural difficulties or dyslexia.

4

Telegraph Guide to Special Educational Needs Schools 2011, **Trotman**
A guide for parents/carers wanting to find a school for a child with special educational needs. Lists both private and state-run schools. Also covers areas such as the assessment and statementing of a child, as well as practical and legal issues involved in securing good provision.

Gabbitas Educational Consultants (ed.) *Schools for Special Needs*, **Kogan Page**

Independent schools

Which School? Guide to independent schools, **John Catt Educational, Annual**
A directory of over 2000 British independent schools; includes nursery, preparatory, junior and senior schools, day and boarding schools.

Boehm, K. and Lees-Spalding, J. (2009) *Telegraph Guide to Independent Schools 2010*, **Trotman**
This provides detailed profiles on over 500 British fee-paying schools across the UK and Europe.

Gabbitas Educational Consultants (ed.) *The Independent Schools Guide*, **Kogan Page, Annual**
This gives detailed information on over 2000 schools.

Also look at the:

Boarding School Association, www.boarding.org.uk

In addition, parents often have anxieties and concerns about the whole process of their child starting school, either for the first time as a 4-year-old or a new school for whatever personal or family reasons. In addition, there is the transition of children from primary to secondary schools. There are many books that deal with coping with a new school. Below are a few suggestions, but you may find alternatives on your library shelves or in your local bookshop.

Potter, M. (2011) *A Parent's Survival Guide to Starting Secondary School: ease the transition for you and your child*, **A&C Black**

Garnett, S. (2001) *When Your Child Starts School: a handbook for concerned parents*, **How To Books Ltd**

Stewart, K. and Ishka, E. (2010) *Supporting the Move to Secondary School: a handbook for parent and pupil*, **Emerald Guides**
The interesting fact about this book is that the co-author Elizabeth Ishka is 12 years old and has moved school six times.

The law on education

Booth, C., Widdrington, T. and Hancox, N. (eds) *The Law of Education*, 6 looseleaf vols, Butterworth Lexis Nexis

Hancox, N. (ed.) *Education Law Manual*, Bloomsbury

Whitbourn, S. (2002) *Special Educational Needs and Disability in Education – a Legal Guide*, Bloomsbury

For publications on aspects of education law and policies look at **www.education.gov.uk/publications**. Many are available to freely download.

Statistics and research

League Tables
    www.education.gov.uk/researchandstatistics

For other statistics and research look at **www.education.gov.uk/rsgateway**.

Websites and organizations

Advisory Centre for Education (ACE)
    1c Aberdeen Studios, 22 Highbury Grove, London, N5 2DQ
    Advice line: Tel: 0808 800 5793
    www.ace-ed.org.uk
    This provides a wide range of publications, some of which are free to download. Excellent and well worth a visit.

BBC Schools
    www.bbc.co.uk/schools
    Learning resources for home and schools.

British Council
    www.britishcouncil.org

Department for Education
    www.education.gov.uk

Department for Education Northern Ireland
    www.deni.gov.uk

Education Guardian
    http://education.guardian.co.uk
    Excellent site.

Education Otherwise
PO Box 325, Kings Lynn, PE34 3XN
Tel: 0845 478 6345
www.education-otherwise.org
Provides support, advice and information for families considering home-based schooling.

General Teaching Council for England
www.gtce.org.uk

National Curriculum online
http://curriculum.qcda.gov.uk

National Union of Teachers
www.teachers.org.uk
Excellent website for education issues and more.

Ofsted (Office for Standards in Education)
www.ofsted.gov.uk

Online Publications for Schools
http://publications.teachernet.gov.uk

Qualifications and Curriculum Development Agency
www.qcda.gov.uk

RE Today Services
www.retoday.org.uk

Scottish Executive Education Department
www.scotland.gov.uk/Topics/Education

Welsh Assembly Government
http://new.wales.gov.uk
Select Education and Skills.

Section 2 General Sources

BOOKS

Typical questions
- Who publishes books for children on geography?
- Are there any children's books linked to the curriculum?
- Can you recommend some books for our school project?

Considerations
There are hundreds, if not thousands, of books suitable for children on all subjects, and the quality and standard these days is, in the main, exceptional. There are umpteen books suggested in this guide, but there are a dozen more for every subject that would be equally suitable. With this in mind, it is worth mentioning that there are publishers who specialize in producing books that support and complement the curriculum and for that reason are worth looking at. However, bear in mind that the two listed below are only two examples and it is worth checking other publishing houses. To find out contact details and web addresses use *Directory of UK and Irish Publishers*, joint publication by the Booksellers Association and Nielsen Book Data.

Specific children's publishers
Evans Publishing Group
> www.evansbooks.co.uk
>
> Specializes in books and resources for all areas of the national curriculum, from Foundation Stage to KS4. It has some excellent titles for all ages, categorized by curriculum subject and age. If you're in need of ideas for books to buy for school or home it's well worth looking at the website.

Lerner Books
> www.lernerbooks.co.uk
>
> Books for schools and libraries. Each title is reviewed by teams of teachers and libraries in the UK, who verify that each book is relevant to the national curriculum and the Scottish guidelines. Titles cover Literacy, Science, Art, History, Design and Technology and Geography.

DICTIONARIES

Typical questions

- How do you spell 'friends'?
- What's another word for 'scared'?
- What do you call a baby swan?
- How many 't's' in motorway?

Considerations

Dictionaries are fantastic tools for those who can spell and read fluently, but can offer little help to the 'bad speller', dyslexic or struggling child. With this in mind, the use of dictionaries to find out the meanings of words or to check the spelling of a word should be a shared task. It would be advisable to have age-appropriate dictionaries available, as these are less daunting in appearance. There are also many available with illustrations. There are some suggestions below. Queries to do with 'words' should not be underestimated and should be taken seriously – after all, words and language are the backbone of all our learning. Instead of simply telling the child how to spell the word, show the child how to look up words in a dictionary, or how to find alternative words in a thesaurus. It may not click the first time, or even the fifth, but this is an important part of the learning process and is also a very important part of what we as 'educators' should offer. Also bear in mind that dictionaries can be subject specific, such as the *Usborne Illustrated Dictionary of Science: a complete reference guide to physics, chemistry and biology*, **Usborne, 2007**. This has beautiful diagrams, clear text and cross-referencing.

There is also a fantastic website from Oxford University Press called **Children's Dictionaries, http://oxforddictionaries.com/page/fun**, which provides a set of fun activity sheets to do with children's dictionaries and words. It is an excellent resource for schools and home.

Where to look

Allen, R. (2009) *Oxford English Dictionary for Schools*, **Oxford University Press**

Allen, R. and Delahunty, A. (eds) (2007) *Oxford Primary Dictionary*, **Oxford University Press**

English Resources for Dictionaries and Words
http://oxforddictionaries.com/page/englishresources
A great set of worksheets to complement the *Oxford English Dictionary for Schools*. Excellent.

Corbeil, J.-C. and Archambault, A. (1993) *Oxford Children's Visual Dictionary,* **Oxford University Press**

An A–Z pictorial dictionary. The only text is the labels. It is beautifully illustrated and demonstrates perfectly the power of the image to convey information.

Foster, J. (2009) Oxford First Rhyming Dictionary, Oxford University Press Rhyme Zone
www.rhymezone.com

Type in a word to find dozens of rhyming words.

Oxford Illustrated Children's Dictionary, **Oxford University Press, 2010**

Oxford Illustrated Children's Thesaurus, **Oxford University Press, 2010**

This has 40,000 synonyms, antonyms and examples, with a great layout.

ENCYCLOPEDIAS

Typical questions

- I need one page on the Romans.
- Have you got a few facts on volcanoes?
- Are there any fact websites for children?
- Why is the grass green?

Considerations

In reality, encyclopedias should be our first port of call when we are faced with fact-based enquiries. However, in this electronic age they are not only often forgotten in the race to enter our search term into Google but are increasingly difficult to obtain from publishers, who seem reluctant to reprint them or to bring out new editions. Encyclopedias offer scholarly definitions and information, well written and researched, and for these reasons should not be overlooked. However, an important caveat is to exercise caution when using older editions – countries change names, boundaries are moved, science discovers and revokes. At least make sure that your library has access to one up-to-date encyclopedia; if not a printed copy, bookmark one of the suggestions below. That having been said, there are still some encyclopedias that are fantastic, even though they may be five or ten years out of date; so long as you are aware of the changes that could affect the information, many of them are worth their weight in gold.

Where to look

Homework Encyclopaedia, **Dorling Kindersley, 2011**
> There are two age-related versions of this: 5 to 7 years and 9 to 11 years.

Llewellyn, C. (1997) *Children's Picture Encyclopaedia*, **Dorling Kindersley**
> This is for younger children, with an A–Z arrangement of labelled pictures with small amounts of text.

Usborne Internet-linked Children's Encyclopaedia, **Usborne, 2011**

Wow! The visual encyclopaedia of everything, **Dorling Kindersley, 2008**
> The photography and pictures in this encyclopaedia are breath-taking. Small amounts of text complement the visual information.

Encyclopaedia Britannica now has an online version for children called **Britannica Online for Kids (http://kids.britannica.com)**. The information can be searched under two age groups, 6–10 years and 11–14 years. In addition, it enables you to browse by subjects. It is also aligned to the school curriculum. A free trial is available before you subscribe.

For libraries and schools:

Britannica Online Library Edition
www.library.eb.co.uk
For subscription charges, contact Enclyclopeadia Britiannica (UK) Ltd
Tel: 020 7500 7000

Encyclopedia.com
www.encyclopedia.com
An impressive free encyclopaedia that allows searching of more than 100 encyclopedias and dictionaries, many of which are well known and trusted titles. Excellent.

Britannica Online School Edition
www.school.eb.co.uk
You can search for Primary (Primary), Secondary (Student) or Teacher (Enhanced Student). There is a teachers' resources area for links with the curriculum, and resources can be saved to the personal workspace facility.

Wikipedia
http://en.wikipedia.org
The 'marmite' of encyclopedias. Users, librarians and teachers either love it or loathe it. Its coverage is amazing. But, with the articles written and edited by anyone who wants to contribute, I am always slightly concerned about using it for topics of which I have no knowledge whatsoever.

FACT BOOKS

Typical questions

- What is the biggest mountain in the world?
- Who is the tallest person in the world?
- How many people live in the world?

Considerations

There are hundreds of fact books available and your library will probably have a selection. Most are suitable to use both for and by children, especially with guidance. In these circumstances, it is best to be familiar with what your library has and to assess which one(s) are more suitable for children. Alternatively, invest in a few that have been specially published with children in mind.

Where to look

Ash, R. *Top 10 of everything 2011*, Hamlyn

Ash, R. (2009) *Whitakers' World of facts*, A&C Black
Divided into 20 sections, including buildings, space and sports. It has data from authoritative sources, with detailed lists and charts.

*Cook, C. (ed) *Pears' Cyclopaedia*, Penguin, Annual
A concise and informative encyclopedia, offering facts and some unusual gems.

*Fact Monster
www.factmonster.com
This includes world atlas, almanac, dictionary and encyclopedia searching using the Columbia Encyclopaedia. Excellent and highly addictive!

Guinness Book of Records, Guinness World Records Ltd, Annual
www.guinnessworldrecords.com

Rooney, A. (2008) *1001 horrible facts*, Arcturus
A team of cartoon characters guides you through a host of gross truths.

LANGUAGE DICTIONARIES

There is a place in libraries and schools for bilingual language dictionaries for children. Various titles are mentioned in **Part 2 – Modern Foreign Languages (MFL)**. However, languages that are spoken at home are equally important. It is advisable to find out what languages are spoken in your area and to have some suitable language dictionaries available, such as *Milet bilingual visual Dictionary English Gujarati*, 2001. See also **Part 2 – Welsh and Gaelic**.

ONLINE LIBRARIES

Typical questions

- Can I access reference books from home?
- Have you got the Oxford Dictionary online?
- Have you got a homework helper online?

Considerations

Below are subscription websites that some libraries have. They provide access to electronic versions of reference books, often allowing library users to use them from home via their library tickets. Many of these subscriptions are fantastic and it is well worth finding out if your library subscribes to any of them and how you can access them. For homework they are invaluable and offer an out-of-hours reference library.

Examples include:

Credo
http://corp.credoreference.com
This provides access to the content of over 551 reference titles from over 70 established publishers. It covers every major subject and includes Cambridge University Press, Routledge, Springer and Elsevier, amongst others. You can find out if your library subscribes on the home page. Excellent.

Gale Virtual Reference Library
http://gale.cengage.com
Online access to selected reference books published by Gale, Macmillan Reference and Scribners, amongst many others.

Oxford Reference Online
www.oxfordreference.com
This has access to over 100 reference books from 26 reference publishers, including Oxford University Press, on a wide range of subjects. Oxford University Press online resources are widely available in UK public libraries. To find out what's available in your library authority visit **www.oup.com/uk/academic/online/library**. Most public library authorities subscribe, which means that we all have access to an extensive reference resource from the comfort of our own homes, available simply via a library card. Excellent.

News database
INFOTRAC

http://infotrac.galegroup.com

INFOTRAC provides access to current and historical full-text articles from 50 journals and 10 newspapers. These include selected national daily and Sunday newspapers as well as popular journals such as: *Lancet, Good Housekeeping, Animals, The Bookseller, British Journal of Psychology, The Literary Review, Computer Weekly, Community Care, Design Week* and others. You can search a specific journal or all journals. Many public libraries subscribe and searching via a library card in your own home is available. Excellent for homework, current affairs and many of the school subjects and issues throughout this book.

Tips and pitfalls

Remember that you are dealing with young people and children. Don't expect them to know how to use dictionaries or encyclopedias: it may be second nature to you, but it requires new skills for them. Have patience and be prepared to guide and teach children how to look for information, how to use books (the contents page, the index, alphabetical order, subject groupings) and how to gather material from many different sources. Many children are great on computers when it comes to games, but are lacking in knowledge and skills when it comes to using them for information. Children believe that they can type anything into Google and it will promptly display the correct answer. Inspire them to think beyond using Google or photocopying a page of text to stick in their books. Challenge them to use online resources such as Encyclopaedia Britannica, specific quality websites such as those mentioned throughout this book, and reference books. Demonstrate how, by doing this, their project or homework is enhanced and their sense of achievement will be huge. What's more, learning through research is fun, and a skill that lasts way beyond school. Don't expect skills to be developed overnight – be prepared to repeat yourself many times (they are, after all, children!). However, do avoid taking over the project, and make it clear that you are there to help. At times avoid interfering even when you think that you know better: children need to learn by trial and error. Instead, offer suggestions and show enthusiasm for trying and thinking.

SEARCH ENGINES

Typical questions

- Are there any search engines specifically for children?
- Do search engines for children definitely filter inappropriate material?

Considerations

Search engines for children are a good idea and a welcome addition to searching the web – but do not be complacent when it comes to safety. Some searches using such search engines can still retrieve unsuitable material. Parents beware! For further information on internet safety look at **Part 3 – E-safety**. Some search engines for children have been tested, but to be honest, it's difficult to rank them because the quality and quantity of the sites retrieved will, in the main, reflect the child's search – some subjects simply always get better results, others are consistently poor. The bonus offered by search engines for children is that generally speaking the sites *are* for children, which reduces the frustration some children experience when searching homework topics. If the question is quantity – well, how many sites does one child really need on the Vikings? A result of five or six is plenty for most subjects, so long as they are informative, current and clear.

Try:

Ask Kids
> **www.askkids.com**
> From the Ask site. This provides access to web pages, movies, games and images. Allows the searcher to limit by age and/or subject.

GoGooligans
> **www.gogooligans.com**
> Possibly one of the better search engines for children.

KidRex
> **www.kidrex.org**
> Based on a Google custom search engine.

Qunitura Kids
> **http://quinturakids.com**
> Based on Yahoo! for Kids. The word cloud is particularly impressive but the results are not too dissimilar to any of the other search engines listed.

Yahooligans
> **www.yahooligans.com**

TELEPHONE DIRECTORIES

Typical questions

- Have you got the phone number for ... ?
- What's the code for London?

Considerations

Sometimes all you may need is this amazing, underrated tool, which lurks in the majority of homes. This is great for those queries such as 'Where do I buy my children's uniform from?' It is great too to demonstrate to children alphabetical ordering and how this facilitates finding information. Telephone directories have an alphabetical classified (subject/business) section and a residential A–Z of names. However, do remember that businesses pay to be included in the Yellow Pages, which means that some are not there, and that residents can choose to be 'ex-directory' and therefore are not listed in the White Pages.

Section 3 General Knowledge

DATES, CALENDARS AND ANNIVERSARIES

Typical questions

- What day of the week was I born?
- Can you tell me a historical event on my birthday?
- What time is it in China now?

Considerations

When answering this type of question it is sensible to consider the age of the enquirer and the level of information that would be appropriate. Some questions are straightforward and simply need one of the sources below, but others require guidance. Choose birthday history sites with care, as many have sponsorship and trivia that may be inappropriate when dealing with children.

Where to look

Calendars

Westrheim, M. (1993) *Calendars of the World: a look at calendars and the ways we celebrate*, **One World**

Covers a diverse range of calendar systems.

Whitaker's Almanac **(Annual), A&C Black, 1868–**

This has a section called 'Calendar for any year 1780–2040', in which the day of any week of any year can be identified.

Time zones

As well as using *Whitaker's Almanac* for time zones, you can take a look at some of the following:

WorldTimeServer.com enables you to type in any country or major city to find out the current time. It also has a Time Zone converter, **www.worldtimeserver.com.**

Greenwich Mean Time
www.greenwichmeantime.co.uk

This enables you to know the current time in the world's major cities and every country in the world. It also explains Greenwich Mean Time (GMT).

Anniversaries and birthdays

Whitaker's Almanac has a section on wedding anniversaries and you could use **www.hintsandthings.co.uk/library/anniversary.htm**, which provides a list of anniversaries and the particular items associated with them.

There are many birthday sites to choose from and they tend to come and go. The celebrity birthday list, **www.celebritybirthdaylist.com**, also has an interesting section called 'This Day in History', which gives one major event for a particular date and lists of famous birthdays and deaths throughout history. Very addictive.

DISCOVERIES, INVENTIONS AND HOW THINGS WORK

Typical questions

- Who invented the computer?
- Can you tell me some medical discoveries?
- When was the telephone invented?

Considerations

Contrary to popular belief, it is not always easy to find out who or when discoveries or inventions were made! Of course, this is not true for all. This is a subject that could take the enquirer to all sorts of detail, in which case it is important to consider how much is required for the specific question. Young children usually require the facts and good images or pictures, so choose your sources well. Older children may require more detail and, again, related images. Encyclopedias will have many inventions covered, so it is worth checking there first.

Where to look

Discoveries

Ardagh, P. (2006) *Science Museum WOW discoveries that changed the World*, Macmillan Children's Books

Bridgman, R. (2006) *1000 Inventions And Discoveries*, Dorling Kindersley in association with the Science Museum
Timeline of key events that formed the backdrop to various inventions and discoveries. Beautiful images complement text and archive material. It has inventions and discoveries from earliest times through to the scientific revolution and the information age.

Chrisp, P. (2010) *The Most Brilliant Boldly Going Book of Exploration ever by the Brainwaves*, Dorling Kindersley
Wonderfully illustrated and written for children, taking them on an adventure of exploration and discovery.

Gribbin, M. and Gribbin, J. (2004) *Dazzling Discoveries: the explosive story of science*, Puffin

Royal Geographical Society (2010) *Explorers: great tales of adventure and endurance*, Dorling Kindersley
This book encompasses explorers from the earliest times to those discovering the secrets of the solar system. It has a foreword by Sir Ranulph Fiennes.

Websites

Explorers

www.enchantedlearning.com/explorers

This provides succinct information on explorers and their discoveries, including the more obscure. Select either alphabetically or by country or century.

Inventions

The **Inventions that Changed the World** series from Heinemann Raintree is worth looking at. Titles include:

Raum, E. (2008) *The History of the Camera*, **Heinemann Raintree**

Raum, E. (2008) *The History of the Car*, **Heinemann Raintree**

Raum, E. (2008) *The History of the Computer*, **Heinemann Raintree**

Raum, E. (2008) *The History of the Telephone*, **Heinemann Raintree**

Raum, E. (2008) *The History of the Television*, **Heinemann Raintree**

Each book in the series looks at the history of an important invention. It shows what life was like before the invention existed and how the invention developed. The books are suitable for KS1 and KS2.

Websites

About.com

http://inventors.about.com/education/inventors

This provides the history of famous inventions and inventors, an A–Z list and an inventions timeline from the 10th century onwards. There are also some images available. Very useful.

History Learning Site

www.historylearningsite.co.uk

This has lots on inventions and discoveries of the 20th century. It provides a list of inventors from 1900 to 1999 and a list of inventions from 1900 to 1990. It also has detailed sections on specific inventions and inventors.

Invent Now

www.invent.org

Search the 'Hall of Fame' by inventor, or invention or view the complete list. For each inventor profile it has a small section called 'Invention Impact', which is unique and very useful.

$Inventions at Play
www.inventionatplay.org/index.html
A fantastic site for children not only to find out information about inventors and inventions but to have fun too. The games and activities are all to promote inventive thinking.

Inventors and What They Invented
www.design-technology.info/inventors
A list of inventors and what they invented. Excellent.

Technology at Home
www.pbs.org/wgbh/aso/tryit/tech
An activity to demonstrate how much use we make of technologies invented and developed in the 20th century. Also has lots of information on the people and their inventions.

Women Inventors
www.factmonster.com
Select People, then Women of Influence, followed by Mothers of Inventions. This provides a list of children's items invented by mothers.

Zoom Inventors and Inventions
www.enchantedlearning.com/inventors
Useful for very succinct information, with a timeline, themes, geographical and A–Z list.

How Things Work

*Macaulay, D. (2010) *The Way Things Work*, **Dorling Kindersley**
Absolutely invaluable for understanding how things in our everyday life work. It is divided into six parts: the mechanics of movement; harnessing the elements; working with waves; electricity and automation; digital domain and the invention of machines. This guide explains through accessible text and wonderful, often humorous illustrations, the principles of hundreds of pieces of machinery, technology and science. This should be on every child's reference shelf. It was first published in 1988 and has stood the test of time, with numerous new editions and reprints.

Websites

How Products Are Made
www.madehow.com
This has seven volumes of products arranged alphabetically, giving details

of the history and manufacturing process, with diagrams. Bear in mind that it is American.

How Things Work: how everyday things are made
http://manufacturing.stanford.edu
This describes and shows through short clips how things are made. Although it has an American bias for some products, it is absolutely fascinating and well worth a visit. It includes products such as glass bottles, airplanes, wool, crayons and jelly beans.

FLAGS

Typical questions

- What does the flag of Egypt look like?
- I'm doing an art project. Have you any pictures of the Union Jack?
- Which flags are green, white and yellow?
- Why do we have flags?

Considerations

Just in case you're caught out by a very smart 9-year-old the study of flags is known as vexillology, from the Latin *vexillum*, for flag or banner. The subject of flags is relatively straightforward and once you have one or two good sources you should need nothing else. The secret is to make sure that they are kept up to date.

Where to look

Printed sources

*Complete Flags of the World (2008), **Dorling Kindersley**

This is excellent for children because of the practical layout. This edition is published in association with the Flag Institute and provides the history, design development, significance of colours, symbols etc. and changes for each flag. It also includes flags of major international organizations, plus key flags in world history. For some countries it would be sensible to cross-reference to one of the websites listed below for any changes since 2008.

Johnson Barker, B. (2009) *The Complete Guide to Flags of the World*, **New Holland**

Websites

Flag Detective

www.flags.av.org/flags

This is not only informative but great fun for those enquiring minds. This allows you to search different flag designs and types and then select colours. The site will then tell you which country your flag belongs to.

Flags of the World

http://flagspot.net

This is an excellent site to search by country or subject, e.g. Historical Flags of the World, as well as for searching by maps. Well worth a visit.

Flags of the World @ Wikipedia is useful too, providing pictures and information on international, national and official flags. You won't believe how many and how much we use flags until you read this!

World Flags Database
   www.flags.net

MONEY

See also: **Part 2 – PSHE (Personal, Social and Health Education)**

Typical questions

- What currency is used in Italy?
- What was £1 worth 10 years ago?
- Do you have any pictures of banknotes from Greece?

Considerations

The queries you can expect will often be related to finding out about the coinage of other countries, what it is called and what it looks like. Equally, the value of money in past times is often popular to include in projects. Both are relatively straightforward and the suggestions below should be sufficient. On the off chance that you are asked for the exchange rate between two currencies, which could be a query from a modern language pupil at secondary school about to do their language exchange trip, I have included a currency converter. Try **Currency Converter, www.iccfx.com** or **Current Exchange Rates, www.oanda.com**. A lot of excellent resources are mentioned in **Part 2 – PSHE**.

Where to look

Current Value of Old Money

> **www.projects.ex.ac.uk/RDavies/arian/current/howmuch.html**
> This has a number of useful sections explaining the origins and history of money; especially child friendly is the section on 'The Vikings and Money'.

Food prices throughout history

> **www.foodtimeline.org/foodfaq5.html**
> Select Looking for other Countries, then United Kingdom. This has some interesting data for school projects. However, I would add a word of caution: some of the data is presented in spreadsheets and the child will need to be guided in its use. Especially useful are the 'Cost of Groceries 1914, 1950, 1975 and 2000'; 'Cost of Living in Jane Austen's England' and the excellent 'War Time Cost of Living'. The last of these three provides pictures and definitions of the coinage in the 1940s, how much things cost and how much people earned for certain jobs. Well worth a visit.

Purchasing power of British Pound

> **www.measuringworth.com**

Select Purchasing Power UK £ from the contents list. Then type in £ amount, original year and desired year.

Tips and pitfalls

For pictures of coins and notes try using some of the resources mentioned in **Part 4, Section 1 – Collecting Things**.

MYTHS AND LEGENDS

Typical questions

- Have you any stories of Welsh legends?
- Who was Arthur?
- Can you tell me about the Minotaur?
- Do you have any Indian legends?

Considerations

Myths, legends and folklore are always very popular not only for school projects but also for children to read for pleasure. The children's library will probably have a selection of books covering various myths and well known legends from a variety of countries. I have included below some of the best, but of course this can be very subjective. Also, many of the titles below are now, sadly, out of print. However, new titles are regularly replacing the old. The list below will, hopefully, give you a flavour of the types of books that prove useful. For the more obscure legends and myths you may need to use other sources. Some of the suggestions listed below offer extensive lists, with stories and definitions. This is an area where I would suggest that you make sure to bookmark good sources that answer regular enquiries.

For local myths and legends try using the resources in your local history collection. Most areas have a few local legends and stories and it is worth knowing what they are, and maybe keeping some photocopies, or references to them, to share with children.

Where to look

The Kingfisher Book of Mythology: gods, goddesses and heroes from around the World, **Kingfisher, 2001**
This includes a very useful chapter on what is a myth? and a glossary of over 500 mythological characters.

McCaughrean, G. and Brassey, R. (1999) *Britannia: 100 great stories from British history*, **Orion Children's Books**
One hundred stories from early times up to 1993. A wonderful, adventurous story book that leaves children eager for more legends. Luckily, there is a list of further reading included. Excellent. No longer in print but well worth looking for.

McKenzie, M. et al. (2011) *Mythologies of the World: illustrated guide to mythological beliefs and customs*, **Checkman Books**

An excellent book for the older child. It gives an overview of the earliest roots of mythology and the beliefs and traditions of indigenous peoples. It explores the mythologies of Mesopotamia, Egypt, Rome, Northern Europe, Central and Eastern Europe, Africa, India, China and Japan, North and Central America, South America and Oceania.

Neil, P. (2011) *Mythology*, Dorling Kindersley, Eyewitness guides
This looks at the stories told by different cultures to explain the mysteries of the world.

***Stories from Ancient Civilisations*, Evans, 2007–**
These are beautifully illustrated anthologies that bring together myths from ancient civilizations from around the world. Additional boxed text provides crucial background information on the myths and characters in the stories. A glossary and index are included. Titles include African Myths, Vikings, Egypt, Greece, Indian Myths and Rome.

Swindells, R. (2000) *The Orchard Book of Egyptian Gods and Pharaohs*, Orchard Books

Also:

McCaughrean, G. (1992) *Orchard Book of Greek Myths*

McCaughream, G. (2003) *Orchard Book of Roman Myths*

McCaughrean, G. (2005) *Orchard Book of Greek Gods and Goddesses*

Swindells, R. (2004) *Orchard Book of Viking Stories*

Wilkinson, P. and Philip, N. (2007) *Mythology: world myths, gods, heroes, creatures, mythical places*, Dorling Kindersley, Eyewitness companions

The **Graphic Universe** series from Lerner Books uses pictures and text by experienced graphic novel authors and artists to create a range of graphic novels covering myths from around the world. These are popular with children across the board, but can be particularly appealing to the reluctant reader. They are certainly worth having on the library shelves. For a list of titles visit **www.lerner.co.uk.**

Websites
Big Myths
http://mythicjourneys.org/bigmyth
Myths from around the world are told through animation and are

accompanied by an overview of the culture, the pantheon of the gods and a series of exercises based on the culture. Includes a teachers' guide.

Greek Mythology
www.mythweb.com
This provides definitions of the main gods and heroes from Greek mythology, using cartoon characters.

Timeless Myths
www.timelessmyths.com
This is an excellent site. Select from Classical Mythology, Norse Mythology, Celtic Mythology and Arthurian Legends: within each of these there is a feast of information, stories and definitions. There is also a search facility. Well worth a visit.

OLYMPICS

Typical questions

- When do the 2012 Olympics start?
- Where are the next Olympics in 2016?
- Who won the men's 100m gold medal in 2008?
- How did the Olympics start?

Considerations

At the time of going to print this will probably be a very popular subject, due to the surge of interest generated by the London Olympics 2012. The website below offers, in my opinion, practically all you need to answer most queries. For up-to-date news stories and recent articles relating to London 2012 try INFOTRAC news database. This has access to current and historical full-text articles from 50 journals and 10 newspapers. See **Part 1 – Online Libraries** for full details. Your public library may subscribe and you may be able to access it from home via your library card.

Where to look

The Official Countdown to the London 2012 Games, **Carlton Books, 2010**
> Covers the sports, the sports stars, records, puzzles and games. Very well presented and probably well worth having over the next year.

Websites

Fact Monster
> **www.factmonster.com**
> Click on Sports, select Olympic Games. This is very useful for the history of the Olympics. It covers the summer Olympics since 1896 and the winter Olympics since 1924.

Olympic.org Official Website of the Olympic Movement
> **www.olympic.org**
> This includes all the sports, the countries, the history, the medallists and much more. Fantastic!

Road to 2012
> **http://roadto2012.npg.org.uk**
> An interesting and different angle to the 2012 Olympics. This is the story that explores the journey to 2012 through commissioned photographs of athletes and organizers and behind-the-scenes stories and interviews.

POPULATION

Typical questions

- What is the population of Egypt?
- How many people live in London?
- Which country has the most people?
- What is the world population?
- How many people live in Aberystwyth?

Considerations

Population statistics can be requested for a plethora of reasons. It could be a project looking at the local area or in the context of looking at world issues. The secret is to find out what they are needed for and the level required and to keep it as straightforward as possible. Publications such as *Annual Abstract of Statistics* or *Social Trends* or *Regional Trends* are excellent sources and, with guidance, are relatively child friendly. Developing the information skills of young people is part of the enquiry-answering process. Also, don't forget, for quick reference, sources such as *Whitakers*, **A&C Black, Annual**.

Where to look

UK population

Annual Abstract of Statistics, **Palgrave Macmillan, Annual**

Social Trends, **Palgrave Macmillan, Annual**

Regional Trends, **Palgrave Macmillan, Annual**

Also available from **www.statistics.gov.uk**.

Census

The 2001 Census data is available on the **National Statistics Neighbourhood Statistics** website, **www.neighbourhood.statistics.gov.uk**. This enables you to search by postcode and provides a wealth of local area data, including population. Absolutely fascinating and very suitable for local area questions or projects.

Populations of other countries

Nation Master
> **www.nationmaster.com**
> This provides country populations. Select Countries A–Z, then select the country required from the list. This will provide the country population

figure and capital population figure. Lots more information available too, if required.

United Nations Population Information Network (POPIN)
www.un.org/popin
Very detailed, but very useful for population projections and projects on globalization.

SPACE, ASTRONOMY AND THE SOLAR SYSTEM

See also: **Part 2 – Science**

Typical questions

- What are the names of the planets?
- How far away is the Earth from the sun?
- Who was the first man on the moon?

Considerations

This is a huge subject area, and very popular too. There are hundreds of books published on space and the solar system. Using the books in your library will in most cases find the answers to queries, and enough information for projects.

Where to look

Couper, H. and Henbest, N. (2009) *Encyclopaedia of Space*, Dorling Kindersley

★Gifford, C. (2001) *The Kingfisher Facts and Records Book of Space*, Kingfisher
This is divided into five sections – solar system; sun and stars; universe; sky watching; people and space. It is a beautifully illustrated, informative book for children. It includes a glossary.

Kerrod, R. (2004) *The Oxford Children's A–Z of Space*, Oxford University Press

★Miles, L. and Smith, A. (2009) *Usborne Book of Astronomy and Space*, Usborne
Covers the solar system, the stars and star constellations.

Mitton, J. and Mitton, S. (2000) *Marshall Children's Guide to Astronomy*, Marshall Publishing
This covers the universe, the stars, the solar system, sky watching and space exploration.

Moore, Sir Patrick (2010) *First Book of Stars*, Amberley Publishing
Excellent.

Murphy, G. (2010) *Science Museum Space, Black Holes and Stuff,* **Macmillan Children's Books**

This is an informative book that covers black holes, eclipses and constellations in a humorous way. Particularly appeals to boys.
Another similar in style title appealing to boys is:

Poskitt, K. (2009) *Gobsmacking Galaxy,* **Scholastic**

Riley, P. (2010) *Earth, Moon and Sun,* **Franklin Watts, Essential Science series**

This gives facts and ideas on how to do practical investigations.

Stott, C. (2010) *Wow! Space,* **Dorling Kindersley**

Websites

Discovering Space

www.bis.gov.uk/ukspaceagency/discover-and-learn/discovering-space

Explore the Universe, Big Bang and Our Solar System with the UK Space Agency.

European Space Agency for Kids

www.esa.int/esaKIDsen

A wonderful site from the European Space Agency looking at Our Universe, Life in Space and the Earth.

Kids Astronomy

www.kidsastronomy.com

This includes an astronomy dictionary. There are also worksheets on the solar system, stars, deep space and more. Click on Teachers Resources.

Nasa (National Aeronautics and Space Administration)

http://solarsystem.nasa.gov/index.cfm

Select Kids, then A Kid Friendly Solar System. This is very clear and informative. Also has available to print out 'Our Solar System Lithograph'.

Our Solar System

www.enchantedlearning.com/subjects/astronomy

This has lots of information.

The Solar System

www.bbc.co.uk/science/space/solarsystem

Enables you to explore the solar system through video clips from BBC programmes.

Solar System
www.factmonster.com
Click Science, select Astronomy and Space.

Solar System
www.nasa.gov/audience/forstudents/k-4/index.html
This has a vast amount of information about the solar systems. Select Find it Fast!, then Our Solar System.

Solar System Live
www.fourmilab.ch/solar

WEATHER

Typical questions

- What is a hurricane?
- How can I find out about floods?
- What is the temperature in France?
- How do we measure rainfall?

Considerations

Even children find the weather fascinating and it is very popular for primary level (KS2) projects or for KS3 and KS4 GCSE geography projects. The main consideration is to understand the level of information required. Extreme weather disasters are well covered by newspapers, and for GCSE it may be appropriate to suggest using INFOTRAC, the news database for up-to-date articles. See **Part 1 – Online Libraries**. If that or similar are not available, some of the excellent websites listed in **Part 2 – Geography** will certainly provide information.

Where to look

Encyclopaedia of Weather and Climate Change: a complete visual guide, Thomas Reed Publications, 2011

Hamblyn, R. (2010) *Met Office Pocket Cloud Book: the definitive guide to cloud types and skies,* David and Charles plc

*The Met Office (2010) *The Met Office Book of the Weather: UK weather month by month,* David and Charles plc

*The Met Office (2008) *Weather,* Dorling Kindersley, Eyewitness Companions series

Websites

BBC Weather
www.bbc.co.uk/weather
Provides lots of reports and articles on weather topics.

Climate Change
http://wwf.panda.org
This is the website of the WWF. Select Our Earth, then Climate.

Climate Science
www.sciencemuseum.org.uk/ClimateChanging/ClimateScienceInfoZone. aspx

Fact Monster

www.factmonster.com

Click on Science, select Weather.

$Met Office

www.metoffice.gov.uk

An excellent site providing a wealth of information on all aspects of the weather. In addition it has an Education section specifically for teachers and children. For teachers it provides lesson plans for KS1, KS2 and KS3 and a section covering in-depth topics: Climate, Extreme Weather, Understanding Weather and the Water Cycle. It also has posters to download. This section would be invaluable for parents and librarians alike helping with homework. For KS3 pupils there is a section covering case studies of specific extreme weather events and I would suggest that these are useful for KS2 pupils too.

WEIGHTS AND MEASURES

Typical questions

- How do you convert ounces to grams?
- What is six feet in metres?
- What is a tonne?
- What is a baker's dozen?
- What unit do we use to measure liquid?

Considerations

Units of measurement can often be confusing for children – and for some adults too! The most sensible suggestion is to keep a list of basic units of measurement and their conversions at hand. Many of the everyday measurements are listed in diaries and it is worth all of us checking what gems we carry around with us. For parents, I would suggest that, having found such a list, you keep it safe for the numerous questions and times you may need to refer to it.

Where to look

Whitaker's Almanac, A&C Black, Annual

*The **Measure It** series from Heinemann Raintree explores different types of measurement and shows how to measure using rulers, scales, speedometers and thermometers. All titles are suitable for ages 8–10, but to behonest they are a great way for all ages to get to grips with measurement and should not be ruled out for older children. The titles in the series include:

Somervill, B. and Rand, C. (2011) *Measure It: distance, area and volume*, **Heinemann Raintree**

Somervill, B. and Rand, C. (2011) *Measure It: mass and weight*, **Heinemann Raintree**

Somervill, B. and Rand, C. (2011) *Measure It: speed and acceleration*, **Heinemann Raintree**

Somervill, B. and Rand, C. (2011) *Measure It: temperature*, **Heinemann Raintree**

Somervill, B. and Rand, C. (2011) *Measure It: time*, **Heinemann Raintree**

Websites

Online Conversion

www.onlineconversion.com

This converts anything to anything else. Very impressive and intriguing. Did you know that one dash is equivalent to 12 drops? Well worth a visit.

Weights and Measures for Kids

www.cdfa.ca.gov/dms/kidspage/kidsindex.htm

This is very useful for providing the history of weights and measures and definitions. The use of brightly coloured pictures helps to keep the subject interesting. It is an American site, so keep this in mind.

PART 2
School Subjects

AN OVERVIEW OF THE NATIONAL CURRICULUM

Typical questions

- What is the National Curriculum?
- What does KS2 mean?
- What topics does my child study for history at primary school?
- What do targets mean?

Considerations

Firstly, this is in reality a difficult subject, despite the fact that the term 'national curriculum' has become embedded in our education system for the last two decades. It is constantly changing. Indeed further reform is on the agenda at this very moment and changes have taken place throughout 2011. It also requires a certain level of knowledge and patience to find out the 'nitty gritty'. Below, the basics are given together with websites where you can find out more detail. The information is organized by the four countries – England, Wales, Scotland and Northern Ireland – that make up the United Kingdom.

England

What is the National Curriculum?

State or 'maintained' schools in England must teach a range of subjects according to targets set by the National Curriculum. This was established in 1989 to ensure the same standards of teaching and learning across the nation.

> The National Curriculum sets out the stages and core subjects your child will be taught during their time at school. Children from 5–16 in maintained or state schools must be taught the National Curriculum.
> (www.direct.gov.uk, Education and Learning)

The National Curriculum covers learning for all children aged 5 to 16 in state schools and sets out which subjects should be taught; the knowledge, skills and understanding a child should achieve in each subject according to their age; targets for each subject; and how information on each child's progress is assessed and reported to parents.

What are the Key Stages?

The National Curriculum is divided into the Early Years Foundation Stage (EYFS) and four Key Stages. These are:

Stage	Child's age	School year
EYFS	3–5 years	Pre-school and Reception
Key Stage 1 (KS1)	5 –7 years	Years 1 and 2
Key Stage 2 (KS2)	7–11 years	Years 3, 4, 5 and 6
Key Stage 3 (KS3)	11–14 years	Years 7, 8 and 9
Key Stage 4 (KS4)	14–16 years	Years 10 and 11

What Subjects are Taught?

The compulsory National Curriculum subjects for Key Stages 1 and 2 are: English, Maths, Science, Design and Technology, Information and Communications Technology (ICT), History, Geography, Art and Design, Music and Physical Education (P.E.). Schools also have to teach religious education, though parents have the right to withdraw children for all or part of the religious education curriculum. In addition, schools are advised to teach Personal, Social and Health Education (PSHE) and Citizenship, together with at least one Modern Foreign Language (MFL). These are sometimes taught under different names, depending on the school. The statutory subjects for KS3 are: Art and Design, Citizenship, Design and Technology, English, Geography, History, ICT, Maths, MFL, Music, P.E. and Science. The teaching of careers education, sex education and religious education is also statutory. The statutory subjects that all pupils must study at KS4 are Citizenship, English, ICT, Maths, P.E. and Science. The teaching of careers education, sex education, work-related learning and religious education is also statutory. All National Curriculum subjects follow a **programme of study**, which is part of the statutory order, meaning it must be taught to all pupils. To find out what is included in each subject's programme of study look at:

http://curriculum.qcda.gov.uk/key-stages-1-and-2/subjects/index.aspx
http://curriculum.qcda.gov.uk/key-stages-3-and-4/subjects/index.aspx

What are National Curriculum Levels?

Key Stages 1, 2 and 3 are all linked to a series of eight levels. These are used to measure a child's progress compared to children of the same age across the country. The levels are:

Levels 1–3 in Key Stage 1	Most pupils are at Level 2 by the end of KS1
Levels 2–5 in Key Stage 2	Most pupils are at Level 4 by the end of KS2
Levels 3–8 in Key Stage 3	Most pupils are at Level 5/6 by the end of KS3

What are Assessments?

At the end of KS1, KS2 and KS3 children are assessed. These assessments are usually called SATs (Standard Assessment Tasks or Tests). At the end of KS1 (Year 2, age 7) the children are assessed by their teacher, along with informal tests in Literacy, Maths and Science. At the end of KS2 (Year 6, age 11) children are assessed through national tests in English, Maths and Science. At the end of KS3 (Year 9, age 14) the children are assessed by their teachers. In KS4 (Years 10 and 11, age 14–16) teachers assess their pupils, along with external examinations. For further and detailed information try the following excellent websites:

BBC Schools Parents
  www.bbc.co.uk/schools/parents/national_curriculum_key_stages

Directgov
  www.direct.gov.uk/en/EducationAndLearning/index.htm
  Go to Schools (Parents section) then Exams, tests and the curriculum.

National Curriculum
  http://curriculum.qcda.gov.uk
  Was due to change in autumn 2011.

Wales

What is the School Curriculum in Wales?

The school curriculum in Wales was implemented in September 2008. It comprises: the Foundation Phase, Skills Development, National Curriculum, Personal and Social Education, Sex Education, Careers and the World of Work and Religious Education.

Since 2008, Wales has been undergoing the phasing out of the KS1 strand and replacing it with the introduction of the Foundation Phase. By autumn 2011 this will be fully implemented.

> The Foundation Phase is based on the principle that early years' provision should offer a sound foundation for future learning through a developmentally appropriate curriculum.
>
> (Welsh Assembly Government [Llywodraeth Cynulliad Cymru]
> http://wales.gov.uk)

The national curriculum for KS2, KS3 and KS4 has also been revised and restructured with the final phase starting in September 2011.There is a very useful document called *Making the Most of Learning – Implementing the Revised Curriculum*, which can be downloaded from **http://wales.gov.uk** (select Education and Skills, then Schools, then National Curriculum – Key Stages 2, 3 and 4).

What are the Key Stages?

The Foundation Phase combines Early Years (3–5 years) and Key Stage 1 (5–7 years) of the National Curriculum. There is a statutory framework to support this new Foundation Phase called *Framework for Children's Learning for 3–7 years old in Wales*. The document can be downloaded from **http://wales.gov.uk/topics/ educationandskills/earlyyearshome/foundation_phase/?lang=en.**

Stage	Child's age	School year
Foundation Phase	3–5 years	Pre-school and Reception
Foundation Phase	5–7 years	Years 1 and 2
Key Stage 2 (KS2)	7–11 years	Years 3, 4, 5 and 6
Key Stage 3 (KS3)	11–14 years	Years 7, 8 and 9
Key Stage 4 (KS4)	14–16 years	Years 10 and 11

What Subjects are Taught?

The Foundation Phase has seven areas of learning: Personal and Social Development, Well-being and Cultural Diversity; Language, Literacy and Communication Skills; Mathematical Development; Welsh Language Development; Knowledge and Understanding of the World; Physical Development; and Creative Development. The subjects for KS2 are: English, Welsh, Maths, Science, Information and Communications Technology (ICT), Design and Technology, History, Geography, Art and Design, Music and Physical Education (P.E.). For KS3 the subjects are the same as KS2 with the addition of a Modern Foreign Language (MFL). For KS4 the statutory subjects are English, Welsh, Maths, Science and P.E.

What are the National Curriculum Levels and Assessments?

The latest information regarding school achievement levels and pupil assessments can be found in the document *Statutory Assessment Arrangements for the School Year 2010/2011*, **www.wales.gov.uk/topics/educationandskills/schoolshome/ curriculuminwales/statutoryassessment/statutoryassessment1011/?lang=en.**

For further research and analysis of assessments the **Learning and Skills Observatory Wales (LSO)** portal provides access to detailed information and statistics, **www.learningobservatory.com/english.**

Scotland

What is the Curriculum in Scotland?

Firstly, the curriculum is known at the Curriculum for Excellence.

The 3–18 curriculum aims to ensure that all children and young people in Scotland develop the attributes, knowledge and skills they will need to flourish in life, learning and work. The knowledge, skills and attributes learners will develop will allow them to demonstrate four key capacities – to be successful learners, confident individuals, responsible citizens and effective contributors.

(Learning and Teaching Scotland [Ionnsachadh agus Teagasg Alba], www.ltscotland.org.uk)

What are the Key Stages?

Scotland has a flexible approach to children starting school, from 4½ to 5½ years old. This means that some children who are not yet ready for school get an extra year at nursery. Children remain at primary school for seven years and there are four compulsory years at secondary school.

Stage	Child's age	School year
Early – pre-school years and P1	4–6 years	Primary 1 (P1)
First – to end of P4	5–7 years	Primary 2 (P2)
First – to end of P4	6–8 years	Primary 3 (P3)
First – to end of P4	7–9 years	Primary 4 (P4)
Second – to end of P7	8–10 years	Primary 5 (P5)
Second – to end of P7	9–11 years	Primary 6 (P6)
Second – to end of P7	10–12 years	Primary 7 (P7)
Third and Fourth – S1 to S3	11–13 years	S1 (First Year)
Third and Fourth – S1 to S3	12–14 years	S2 (Second Year)
Third and Fourth – S1 to S3	13–15 years	S3 (Third Year)
Senior	14–16 years	S4 (Fourth Year)

What Subjects are Taught?

Building the Curriculum 1 focuses on the curriculum areas which contribute to developing the four capacities mentioned above. The eight curriculum areas are: Expressive Arts, Health and Well-being, Languages, Mathematics, Religious and Moral Education, Sciences, Social Studies and Technologies. To find out what is included look at **www.ltscotland.org.uk/understandingthecurriculum/ howisthecurriculumstructured/curriculumareas/index.asp**.

What are the Curriculum for Excellence Levels and Assessments?

The Curriculum for Excellence has five levels of learning. The 'experiences and outcomes' for the first four levels can be viewed at: **www.ltscotland.org.uk/ Images/all_experiences_outcomes_tcm4-539562.pdf**, with the fifth level (the senior phase) progressing and resulting in qualifications.

Level	Stage
Early	The pre-school years and P1
First	To the end of P4
Second	To the end of P7
Third and Fourth	S1 to S3
The fourth level broadly equates to Scottish Credit and Qualifications Framework Level 4	
Senior Phase	S4 to S6 and college
Standard Grade (Foundation Level) or Access 3 Standard Level (General Level) or Intermediate 1 Standard Grade (Credit Level): Intermediate 2	

What are experiences and outcomes?

The title 'experiences and outcomes' recognizes the importance of the quality and nature of the learning **experience** in developing attributes and capabilities and in achieving active engagement, motivation and depth of learning. An **outcome** represents what is to be achieved.

(www.ltscotland.org.uk)

Northern Ireland

What is the Curriculum in Northern Ireland?

A revised curriculum was introduced in 2007/2008 and now applies to all 12 years of compulsory education. The **Education (Curriculum Minimum Content) Order (Northern Ireland) 2007** states exactly what the curriculum in Northern Ireland must have as a minimum. It specifies the Areas of Learning from Foundation Stage to KS4 and what is considered a contributory element to this learning, i.e. skill or subject. It also specifies in detail the progression that each pupil should make for each skill/subject, at each stage, i.e. Foundation Stage, KS1, KS2, KS3 and KS4. This is very useful and every parent in Northern Ireland should consider this no-frills government document essential reading. It can be found at **www.deni.gov.uk/nisr_20070046_en.pdf**.

The emphasis of the revised curriculum is on the development of skills and capabilities for life-long learning and for contributing effectively to society. These whole curriculum skills and capabilities consist of Cross-Curricular Skills and Thinking Skills and Personal Capabilities. They are embedded throughout the revised Northern Ireland curriculum at each key stage and pupils should have opportunities to acquire, develop and demonstrate these skills in all areas of the curriculum.

(Northern Ireland Curriculum, www.nicurriculum.org.uk)

What are the Key Stages?

The curriculum is organized into blocks of years called Key Stages. The following table shows how this is arranged in Northern Ireland.

Stage	Child's age	School year
Foundation	3–4 years	Pre-school and Reception
Key Stage 0/Reception	4–5 years	Reception
Key Stage 1 (KS1)	4–8 years	Years 1 and 2, 3, 4
Key Stage 2 (KS2)	8–11 years	Years 5, 6 and 7
Key Stage 3 (KS3)	11–14 years	Years 8, 9 and 10
Key Stage 4 (KS4)	14–16 years	Years 11 and 12

What subjects are taught?

Pupils work within the framework of the skills and capabilities development mentioned above.

The Cross-Curricular Skills are Communications; Using Mathematics; Using ICT. These are the skills through which young people access knowledge and develop understanding. The emphasis is placed on transferring, applying and using skills effectively, throughout the curriculum. Pupils should be provided with a range of learning opportunities to acquire and develop cross-curricular skills in a variety of contexts. The areas of learning for Foundation, Key Stage 1 and Key Stage 2 are Language and Literacy; Mathematics and Numeracy; the Arts; the World around Us; PDMU (Personal Development and Mutual Understanding); P.E. (known as PDM, Physical Development and Movement for Foundation Stage); Religious Education. In Key Stage 3 the areas of learning are English; Mathematics; the Arts; Learning for Life and Work; Modern Languages; Environment and Society; Science and Technology; Physical Education; and Religious Education. In Key Stage 4 the areas of learning are Language and Literacy; Mathematics; Modern Languages; the Arts; Environment and Society; Science and Technology; Learning for Life and Work; Physical Education; Religious Education. For more detail look at:

> www.nicurriculum.org.uk/foundation_stage
> www.nicurriculum.org.uk/key_stages_1_and_2
> www.nicurriculum.org.uk/key_stage_3
> www.nicurriculum.org.uk/key_stage_4.

The Thinking Skills and Personal Capabilities provide the ability to think both critically and creatively and to develop personal and interpersonal skills and dispositions essential for functioning effectively in a changing world. They are at the heart of the curriculum from Foundation Stage to Key Stage 4. For more detailed information on what this entails in the classroom look at *Thinking Skills and Personal Capabilities Guidance* booklet, www.nicurriculum.org.uk. Select required Key Stage, then Thinking Skills.

What are the Curriculum Levels and Assessments?

The following are the expected levels of progression for Cross-Curricular Skills.

Levels by Key Stage	Expected levels
Levels 1–3 in Key Stage 1	Level 2 by the end of KS1/Year 4
Levels 1–5 in Key Stage 2	Level 4 by the end of KS2/Year 7
Levels 1–7 in Key Stage 3	Level 5 by the end of KS3/Year 10
GCSE in KS4	

In addition, individual pupils should progress by at least one level between each Key Stage. In Irish medium schools and units, where Communication is assessed in both English and Irish at the end of Key Stage 2, Level 4 is the expected level in both languages. For more detailed information take a look at *Guide to Assessment: supporting schools in meeting statutory requirements for assessment and reporting: foundation stage to key stage 3*, **www.nicurriculum.org.uk/docs/assessment/Guide_to_ Assessment_ 9March.pdf.**

For further detailed information try the following excellent websites:

BBC Schools Northern Ireland
www.bbc.co.uk/northernireland/schools

Council for the Curriculum, Examinations and Assessment
www.rewardinglearning.org.uk

Department of Education Northern Ireland
www.deni.gov.uk

Northern Ireland Curriculum
www.nicurriculum.org.uk

Tips and pitfalls

For those answering queries regarding the curriculum and programmes of study, avoid giving advice and getting into parent–pupil–school disputes or discussions. Always use official or quality sources of information and make sure they are up to date. You can only provide the information as it is and suggest further sources.

ART

See also: **Part 4, Section 1 – Drawing and Painting**

Typical questions

- Where can I get pictures of primitive art?
- What is sculpture?
- Who is Paul Klee?
- Can you give me the name of a woman artist?

Considerations

This is a vast subject for all, and equally so for those studying towards any examination. The main consideration is the level of information you need to provide and it is wise to probe the enquirer further. Many questions may be related to homework or course work, but others may simply be interest, curiosity or wanting to know how to draw something. See also: **Part 4, Section 1 – Drawing and Painting**.

Vast numbers of art encyclopedias and information books are available, so start with what your library already has; this includes using the general non-fiction/reference section if you don't find what you are looking for straight away. The suggestions below all relate to excellent publications produced specially for children, but don't rule out other general dictionaries such as *Oxford Dictionary of Art and Artists* (2009), 4th edition, Oxford University Press; *Concise Oxford Dictionary of Art Terms* (2010), 2nd edition, Oxford University Press; or, for the more specific techniques, query *The Search Press Guide to Painting Techniques*, Search Press, 2011 or *The Colour Sourcebook*, Flame Tree Publishing, 2007. You could also use the vast online **Art Encyclopaedia, www.artcyclopaedia.com**, which includes articles, news and links and is searchable by artist's name, medium, subject and nationality.

Programme of study

To find out exactly what is studied at each level use the **programme of study** within the curriculum. These are slightly different for each of the four countries of the United Kingdom. However, there are excellent guidelines given on the web pages listed below and they are well worth consulting to understand exactly what your child will be doing in class.

England

http://curriculum.qcda.gov.uk/key-stages-1-and-2/subjects/index.aspx
http://curriculum.qcda.gov.uk/key-stages-3-and-4/subjects/index.aspx

Wales
http://wales.gov.uk/topics/educationandskills/schoolshome/
curriculuminwales/arevisedcurriculumforwales/nationalcurriculum/
?lang=en

Scotland
www.ltscotland.org.uk/understandingthecurriculum/
howisthecurriculumstructured/curriculumareas/index.asp

Northern Ireland
www.nicurriculum.org.uk/foundation_stage
www.nicurriculum.org.uk/key_stages_1_and_2
www.nicurriculum.org.uk/key_stage_3
www.nicurriculum.org.uk/key_stage_4

Subject specifications

For **subject specifications and past papers** at GCSE and other levels it is essential to use the correct examination board specifications. It is important for pupils to check this with their teachers and make a note. How to access specifications and past papers for this subject can be found in **Part 3 – Examinations, Assessments and Revision.** Using past papers is an important part of revision, so it is worth encouraging pupils to use this valuable resource.

Where to look

Children's Book of Art: an introduction to the world's most amazing paintings and sculptures, **Dorling Kindersley, 2009**

Finger, B. (2010) *13 Modern Artists Children Should Know,* **Prestel Verlag**
Introduces young readers to modern art, from Cubism to cartoons, and shows 13 artists' best works. It has a timeline of what was happening in the world when each artist lived.

Schuenemann, B. (2010) *13 Women Artists Children Should Know,* **Prestel Verlag**

Wenzel, A. (2010) *13 Artists Children Should Know,* **Prestel Verlag**

The *Look!* series:

Wolfe, G. (2003) *Look! zoom in on art,* **Francis Lincoln**
This encourages children to look at painting from different perspectives.

Wolfe, G. (2006) *Look! Body language in art,* **Francis Lincoln**
This focuses on how artists use body language to tell stories.

Wolfe, G. (2008) *Look! Drawing the line in art*, Francis Lincoln

Wolfe, G. (2010) *Look! Really smart art*, Francis Lincoln
This looks at the secret skills artists use to make us see their paintings differently.

For GCSE pupils

Pipes, A. (2008) *Foundations of Art and Design*, Laurence King Publishing, 2nd edition
This is an introduction to the visual language of art and design. Part 1, The Elements covers points and lines; shape; texture; space; time and motion; value and colour. Part 2, Rules covers unity and harmony; balance; scale and proportion; contrast and emphasis; and rhythm. Excellent.

Websites

$A. Pintura, Art Detective
www.eduweb.com/pintura/index.html
This is an interesting online game about art history and composition. Find out the mystery of Grandpa's painting found in the attic by examining paintings by famous artists, as well as looking at composition, style and subject. There are also teachers' resources available.

Access Art
www.accessart.org.uk

Art
www.ngfl-cymru.org.uk/index-new.htm
Click on KS1, KS2, KS3 and KS4 under Teaching Resources, then click on Art. This offers lesson plans and resources on a wealth of curriculum art topics. Fantastic for parents and teachers alike.

$Artisancam
www.artisancam.com
This is an amazing site for children and teachers, indeed anyone interested in knowing more about living artists. There are videos from an impressive list of contemporary artists which show the artist and provide interviews on why and what inspired some of their most popular or well known works. It has a fantastic section for teachers, providing cross-curricular links to the artist, techniques and influences and even has suggested classroom lessons that follow the curriculum. The activities section is simply brilliant. I challenge anyone not to love this site. Excellent.

Artist's Toolkit

www.artsconnected.org/toolkit/index.html

Enables art students and teachers to explore how visual elements and principles of line, colour, shape and space can be used to create works of art. There are also videos of artists in action and a facility to create your own art.

Artyfactory

www.artyfactory.com

Very good for information and pictures on African masks, ancient Egyptian art, still life, pen and ink drawing, perspective drawing, pencil portraits, Pop Art, drawing animals and portrait painting. Also gives some suggested lessons for some of the above. Well worth a visit.

CLEO (Cumbria and Lancashire Education Online)

www.cleo.net.uk

This provides online resources for use in school and at home as well as giving support to teachers. It has a wide range of resources, but qualitywise they are a mixed bag. However, some are excellent, so it is worth trying. Select Art and Design, then the relevant Key Stage.

Crayola

www.crayola.com (American)

This is an excellent site for parents and teachers alike. Click on Educators to discover hundreds of lesson plans with great ideas and how to achieve them, as well as details of how to do various art techniques and tips for achieving. Click on Parents to find a wealth of colouring pages, craft ideas and loads of printable material. Well worth a visit.

Culture 24

www.24hourmuseum.org.uk

A gateway to over 3000 museums and galleries. Enables you to search for galleries and art exhibitions from around the country. There is a section for teachers too.

Everything Art

www.smithsonianeducation.org/students/explore_by_topic/
everything_art.html

An interesting site from the Smithsonian Museum, USA, which offers art topic ideas for young people.

The Guggenheim Collection

www.guggenheimcollection.org/index.html

This features highlights from the collection, searchable by artist, date, title, movement, medium or concept. Extensive, yet this is not even the museum's full collection!

$I am an Artist

www.iamanartist.ie/index.aspx

An Irish site. The project ideas for at home and for teachers are brilliant. It provides downloadable lesson plans and ideas as well as links to relevant websites. An excellent feature is the Project Ideas for things to do at home – children will love this!

$Inside Art

www.eduweb.com/insideart/index.html

Another fun site. Uses the idea of falling into a Van Gogh painting to learn about the techniques and style of the artist.

Learning Art and Images

www.bl.uk/learning/artimages/index.html

A fantastic collection of resources; lots of information, sound recordings, pictures, videoclips and more.

The Louvre

www.louvre.fr/llv/commun/home_flash.jsp

National Gallery

www.nationalgallery.org.uk

Has an excellent section called Explore the Paintings. It has an Artist A–Z, a Browse by Century and 30 'must see' paintings.

National Maritime Museum

www.nmm.ac.uk

This has a fantastic set of interactive resources searchable by Key Stage (starting from early years, up to and beyond KS4), curriculum subject, e.g. Art and Design, and by theme. Excellent.

National Portrait Gallery

www.npg.org.uk

This has an absolutely brilliant digital resources section to support school and home learning. There are resources specifically for teachers at primary and secondary level, covering popular topics. There is also a wonderful section on Interviews with Artists and Sitters, all transcribed from video and historic recordings. It also has a section of Special Educational Needs topics. Well worth a visit and highly recommended.

Primary School Teaching Ideas

www.teachingideas.co.uk

Select Art for loads of activities and lesson plans. Also select Early Years, then Art, for young children. Excellent.

Saatchi Gallery

www.saatchi-gallery.co.uk/schools/info.htm

This has some lesson plans for teachers, with ideas and suggestions for pupils and teachers alike for GCSE work.

ShowMe

www.show.me.uk

Select Pick a Topic, then choose Art and Design. You will be taken to a vast wealth of related art projects and games; all collected from museums and galleries throughout the UK. There is a section on Teachers' Resources and a section for parents too. Excellent.

Tate Gallery

www.tate.org.uk

This has a Learn Online section where you can find in-depth information on artists and works in the Tate Collection. Click on Works in Focus.

Victoria and Albert Museum

www.vam.ac.uk

This has a brilliant Learning Resources Finder, which allows searching by Key Stage of pupil (including pre-school, further education and families), by subject, by resource type or by keyword. Look under Education then Teachers' Resources, or you can search the alphabetical subject index of the Collections section.

Web Gallery of Art

www.wga.hu/index.html

This is a virtual museum and searchable database of European painting and sculpture from the 11th to mid-19th centuries. An art history resource for students and teachers. Excellent.

Web Museum, Paris

www.ibiblio.org/wm/paint

This provides heaps of information on types of painting and artists. It is exceptionally useful for school projects. There are some images, but mostly text. Definitely one to bookmark.

Winsor and Newton

www.winsornewton.com/resourcecentre

Very useful for information on materials and painting techniques. Particularly useful is the Artists' Glossary.

Tips and pitfalls

Please refer to **Part 3 – Examinations, Assessments and Revision** for syllabus and examination past papers. Don't forget to refer parents and pupils to the general art books outside the children's library. For the serious GCSE pupil, it may be possible to visit specialized art libraries that you may be lucky enough to have in your region. If so, remember to keep contact details, opening hours and conditions of use handy. You may also want to check in *Libraries and Information Services in the United Kingdom and Republic of Ireland*, **Facet Publishing, Annual**.

CITIZENSHIP

See also: **Part 1, Section 3 – Weather; Part 2 – Geography**

Typical questions

- What is citizenship?
- How do I find out about human rights for children?
- Do you have any information on water issues?
- I need to understand the election process; can you help?

Considerations

Before trying to tackle this subject it is useful to have a little understanding of what is meant by citizenship.

> Citizenship is taking an active part in society. It is about how we live together in our communities and about how we 'get on' locally, nationally and globally. It is about ensuring that everyone has the knowledge and skills to understand, engage with and challenge the main pillars of our democratic society – politics, economy and the law.
>
> (Citizenship Foundation, www.citizenshipfoundation.org.uk; has excellent further information on 'What is Citizenship Education?')

For more information on what exactly citizenship means today in education, visit

www.education.gov.uk/schools/teachingandlearning/curriculum/subjects/a0 064859/citizenship.

Programme of study

To find out exactly what is studied at each level use the **programme of study** within the curriculum. These are slightly different for each of the four countries of the United Kingdom. However, there are excellent guidelines given on the web pages listed below and they are well worth consulting to understand exactly what your child will be doing in class.

England
> **http://curriculum.qcda.gov.uk/key-stages-1-and-2/subjects/index.aspx**
> **http://curriculum.qcda.gov.uk/key-stages-3-and-4/subjects/index.aspx**

Wales
> **http://wales.gov.uk/topics/educationandskills/schoolshome/ curriculuminwales/arevisedcurriculumforwales/nationalcurriculum/ ?lang=en**

Scotland
www.ltscotland.org.uk/understandingthecurriculum/
howisthecurriculumstructured/curriculumareas/index.asp

Northern Ireland
www.nicurriculum.org.uk/foundation_stage
www.nicurriculum.org.uk/key_stages_1_and_2
www.nicurriculum.org.uk/key_stage_3
www.nicurriculum.org.uk/key_stage_4

Subject specifications

For **subject specifications and past papers** at GCSE and other levels it is essential to use the correct examination board specifications. It is important for pupils to check this with their teachers and make a note. How to access specifications and past papers for this subject can be found in **Part 3 – Examinations, Assessments and Revision**. Using past papers is an important part of revision, so it is worth encouraging pupils to use this valuable resource.

Where to look

Global Questions series, Franklin Watts Publishers, 2010
Provides an in-depth look at major social and political issues, examines the historical background to these issues and explores how we are dealing with them. Titles include: *What are human rights?*, *Why do people make and sell drugs?*, *Do animals have rights?*

Rowe, D. (2001) *Introducing Citizenship*, **A&C Black**
A practical handbook for primary schools.

Rowe, D. and Newton, J. (1995) *You, Me, Us! A citizenship pack for primary schools*, **Home Office**
This is now out of print but is available to download freely from **www.citizenshipfoundation.org.uk/main/resource.php?s116**.

Thorpe, T. (2008) *Understanding Citizenship: Book 1*, **2nd edition, Hodder Education**

Thorpe, T. (2008) *Understanding Citizenship: Book 2*, **2nd edition, Hodder Education**

Thorpe, T. (2008) *Understanding Citizenship: Book 3*, **2nd edition, Hodder Education**

Thorpe, T. and Gibbings, J. (2008) *Understanding Citizenship: teachers' resource*, 2nd edition, Hodder Education

Thorpe, T. (ed.) (2011) *Young citizen's passport, England and Wales*, 15th edition, Hodder Education
Explains simply those parts of the law that have most relevance to the everyday life of young people in England and Wales.

Websites

These are websites that cover a range of topics on the Citizenship curriculum.

Ask Cedric

www.tradingstandards.gov.uk/advice/advice-cedric.cfm
This is from the Trading Standards Institute. It provides hundreds of ideas for teachers on citizenship, arranged by Key Stages, as well as lots of links for pupils.

Christian Aid

http://learn.christianaid.org.uk
This has lots of resources on an extensive list of topics/issues for teachers and youth leaders, but could be used by teens and parents as well.

Citizen Power

www.channel4.com/learning/microsites/C/citizenpower/index2.htm
This is an excellent animated site covering Who Rules?; Your Voice Counts; Your Rights; War and Peace; Animals and Us; Crime and Punishment; One World; and Media Matters. It includes information and games.

Citizenship Foundation

www.citizenshipfoundation.org.uk
As well as the resource mentioned above in 'Considerations', this website includes an alphabetical list of resources and teaching materials, which are excellent.

CitizenX

www.bbc.co.uk/schools/citizenx
This starts by asking 'What does it mean to be a citizen?' and then helps to explain what it means to individuals. It has four sections: Being a citizen; Local citizen; National citizen and International citizen. For each there are facts, information, activities and a quiz. Excellent.

CLEO (Cumbria and Lancashire Education Online)

www.cleo.net.uk

This provides online resources for use in school and at home as well as giving support to teachers. It has a wide range of resources, but qualitywise they are a mixed bag. However, some are excellent, so it is worth trying. Select Citizenship, then the relevant Key Stage.

Global Footprint

www.globalfootprints.org/teachers/index.htm

GoGivers

www.gogivers.org/index.cfm

This covers the KS1 and KS2 lessons on Citizenship and PSHE. It has a great list of topics: Diversity and Cohesion; Feelings; Friendship and Care; Global Issues; Keeping Safe; Making a contribution; Money; Rights and Responsibilities; Sustainability and Values. It also has a KidsZone for related games and an excellent Parents' area on how to help your child through everyday family life and to encourage good citizenship.

National Maritime Museum

www.nmm.ac.uk

This has a fantastic set of interactive resources searchable by Key Stage (starting from early years, up to and beyond KS4), curriculum subject, e.g. citizenship, and by theme. Excellent.

Newsround Extra Stuff

www.bbc.co.uk/newsround/13948446

This has lots of well-presented newsround specials covering subjects such as growing up in a war zone, child poverty and more.

Oxfam – Global Citizenship

www.oxfam.org.uk/education/gc

This gives information, support and ideas for developing a global citizenship approach in school. There are also resources for Citizenship. Click on Curriculum in Resource: Quick Find for excellent lesson plans and activities for use at school or at home.

Primary School Teaching Ideas

www.teachingideas.co.uk

Select Citizenship for loads of activities and lesson plans. Excellent.

Save the Children

www.savethechildren.org.uk/en/online-library.htm

Packed with publications and resources on issues relating to children worldwide. Excellent.

We Are From
www.channel4.com/learning/microsites/W/wearefrom/main_flash.html
Find out about living in different European countries. Also has a good set of worksheets to use.

Animal rights

Royston, A. (2010) *Animals Under Threat*, Raintree

Spilsbury, L. and Spilsbury, R. (2007) *Animals and Us*, Evans Publishing, Start-Up Citizenship series
This is designed especially for KS1 pupils to understand animal welfare issues, with large, clear text and photographs.

Websites
Animal Welfare
www.co-operative.coop
Select Food, then Food Ethics, then Animal Welfare.

RSPCA
www.rspca.org.uk
Select Educating, then Teachers, for lots of resources on the welfare of animals, listed by Key Stages. Suitable for parents too.

Farming, food and water
BananaLink
www.bananalink.org.uk
Looks at fair trade in the banana industry.

Cafod
www.cafod.org.uk/resources
Select either Primary Schoolteachers or Secondary Schoolteachers for material on issues such as climate change, food and hunger, and health and water. Cafod is a Catholic organization for overseas development.

Cool Planet
www.oxfam.org.uk/coolplanet
Oxfam's site for children, looking at food from around the world, their countries and issues. It has lots of stories and quotes to support school projects and citizenship discussions. Useful for KS2 and KS3 children.

Dubble
www.dubble.co.uk
Comic Relief fair trade chocolate.

Ethical Trading
www.co-operative.coop/food/ethics
Select Ethical Trading. Looks at fair trade and fair-trade products.

Fairtrade
www.fairtrade.org.uk
Looks at better prices; decent working conditions; local sustainability; and fair terms of trade for farmers and workers in the developing world.

The Food Commission
www.foodmagazine.org.uk/home
The independent watchdog on food issues.

Soil Association Farm Trails
www.farmtrails.org.uk
Learn about organic farming through a series of online farm trails. Click on Curriculum Links for KS2 and KS3. Excellent.

Sustain
www.sustainweb.org
The alliance for better food and farming.

Water Aid
www.wateraid.org
Click on LearnZone, which is an area with activities, games and information for teachers, parents, youth leaders and teens (11 years plus) on water aid. It has facts, statistics, water rights and more.

Human rights and responsibilities

Amnesty
www.amnesty.org.uk/content.asp?/CategoryID=11743
Click on Citizenship. This has lots of downloadable resources, including a number of downloadable books.

Association of the British Pharmaceutical Industry
http://abpischools.org.uk/page/resource/age/subject.cfm
This provides a huge amount of resources for schools and children. Select PSHE/Citizenship 14–16. This covers topics such as Cloning and Stem Cell research. For teachers there is a vast amount of material, including

Curriculum Links which actually link by country, i.e. England, Wales, Scotland and Northern Ireland, and within these by Key Stages. Excellent.

Citizenship

www.bl.uk/learning/citizenship/citizenshiphome.html

This has interactive resources for the issues surrounding citizenship, including our rights and responsibilities as citizens and running campaigns. It makes use of cross-curricular links which show pupils how citizenship comes from all we do.

Save the Children

www.savethechildren.org.uk/en/online-library.htm

Packed with publications and resources to download and searchable by topic. Select either Child Rights and Participation under International, or Child Rights under UK.

Race and racism

Britkid

www.britkid.org

Tackles the issues of race and racism in Britain today, with a host of information for teachers as well.

DESIGN AND TECHNOLOGY

Typical questions

- Do you have any books or information on package design?
- I'm looking for ideas on using textiles?
- What can I make with plastic?

Considerations

Firstly, for those of us who did domestic science, woodwork, technical drawing and needlework at school, Design and Technology encompasses a whole host of 'technologies'. These are graphics, resistant materials (wood, metal and plastics), food technology, textiles technology, electronics, and systems and control. Each of these may be studied in KS2 and KS3 for a period of time and one of the subjects may be studied separately for GCSE, e.g. food technology. For information on what exactly 'design and technology' means today in education, visit **www.education.gov.uk/ schools/teachingandlearning/curriculum/subjects/a0077337/design-and-technology-at**.

Programme of study

To find out exactly what is studied at each level use the **programme of study** within the curriculum. These are slightly different for each of the four countries of the United Kingdom. However, there are excellent guidelines given on the webpages listed below and these are well worth consulting to understand exactly what your child will be doing in class.

England
> **http://curriculum.qcda.gov.uk/key-stages-1-and-2/subjects/index.aspx**
> **http://curriculum.qcda.gov.uk/key-stages-3-and-4/subjects/index.aspx**

Wales
> **http://wales.gov.uk/topics/educationandskills/schoolshome/ curriculuminwales/arevisedcurriculumforwales/nationalcurriculum/ ?lang=en**

Scotland
> **www.ltscotland.org.uk/understandingthecurriculum/ howisthecurriculumstructured/curriculumareas/index.asp**

Northern Ireland

www.nicurriculum.org.uk/foundation_stage
www.nicurriculum.org.uk/key_stages_1_and_2
www.nicurriculum.org.uk/key_stage_3
www.nicurriculum.org.uk/key_stage_4

Subject specifications

For **subject specifications and past papers** at GCSE and other levels it is essential to use the correct examination board specifications. It is important for pupils to check this with their teachers and make a note. How to access specifications and past papers for this subject can be found in **Part 3 – Examinations, Assessments and Revision**. Using past papers is an important part of revision, so it is worth encouraging pupils to use this valuable resource.

Where to look

The A–Z of Modern Design, **Merrell, 2009**

Encyclopedia of modern design in the 20th and 21st centuries.

Fowler, P. and Horsley, M. (1998) *Collins GCSE Design and Technology*, **Collins**

Covers the basic themes for KS3 and GCSE work – designs and designing; basic graphics; technology in society; principles of control; materials and their applications; energy; electronics; digital electronics; mechanisms; pneumatics; structures and project works. For more design and technology books look at **www.collinseducation.com/Secondary/DesignAndTechnology/Pages/Default.aspx**.

Garratt, J. *Design and Technology*, **Cambridge University Press**

This covers the 'design process'; aesthetics; ergonomics; structures; mechanisms; control electronics; electrics; materials and manufactured products.

Websites

General

British Standards Institution

www.bsieducation.org/Education/default.php

British Standards has created an excellent resource to teach children the importance of good design for health and safety. The activities are divided into the 7–11, 11–14 and 14–19 age groups. There are games to play and classroom activities with teachers' notes. Some of the activities have cross-curricular links with Citizenship and Geography. Highly recommended.

CLEO (Cumbria and Lancashire Education Online)
www.cleo.net.uk

This provides online resources for use in school and at home as well as giving support to teachers. It has a wide range of resources, but quality-wise they are a mixed bag. However, some are excellent, so it is worth trying. Select Design and Technology, then the relevant Key Stage.

Design and Technology Association
www.data.org.uk

This provides an overview of design and technology for primary and secondary schools and includes the programme of study divided into 24 schemes of work. It also highlights cross-curricular links. It is useful for both pupils and parents to identify exactly what they should be covering in their subjects.

DesignandTech.com
www.designandtech.com

This covers the subjects: graphics, resistant materials, food and textiles, electronics, systems and control. For each there is a vast amount of information presented in a clear and usable format. 'The Cook's Thesaurus' for Food Technology is just one example of excellence.

Design and Technology GCSE Bitesize
www.bbc.co.uk/schools/gcsebitesize/design

This contains revision notes for electronics, food, graphics, resistant materials, systems and control, and textile technology.

Design and Technology on the Web
www.design-technology.info

This is packed with design ideas and links covering hundreds of designs and the design process. It includes a section on KS3 projects, divided further by school year, i.e. Year 7, Year 8, Year 9, GCSE and homework. It covers graphics, resistant materials (wood, plastics, metal), textiles technology and food technology. There are indexes of designers, inventors and engineers. It also has coursework help, drawing and sketching rules for GCSE and graphics. It includes the GCSE syllabus information for most exam boards. Excellent. Well worth a visit.

Design Technology Department
www.design-technology.org

This has some really useful sections on aspects of design and technology, especially some topic quizzes and revision sheets.

Primary School Design and Technology
www.teachingideas.co.uk/dt/contents.htm
This is wonderful for design and technology ideas to do in the classroom.

realDesign
www.channel4.com/learning/microsites/R/realdesign/index_flash.html
This provides case studies from a number of designers showing how and why they created and designed new products. It has a good set of links and a design toolkit.

TechnologyStudent.com
www.technologystudent.com
This covers all aspects of design and technology and includes an excellent set of links. Well worth a visit.

Warren Design and Technology
www.the-warren.org
Packed with information, worksheets, homework exercises, quizzes and more. This has everything for the design and technology student from Year 7 to GCSE. Excellent.

Electronics

Doctronics
www.doctronics.co.uk/design.htm
A fascinating and informative site on electronics, packed with explanations, diagrams and facts. Excellent.

Food Technology

ActiveKidsGetCooking
http://activekidsgetcooking.org.uk/activekidsgetcooking/welcome.htm
This provides case studies and a host of activities and lesson plans for teachers. There are also Primary and Secondary School awards from ActiveKidsGetCooking and an annual special challenge for schools to take part in.

British Nutrition Foundation
www.nutrition.org.uk
Click on Food in Schools, followed by Curriculum, then The Curriculum to find out what is involved in food and nutrition at schools. The site also has an excellent Teacher Centre with a huge amount of resources, from podcasts to recipes and worksheets. There are some great interactive games that are well worth trying – just click on Play. Excellent.

Food a fact of life

www.foodafactoflife.org.uk

A fantastic website for teaching healthy eating, cooking, food and farming from ages 3 to 16 years.

GrainChain.com

www.grainchain.com

An absolutely wonderful site looking at flour and grain. It is divided by primary school and secondary school resources, and within these by Key Stages. There are also activity sheets and lesson plans for teachers.

Licence to Cook

www.licencetocook.org.uk

Registration is required to use the site, but has lots of information.

Young Veggie

www.youngveggie.org/information/resources.html

Select Project Booklet for Schools. This has been specially written for pupils studying Food Technology. It covers nutrition, menu planning, designing and packaging of vegetarian foods, facts about vegetarianism and alternative sources of protein.

Textiles Technology

Technology Things We Wear

www.bbc.co.uk/scotland/education/as/tech/flash/index.shtml

This is useful for learning about clothing: fabrics, colours and manufacture.

Victoria and Albert Museum

www.vam.ac.uk/collections/fashion/index.html

Fantastic for looking at fabrics and design through the ages.

DRAMA AND THEATRE STUDIES

See also: **Part 4, Section 1 – Acting and Performing; Part 2 – English (Literacy) and English Literature**

Typical questions

- Have you any information on stage lighting?
- Do you have a book on playing . . . ?
- What is a monologue?
- Have you any books on mime?

Considerations

Drama and Theatre Studies covers a wide range of skills and disciplines, so answering queries may often involve a little bit of lateral thinking, especially if you consider that stage management, lighting design, acting, costume and stage make-up are just some of the areas embraced by the subject. As well as queries relating to the subject, there is also the budding young actor who may want to polish their acting skills, find an agent or join a local group. Suggestions for most of these and more can be found at **Part 4, Section 1 – Acting and Performing**.

Programme of study

To find out exactly what is studied at each level use the **programme of study** within the curriculum. These are slightly different for each of the four countries of the United Kingdom. However, there are excellent guidelines given on the web pages listed below and are well worth consulting to understand exactly what your child will be doing in class.

England

> **http://curriculum.qcda.gov.uk/key-stages-1-and-2/subjects/index.aspx**
> **http://curriculum.qcda.gov.uk/key-stages-3-and-4/subjects/index.aspx**

Wales

> **http://wales.gov.uk/topics/educationandskills/schoolshome/**
> **curriculuminwales/arevisedcurriculumforwales/nationalcurriculum/**
> **?lang=en**

Scotland

> **www.ltscotland.org.uk/understandingthecurriculum/**
> **howisthecurriculumstructured/curriculumareas/index.asp**

Northern Ireland
www.nicurriculum.org.uk/foundation_stage
www.nicurriculum.org.uk/key_stages_1_and_2
www.nicurriculum.org.uk/key_stage_3
www.nicurriculum.org.uk/key_stage_4

Subject specifications

For **subject specifications and past papers** at GCSE and other levels it is essential to use the correct examination board specifications. It is important for pupils to check this with their teachers and make a note. How to access specifications and past papers for this subject can be found in **Part 3 – Examinations, Assessments and Revision**. Using past papers is an important part of revision, so it is worth encouraging pupils to use this valuable resource.

Where to look

Balme, C. B. (2008) *The Cambridge Introduction to Theatre Studies*, Cambridge University Press

Cambridge Guide to Theatre, Cambridge University Press, 1995
This is a comprehensive guide to the history and current practice of theatre worldwide. It covers all major playwrights, works, traditions and theories. Very useful for theatre students.

Children's Writers' and Artists' Yearbook, A&C Black, Annual
Lists theatre for children, both London and provincial theatres and touring companies.

Cody, G. H. and Sprinchorn, E. (eds) (2007) *The Columbia Encyclopaedia of Modern Drama*, Columbia University Press

RSC Shakespeare Toolkit for Teachers, A&C Black, 2010
Useful for KS3 English and drama and for KS2 Shakespeare.

Schechner, R. *Performance Studies*, 2nd edition, Routledge
This is written for undergraduates but the style and structure of the text make it useful for GCSE students to dip into.

Stanton, S. and Banham, M. (1996) *Cambridge Paperback Guide to Theatre*, Cambridge University Press

KS2

Grainger, T. et al. (2004) *Creative Activities for Plot, Character and Setting Ages 9–11*, **Scholastic**
This covers structure, character, setting, theme and language and provides drama activities.

Potter, M. (2009) *Inspirational Ideas Drama 9–11; engaging activities to get your class into drama*, **A&C Black**

Costume and make-up

Thudium, L. (1999) *Stage Make-up: the actor's complete guide to today's techniques and materials*, **Random House**
A guide for the student, amateur and professional.

Websites

Make-up

www.themakeupgallery.info
This has 5000 before-and-after images of actresses in character make-up. You can search by type, such as old age; bald; disfigured; or weird; to name but a few. Excellent.

Victoria and Albert Museum Costumes

www.vam.ac.uk/collections/fashion/index.html
This has excellent online resources for discovering the Museum's costume and historical clothing collections.

Plays

The Guide to Selecting Plays for Performance, **Samuel French Ltd, Annual**
Contains cast and story details of around 2000 titles available for amateur performance in the British Isles. It is divided into sections; the titles are indexed according to the number of characters and period and/or type of play to help companies choose a play for production. In addition, individual sections cover full-length plays (including all-male and all-female plays); one-act plays (including all-female and all-male plays); plays for children and young people; pantomimes and Christmas plays and musical plays.

Hooks, E. (ed.) (2007) The Ultimate Scene and Monologue Sourcebook, Back Stage Books
This is an actors' reference to over 1000 scenes and monologues from more than 300 contemporary plays.

Critical Scripts (2011) are plays for KS3 and GCSE from A&C Black
These are by well known authors and designed specifically for secondary schools, accompanied by schemes of work for teachers. The plays include *The Road* by Cormac McCarthy; *Ostrich Boys* by Keith Gray; *Out Day Out* by Willy Russell; *A Christmas Carol* by Charles Dickens.

Plays with Attitude series by Evans Publishing:

Peters, A. F. and Peters, P. (2007) *Kick Off*, Evans Publishing

Peters, A. F. and Peters, P. (2008) *Much Ado about Clubbing*, Evans Publishing

Peters, A. F. and Peters, P. (2007) *Twisted*, Evans Publishing

Peters, A. F. and Peters, P. (2008) *Flipside*, Evans Publishing

Stagecraft

Brewster, K. and Shafer, M. (2011) *Fundamentals of Theatrical Design: a guide to the basics of scenic, costume and lighting design*, Allworth Press

Campbell, D. (2011) *Digital Technical Theatre Simplified Using High Tech on a Low Budget*, Allworth Press

Jones, C. (2005) *Make Your Voice Heard*, Back Stage Books
Looks at voice training.

Kelly, T. A. (2009) *The Back Stage Guide to Stage Management*, 3rd edition, Back Stage Books
Traditional and new methods for running a show, from first rehearsal to last performance.

Journals

The Stage
The Stage Newspaper Publisher
Tel: 020 7403 1818
Weekly
www.thestage.co.uk

Theatre Voice
www.theatrevoice.com

Websites

CLEO (Cumbria and Lancashire Education Online)

www.cleo.net.uk

This provides online resources for use in school and at home as well as giving support to teachers. It has a wide range of resources, but quality-wise they are a mixed bag. However, some are excellent, so it is worth trying. Select Drama, then the relevant Key Stage.

National Drama

www.nationaldrama.org.uk

Select Publications for using drama in the classroom, recognizing talent and linking to community.

National Theatre

www.nationaltheatre.org.uk

Select Discover for a whole host of material on the stage; set and costume design; the theatre; lighting special effects and more. Well worth a visit.

Performing Right Society for Music (PRS)

Copyright House

29–33 Berners St

London W1T 3AB

Tel: 020 7580 5544

www.prsformusic.com/Pages/default.aspx

Royal Shakespeare Company

www.rsc.org.uk

Select Explore or Education for a host of resources on the plays of Shakespeare, as well as the language and the historical context of the plays.

Set and Recommended Texts for KS4

www.acblack.com/drama/Drama-Education-Area-Set-Texts-KS4/content/53

Methuen Drama has collated the set texts and relevant companion texts for each exam board in KS4.

Shakespeare's Globe

www.shakespeares-globe.com

Universal Teacher

www.universalteacher.org.uk/drama/drama.htm

Select Drama. Useful for teachers. Sections such as Drama Techniques are very informative for pupils and well worth bookmarking.

Virtual Library of Theatre and Drama
  www.vl-theatre.com

Tips and pitfalls

Remember to look also at **Part 4, Section 1 – Acting and Performing** of this book. Many of the suggested acting books are listed there to avoid duplication. Also, for those who need specialist books, try French's Theatre Bookshop, which is a specialist theatre and drama bookshop. For more information contact tel: 020 7255 4300.

ENGLISH (LITERACY) AND ENGLISH LITERATURE

See also: **Part 2 – Drama**

Typical questions

- What is persuasive writing?
- How do you spell . . . ?
- My son needs help with using punctuation – any suggestions?
- What exactly does my child do for Literacy at primary school?
- Does my child study English at secondary school?
- Have you got any critical works on *Of Mice and Men*?

Considerations

The English language is vital to all school subjects and everyday life, so it is important to tackle any queries with the importance they deserve. It is essential for children to acquire solid knowledge and understanding (of what is a very complicated language) from an early age – the earlier the better. We live in an increasingly multicultural country and some parts of the UK will encounter, on a regular basis, children who speak English as a second language or whose home language is not English. For them, guidance on the use of grammar, spelling, punctuation and more is vital if they are to be successful at school. Equally, all children need to develop strong literacy skills for success, which is why schools spend a large proportion of time on literacy-based activities. The library should support this work through complementary resources and having an understanding of what literacy (English) entails for all the Key Stages at school. It would be advisable to have some of the suggestions below, or similar titles, on your library shelves. The secret is to opt for books that are bright, clear, simple and have good explanations and examples of English language usage. Although books of this nature are given a targeted age group or Key Stage, I actually think that if the book demonstrates, for example, punctuation in an understandable way, then there is no reason not to use that book with any age group. One of my favourite grammar books remains ***Ladybird Homework Helpers: Grammar and Punctuation for Schools*, Ladybird, 2009** – and I am certainly over 21!

The other aspect of English at school is English Literature. This is studied seriously during KS3 and KS4 and forms part of the GCSE English syllabus. Texts studied will vary from year to year, although not on a year-on-year basis, and within different exam boards. Queries will nearly always centre on analysing the set novels, plays or poems. In this case, you need to look at what your library has on critical works and guidance notes. It may be that your area has some famous authors – such as Bradford and the Brontës – in which case, give consideration to what is being asked for, and not over-enthusiasm as you pile a 16-year-old high with your prized collection.

Programme of study

To find out exactly what is studied at each level use the **programme of study** within the curriculum. These are slightly different for each of the four countries of the United Kingdom. However, there are excellent guidelines given on the web pages listed below and they are well worth consulting to understand exactly what your child will be doing in class.

England
http://curriculum.qcda.gov.uk/key-stages-1-and-2/subjects/index.aspx
http://curriculum.qcda.gov.uk/key-stages-3-and-4/subjects/index.aspx

Wales
http://wales.gov.uk/topics/educationandskills/schoolshome/
curriculuminwales/arevisedcurriculumforwales/nationalcurriculum/
?lang=en

Scotland
www.ltscotland.org.uk/understandingthecurriculum/
howisthecurriculumstructured/curriculumareas/index.asp

Northern Ireland
www.nicurriculum.org.uk/foundation_stage
www.nicurriculum.org.uk/key_stages_1_and_2
www.nicurriculum.org.uk/key_stage_3
www.nicurriculum.org.uk/key_stage_4

Subject specifications

For **subject specifications and past papers** at GCSE and other levels it is essential to use the correct examination board specifications. It is important for pupils to check this with their teachers and make a note. How to access specifications and past papers for this subject can be found in **Part 3 – Examinations, Assessments and Revision**. Using past papers is an important part of revision, so it is worth encouraging pupils to use this valuable resource.

Where to look

General

Coxon, C. (2009) *Help Your Child with Literacy: age range 3–7*, Continuum

Coxon, C. (2009) *Help Your Child with Literacy: age range 7–11*, Continuum
Essential reading for parents, with lots of information on how you can help your child with reading and writing.

Websites

Carol Vorderman's English Homework Help
www.dorlingkindersley-uk.co.uk/static/html/features/made_easy/english.html
This has printable worksheets on punctuation, poems, apostrophes and more. It also has English quizzes.

CLEO (Cumbria and Lancashire Education Online)
www.cleo.net.uk
This provides online resources for use in school and at home as well as giving support to teachers. It has a wide range of resources, but quality-wise they are a mixed bag. However, some are excellent, so it is worth trying. Select English, then the relevant Key Stage.

Exploring Language and Literary Treasures
www.bl.uk/learning/langlit/index.html
Using the wealth of unique and original source materials from the British Library, literary treasures and the history of the English language are explored. There is a huge amount of information, sound recordings, pictures, video clips and more.

Help with English
www.bbc.co.uk/schools/websites/11_16/site/english.shtml
This is packed with topics and English skills to explore. There are also teachers' notes and lesson plans, competitions, writing tips and skills, poetry and much more. Well worth a visit. Try also for the 4- to 11-year-olds: **www.bbc.co.uk/schools/websites/4_11/site/literacy.shtml**.

Homework High
www.channel4.com/learning/microsites/H/homeworkhigh/index.html
Click on English, then choose a category from the list. There is an extensive list covering, for example, punctuation, language structure, handwriting and presentation, fiction etc. The section is based on questions and answers, some of which are very specific. The site is aimed at 11- to 16-year-

olds. It is very useful for those who are struggling with a topic and who may be lucky enough to find a previously asked similar question.

National Maritime Museum
www.nmm.ac.uk
This has a fantastic set of interactive resources searchable by Key Stage (starting from early years, up to and beyond KS4), curriculum subject e.g. English and by theme. Excellent.

Primary School Teaching Ideas
www.teachingideas.co.uk
Select Literacy for loads of activities and lesson plans. Also select Early Years, then Literacy for young children. Excellent.

Universal Teacher
www.universalteacher.org.uk
Useful for KS2, KS3 and GCSE English and English Literature. This has a whole host of tutorials on text, as well as some audio files of readings. Very useful but, sadly, no longer updated.

Punctuation and grammar

The **Grammar Ray** series helps children to identify and understand the different parts of speech that make up English grammar. These are books with three parts. Part 1 introduces the part of speech in a comic-style way, Part 2 is a summary with more information and Part 3 tests knowledge and understanding. Titles include:

Carter, A. (2009) *Adjectives*, **Evans Publishing**

Carter, A. (2009) *Adverbs*, **Evans Publishing**

Carter, A. (2009) *Nouns and Pronouns*, **Evans Publishing**

Carter, A. (2009) *Prepositions*, **Evans Publishing**

Carter, A. (2009) *Punctuation and Sentences*, **Evans Publishing**

Carter, A. (2009) *Verbs*, **Evans Publishing**

The **Words are CATegorical** series introduces young readers (KS1) to different types of words through rhyming verse. They have great titles which really highlight the fun aspect of learning. They include titles such as:

A Lime, a Mime, a Pool of Slime: what is a noun? **Lerner Publishing**

Hairy, Scary, Ordinary: what is an adjective? **Lerner Publishing**

Slide, and Slurp, Scratch and Burp: what is a verb? **Lerner Publishing**

Websites

Fact Monster

www.factmonster.com

Click on Word Wise for spelling and grammar.

Grammar Slammar

http://englishplus.com/grammar/index.htm

Extensive information on grammar. Well worth a visit.

Guide to Grammar and Writing

http://grammar.ccc.commnet.edu/grammar

This is packed with everything you should ever need to ask regarding grammar.

Punctuation

www.edufind.com/english/punctuation/index.cfm

Click on the icons to find out how to use each piece of punctuation. Very easy to use.

Spelling

$Fairground Spells

www.channel4.com/learning/microsites/F/fairground

Some animated spelling games to test your knowledge and skills. Lots of fun for KS2.

Skillswise:Spelling

www.bbc.co.uk/skillswise/words/spelling

This is an excellent site to improve spelling and to test spelling knowledge. It has factsheets, worksheets, quizzes and games to help with common spelling mistakes. There are also notes for tutors that are useful for both teachers and parents.

Spell Check

www.funbrain.com/spell

A game to spot the incorrect spellings, suitable for KS2.

Spelling Rules

wwwfactmonster.com/ipka/A0886509.html

Spelling rules for plural nouns.

Writing

There are lots of resources and ideas in **Part 4, Section 1 – Writing**

Brodie, A. (2009) *Brilliant Ideas To Get Boys Writing 7–9*, **A&C Black**

Collins Easy Learning Writing, **2010**

Grainger, T. et al. (2004) *Creative Activities for Plot, Character and Setting Ages 9–11*, **Scholastic**
This covers structure, character, setting, theme and language and is especially useful for writing and includes traditional tales.

Websites
Better Writing
www.askoxford.com/betterwriting/?view=uk
This has practical guides and tips on grammar, spelling, punctuation, writing and more from Oxford University Press.

Improving Your Writing
www.lancsngfl.ac.uk/curriculum/literacy/lit_site/html/writing/
writing_ict/cover.htm

Writing
www.bbc.co.uk/schools/ks3bitesize/english/writing/index.shtml
Well presented and easy to use, suitable for KS3, this has easy-to-follow notes on aspects of writing; an activity to reinforce; and a test. Excellent.

Writing
www.bbc.co.uk/skillswise/words/writing
Gives information on writing format and structure, proof-reading, planning and much more.

Writing Essays
www.factmonster.com/homework/writingskills1.html
Provides information on how to write a good essay.

Writing Instructions
www.englishonline.co.uk/englishnon/literacy
Everything you need to include and use when writing instructions.

Literature

There are lots of resources and ideas to use in **Part 4, Section 1 – Reading** for children from KS1 to KS4.

For KS1 and KS2

Reading

Oxford Owl

www.oxfordowl.co.uk

A wonderful website from Oxford University Press for parents to help their child's reading and phonics work. It is aimed at the 3- to 7-year-olds and is packed with advice, ideas and activities to do together. Excellent.

Phinn, G. (2000) *Young Readers and Their Books: suggestions and strategies for using texts in the literacy hour,* **David Fulton Publisher**

Although slightly dated, and aimed at primary teachers, this is a wonderful book for parents who want to develop their child's reading as well as select appropriate books to share.

Poetry and poets

Fun Poetry

www.fizzyfunnyfuzzy.com

John Foster – Poet

www.johnfosterchildrenspoet.co.uk

This is a fun site for children to explore poetry.

Rhyme Zone

www.rhymezone.com

Type in a word and find out dozens of rhyming words. Wonderful for poets.

For KS3 and KS4

Authors

The following are a selection of authors studied for English Literature; the list is by no means exhaustive and, of course, it can change. Find out who is studied in your area and bookmark similar sites.

Jane Austen

www.pemberley.com/janeinfo/janeinfo.html

Lots of information on the author; however, not the best layout.

Charles Dickens

www.fidnet.com/%7Edap1955/dickens

This has everything on the author, including novel summaries, characters profiles, Dickens' London and more. Excellent.

William Golding

www.william-golding.co.uk

Click on Resources for notes on *Lord of the Flies*, specially commissioned for teachers.

Lord of the Flies

www.faber.co.uk/site-media/reading-guides/lord_of_the_flies_.pdf

Lord of the Flies game

http://nobelprize.org/educational/literative/golding/index.html

Lord of the Flies: Education Pack

www.pilot-theatre.com/redesign/page.asp?idno=251

A useful set of notes on *Lord of the Flies* from the Pilot Theatre Company.

John Steinbeck

http://as.sjsu.edu/steinbeck/teaching_steinbeck/index.jsp

Fantastic resources from the Martha Heasley Cox Centre for Steinbeck Studies. There is a list of novel titles to select from. For each title there are plot synopsis, major themes, reviews, study guides and lots more. Excellent.

Poetry and poets

Homework High: Poetry

www.channel4.com/learning/microsites/H/homeworkhigh

Click English, then Poetry for hundreds of questions and answers about poetry. Use the 'What do you want to know?' facility to search for answers to specific questions. Excellent.

Representative Poetry Online

http://rpo.library.utoronto.ca

Lots of poets, but not comprehensive. Listed by name, poem title, first line and last line. It also enables searching by keyword. For each there is a vast amount of information.

Rhyme Zone

www.rhymezone.com

Type in a word and find out dozens of rhyming words. Wonderful for poets.

Way with Words

www.channel4.com/learning/microsites/W/waywithwords

Select Poetry and let Benjamin Zephaniah help you to learn about five different poems in a humorous and educational way. Compatible with the curriculum and suitable for Year 7, Year 8 and Year 9. Brilliant.

Understanding texts

Undertanding Texts

www.bbc.co.uk/schools/ks3bitesize/english/reading/index.shtml
This provides help with analysing fiction and non-fiction texts. It provides revision notes, an activity to reinforce, and a test. It is aimed at KS3 but could also be useful for Year 6. Excellent.

Shakespeare

Dickson, A. (2009) *Rough Guide to Shakespeare: the plays: the poems and the life,* **Rough Guides**
The ultimate companion to Shakespeare, covering all 39 plays, Shakespeare's life and theatre, his poetry and some interesting features.

Ganeri, A. (2004) *The Young Person's Guide to Shakespeare in Association with the Royal Shakespeare Company,* **Chrysalis Children's Books**

Matthews, A. (2001) *The Orchard Book of Shakespeare Stories,* **Orchard Books**

Alternative texts:

McDonald, J. (2007) *Henry V: the graphic novel,* **Classical Comics**

McDonald, J. (2007) *Macbeth: the graphic novel,* **Classical Comics**

Vieceli, E. (2007) *Manga Shakespeare: Hamlet,* **SelfMadeHero**

Websites

About Shakespeare
www.shakespeare.about.com
Plenty of articles, quizzes and links to useful sites.

Shakespeare
www.bbc.co.uk/schools/ks3bitesize/english
This provides summaries plus set scenes from the latest set texts, with revision notes and tests. Excellent.

GEOGRAPHY

See also: **Part 1, Section 3 – Weather; Part 2 – Science**

Typical questions

- Have you got any information about volcanoes?
- I need some images of India.
- How do I read a map?
- What is a contour line?

Considerations

Geography now encompasses not only physical and human geography but also environmental geography, social geography, geology and geopolitics. In addition, it includes map-reading and fieldwork skills, not to mention the weather and climate change. With this in mind, the range of enquiries is endless. It is best to make sure that you are clear about the area of geography, the level and the detail required before rushing off to your geography collection. This is not necessarily mentioned by the enquirer, or indeed understood, and may require not only asking further questions but some educated decisions based on the child's age and apparent knowledge. As with all school subjects, certain topics become very popular. At the moment, natural disasters, China and globalization are recurring queries. For these topical projects it is worth keeping a set of resources together, including bookmarking some useful websites.

Programme of study

To find out exactly what is studied at each level use the **programme of study** within the curriculum. These are slightly different for each of the four countries of the United Kingdom. However, there are excellent guidelines given on the web pages listed below and are well worth consulting to understand exactly what your child will be doing in class.

England

> **http://curriculum.qcda.gov.uk/key-stages-1-and-2/subjects/index.aspx**
> **http://curriculum.qcda.gov.uk/key-stages-3-and-4/subjects/index.aspx**

Wales

> **http://wales.gov.uk/topics/educationandskills/schoolshome/**
> **curriculuminwales/arevisedcurriculumforwales/nationalcurriculum/**
> **?lang=en**

Scotland
> www.ltscotland.org.uk/understandingthecurriculum/
> howisthecurriculumstructured/curriculumareas/index.asp

Northern Ireland
> www.nicurriculum.org.uk/foundation_stage
> www.nicurriculum.org.uk/key_stages_1_and_2
> www.nicurriculum.org.uk/key_stage_3
> www.nicurriculum.org.uk/key_stage_4

Subject specifications

For **subject specifications and past papers** at GCSE and other levels it is essential to use the correct examination board specifications. It is important for pupils to check this with their teachers and make a note. How to access specifications and past papers for this subject can be found in **Part 3 – Examinations, Assessments and Revision**. Using past papers is an important part of revision, so it is worth encouraging pupils to use this valuable resource.

Where to look

*Doherty, G. et al. (2010) *Usbourne Geography Encyclopaedia*, **Usbourne**
> This looks at the physical characteristics of earth, as well as taking a continent-by-continent look at the people and government. It has internet-linked websites and a complete world atlas.

*Gifford, C. (2011) *The Kingfisher Geography Encyclopaedia*, **Panmacmillan**
> Covers the physical and human geography of each country of the world.

There are numerous geography series available that have been developed for children, and most cover the range of topics within modern geography, the suggestions below are given as examples.

Geography Now series from Wayland
> This explores the physical features and natural forces of the planet. There are seven books in the series e.g. *Coastlines Around the World*.

Geography Fact Files series from Wayland
> This covers the key themes of physical and human geography. There are four books in the series, e.g. *Deserts*.

Also, don't rule out the **Horrible Geography series by Anita Ganeri**. The series is full of facts as well as fun. Titles include *Freaky Peaks*; *Cracking Coasts*; *Desperate*

Deserts and *Stormy Weather*. For further information see **www5.scholastic.co.uk/ zone/book_horr-geography.htm**.

For local geography try:

Explore Geography series from Heinemann
  Suitable for KS2, this explores local areas. The books look at landscapes, settlements, coasts and compare and contrast local areas.

Websites

CLEO (Cumbria and Lancashire Education Online)
  www.cleo.net.uk
  This provides online resources for use in school and at home as well as giving support to teachers. It has a wide range of resources, but quality-wise they are a mixed bag. However, some are excellent, so it is worth trying. Select Geography, then the relevant Key Stage.

Earth Science for Schools
  www.moorlandschool.co.uk/earth/index.htm
  A straightforward information site covering the Earth's origin, Earth structure, volcanoes and earthquakes, fossil fuels and more.

Geography Pages
  www.geographypages.co.uk
  This has a huge amount of links to resources for KS1 up to GCSE, for both teachers and pupils. However, children will need help to navigate successfully through the many links.

The Geography Site
  www.geography-site.co.uk
  An amazing site covering all aspects of geography: human, physical, environmental and so forth. It is useful for primary and secondary children for information and definitions on many of the topics covered in KS2 and KS3. Well worth a visit.

GeoInteractive
  www.geointeractive.co.uk
  This provides a huge quantity of geography resources for secondary teachers.

Geo Mysteries
  www.childrensmuseum.org/geomysteries/index2.html
  This provides information on rocks and fossils using animation.

GeoResources

www.georesources.co.uk

This is a geography portal for both pupils and teachers, focused on KS3 and GCSE.

Homework High

www.channel4.com/learning/microsites/H/homeworkhigh

Click on Geography. This covers most geo-topics, including ecosystems, weather and population.

Internet Geography

www.geography.learnontheinternet.co.uk

An excellent website for KS3 and GCSE level, but it would also be useful for primary projects and lesson planning too. It doesn't appear to be updated, but this only affects the news area. It also has a good collection of images. Well worth a visit.

National Geographic

www.nationalgeographic.com

This has lots of lesson plans for teachers, but bear in mind that it is an American site. The Kids section is brilliant for schools projects and for interest alike.

National Maritime Museum

www.nmm.ac.uk

This has a fantastic set of interactive resources searchable by Key Stage (starting from early years, up to and beyond KS4), curriculum subject, e.g. Geography and by theme. Excellent.

Primary School Teaching Ideas

www.teachingideas.co.uk

Select Geography for loads of activities and lesson plans. Excellent.

Rader's Geography4Kids

www.geography4kids.com

This site introduces the earth sciences and includes topics such as the earth's structure and atmosphere. There is lots of well presented information, and quizzes to test your knowledge along the way.

Royal Geographical Society

www.rgs.org

This has some great resources although they can be slightly tricky to find. Click on Who are you? then Teacher, then Schools, finally Websites and resources. You'll find some excellent material, podcasts, clips etc. on many KS3 topics.

Science Learning Network
www.sln.org
This has some great resources for popular geography topics under Explore Our Resources.

World Infozone
www.worldinfozone.com
This has lots of information on countries; especially useful are the photos, found in the gallery.

Fieldwork

Virtual Fieldwork
www.georesources.co.uk/indexvf.htm
For those unable to carry out actual fieldwork this offers four fieldwork units covering coastal erosion, sand dunes, a river study and an urban study. For each there are maps, detailed information, diagrams and photos.

Geology

Park, G. (2010) *Understanding Geology: a guide to the world of rocks*, 2nd edition, **Dunedin Academic Press**

For younger children try:

The Rock on! Look at Geology series. Titles include:

Petersen, C. (2010) *Fantastic Fossils*, **Abdo Publishing**

Petersen, C. (2010) *Mighty Minerals*, **Abdo Publishing**

Petersen, C. (2010) *Outrageous Ores*, **Abdo Publishing**

Petersen, C. (2010) *Rockin' Rocks*, **Abdo Publishing**

Petersen, C. (2010) *Super Soils*, **Abdo Publishing**

Websites
Many of the general geography websites listed cover rocks and minerals too.

Geological Society
www.geolsoc.org.uk
Click on Education, then Resources. This has a set of factsheets covering

the main geoscience areas, including earthquakes and tsunamis, which are useful for school topics. In addition it has an online resource aimed at KS3 called *The Rock Cycle*, which uses animations and images to show how surface and deep-Earth processes produce the rocks we stand on.

Geo Mysteries
www.childrensmuseum.org/geomysteries/index2.html
This provides information on rocks and fossils, using animation.

Maps and map-reading

$Ordnance Survey
www.ordnancesurvey.co.uk
Click on Education for a wealth of information. The Teaching Resources section has resources for the many aspects of map work available to download. The MapZone is wonderful for downloads, games and information for projects and fun alike. Well worth a visit.

World Atlas
www.worldatlas.com
This is great for lots of maps, country information and links. It also has printable outline maps, which are good for projects and map tests.

Specific topics

Cool Planet
www.oxfam.org.uk/coolplanet/kidsweb
Oxfam's site for children looking at food from around the world and countries and their issues. There are lots of stories and quotes to support school projects. Very accessible to KS2 children.

Also:

Dartmoor National Park Authority
www.dartmoor-npa.gov.uk
Click on Learning About, then Printable Resources, followed by Leaflets and Factsheets. These cover climate and weather, geology and landscape, and land use and issues, amongst others. There are also junior worksheets and maps to illustrate specific project work, for example, hydrology. Well worth a visit.

Earth Issues
www.panda.org/index.cfm
This has lots of information on issues affecting the planet. Click on Our

Earth to learn about biodiversity, climate change, oceans, seas and coasts and lots more. There are also factsheets, publications and resources for teachers; all of which would be equally useful for pupils and home use.

Fact Monster
www.factmonster.com
Click on Science, select Weather.

Global Eye
www.globaleye.org.uk
This is an outline resource based on the school magazine about global development issues. It is excellent, dividing resources into primary and secondary, and focusing on developing countries and a key topic such as water, oil, population and sustainability to name but a few. Well worth a visit.

GrainChain.com
www.grainchain.com
This covers the science of farming, the farming business and sustainability, the wheat market and more. All designed to follow the curriculum for 11- to 16-year-olds. Excellent.

The Hydrological Cycle
www.nwlg.org/pages/resources/geog/hydro_cycle/index.htm

Oxfam Education
www.oxfam.org.uk/education/
This is packed with resources to cover issues such as climate change, water, fair trade and lots more. There are a range of resources from early years to age 16. The site is also cross-curricular, with a vast number of downloads and lesson plans for all school stages. Excellent.

Pl@net.com
www.channel4.com/learning/microsites/P/planet/menu.html
This covers global and environmental issues. It divides each topic into sections, which is great for projects.

Renewable Energy It's Only Natural for schools
**http://webarchive.nationalarchive.gov.uk/+/dti.gov.uk/
renewables/schools**
This has now been archived, so many of the links may not work, but the eight key renewable energy sources case studies remain available and very useful for school projects, particularly for 11 years plus.

Rivers and Coasts

www.bbc.co.uk/schools/riversandcoasts/index.shtml

Well presented information for KS2 geography using colourful pictures and cartoons. There are lesson plans for teachers and printable worksheets for use at school or home.

Water

www.thameswater.co.uk

Select Community and Recreation, then Water in Schools. This has lots of resources for pupils and teachers looking at the importance of water and its many issues.

Your Ocean

www.nmm.ac.uk/upload/package/52/index.html

Looks at the ocean and the part it plays in our lives. As well as information for children it has resources to complement the KS2 and KS3 geography curriculum and lesson plans for teachers.

Tips and pitfalls

This can be a tricky subject, so start by offering the basics, unless you feel this is not required, and gradually offer information that gives more detail on the topic area. A common mistake we all make with children's enquiries is to give so much detail as to obscure their understanding.

HISTORY

See also: **Part 4, Section 1 – Family History**

Typical questions

- Have you got any information on the Victorians?
- Do you have any stories about the evacuees in the war?
- I need some pictures of Viking longboats.
- I'd like information on medicine in history.

Considerations

The subject of History is vast, and when you're dealing with children, and indeed some adults too, you can find that their knowledge is patchy and sometimes confused, especially when it comes to dates and centuries when things may have happened. So check exactly what is being asked for before rushing off to your history collection. Also, consider the level required. Topics for KS2 and KS3 are more focused on information collection with supportive images, whereas KS4 (GCSE) requires, in addition, analysis and comment. Moreover, do not be tempted to overload the enquirer with everything you have in the hope they will glean from it what they need. Better to point them to specific sources or good websites. For this reason it would be wise to bookmark good websites and to keep notes of good printed sources for popular queries – the same school projects have a tendency to keep reappearing. There are some suggested sources below. However, don't forget also to use some of the suggested sources mentioned in **Part 1 – General Sources**, especially for modern history or current affairs.

Programme of study

To find out exactly what is studied at each level use the **programme of study** within the curriculum. These are slightly different for each of the four countries of the United Kingdom. However, there are excellent guidelines given on the web pages listed below and they are well worth consulting to understand exactly what your child will be doing in class.

England

http://curriculum.qcda.gov.uk/key-stages-1-and-2/subjects/index.aspx
http://curriculum.qcda.gov.uk/key-stages-3-and-4/subjects/index.aspx

Wales

http://wales.gov.uk/topics/educationandskills/schoolshome/
curriculuminwales/arevisedcurriculumforwales/nationalcurriculum/
?lang=en

Scotland

www.ltscotland.org.uk/understandingthecurriculum/
howisthecurriculumstructured/curriculumareas/index.asp

Northern Ireland

www.nicurriculum.org.uk/foundation_stage
www.nicurriculum.org.uk/key_stages_1_and_2
www.nicurriculum.org.uk/key_stage_3
www.nicurriculum.org.uk/key_stage_4

Subject specifications

For **subject specifications and past papers** at GCSE and other levels it is
essential to use the correct examination board specifications. It is important for
pupils to check this with their teachers and make a note. How to access
specifications and past papers for this subject can be found in **Part 3 –
Examinations, Assessments and Revision.** Using past papers is an important part
of revision, so it is worth encouraging pupils to use this valuable resource.

Where to look

*Bingham, J. et al. (2009) *Usbourne Encyclopaedia of World History*,
Usborne
This is a good starting-point, covering from prehistoric times to the 21st
century with a 12,000-year illustrated time chart. It has 700 internet links
to websites offering homework help and more. It also has downloadable
pictures for use in schools and project work.

Matthews, R. (consultant) (2010) *History Timelines*, **Miles Kelly Publishing**
This spans the history of the world from the formation of the Earth to the
modern age. It has over 2000 key dates, with hundreds of illustrations,
diagrams and photos.

Steele, P. (2009) *British History*, **Miles Kelly**
An excellent, accessible reference book that tells the story of thousands of
years of history of the British Isles, from the first inhabitants to the start of
the new millennium.

Also worth looking at are the:

Usborne History of Britain series, www.usborne.com

and

Horrible Histories series from Scholastic
Titles include *Cut-throat Celts*, *Ruthless Romans* and *Terrifying Tudors*, all written by Terry Deary. They put the fun and the gore back into history for children. There are loads of titles; for a full list take a look at **www5.scholastic.co.uk/zone/book_horr-histories.htm.**

Archaeology
Adams. S. (2008) *Archaeology Detectives*, Oxford University Press
This shows how archaeologists interpret a wide range of evidence to piece together the lives of our ancestors.

Archaeology in Education Service
www.canterbury.co.uk/learning/aes

Council for British Archaeology
www.britarch.ac.uk/cba/educate.html
Includes educational resources.

Websites
CLEO (Cumbria and Lancashire Education Online)
www.cleo.net.uk
This provides online resources for use in school and at home as well as giving support to teachers. It has a wide range of resources, but qualitywise they are a mixed bag. However, some are excellent, so it is worth trying. Select History, then the relevant Key Stage.

History for Kids
www.bbc.co.uk/history/forkids

Try also:

BBC History
www.bbc.co.uk/history/
A huge amount of information on different periods of history.

History Learning Site
www.historylearningsite.co.uk
This covers ancient Rome, medieval England, Tudor and Stuart England, Britain 1700–1900, World Wars 1 and 2, British women in the 20th century,

Hitler and Nazi Germany, and Inventions and Discoveries of the 20th century. It includes exam subjects, modern world history 1918–1980 and a history of medicine. Each subject is divided into very specific areas. These subject divisions are amazingly extensive. Excellent.

History on the Net
www.historyonthenet.com
This is an excellent site that covers a vast quantity of history topics suitable for KS2 and KS3. It also has worksheets, a history dictionary, famous battles and timelines and a fantastic set of links.

Homework High
www.channel4.com/learning/microsites/H/homeworkhigh/index.html
Click on History, then choose a category from the list.

Learning History
www.bl.uk/learning/histcitizen/index.html
A fantastic collection of resources; lots of information, sound recordings, pictures, videoclips and more.

$Museum of London
www.museumoflondon.org.uk
This has some fantastic and well presented resources for children, teachers and parents alike. Click on Learning, then Schools, followed by Classroom and Homework Resources. Under the Kids section there are lots of topical games that are not only educational but fun too. Well worth a visit.

The National Archives
www.nationalarchives.gov.uk/education
The National Archives Education Service has a fantastic site with lessons designed for all Key Stages and online resources. It covers history from 1066 to the present. Excellent.

National Maritime Museum
www.nmm.ac.uk
This has a fantastic set of interactive resources searchable by Key Stage (starting from early years, up to and beyond KS4), curriculum subject, e.g. History and by theme. Excellent.

Primary School Teaching Ideas
www.teachingideas.co.uk
Select History for loads of activities and lesson plans. Excellent.

School History
www.schoolhistory.co.uk

I'd be surprised if anyone doing history needed anything more than this site. It lists all the History subjects and topics covered by Primary level, Year 7, Year 8, Year 9 and GCSE, which is invaluable. For each (and it is extensive) it gives information, links and downloadable material. It provides exceptionally well presented lesson plans for teachers and parents and it has a whole section on teaching History that would be invaluable to new/trainee teachers. Highly recommended.

Schools History
www.schoolshistory.org.uk

This is aimed at the KS3 and KS4 history curriculum and offers a vast amount of information on history topics.

Show Me History
www.show.me.uk

Select History, then topic.

Spartacus Educational
www.spartacus.schoolnet.co.uk

A wealth of information on a large list of history topics especially aimed at KS3 and KS4.

Time Traveller's Guides
www.channel4.com/history/microsites/H/history/guides

These cover the Roman Empire, Medieval Britain, Tudor England, Stuart England, Napoleon's Empire, Victorian Britain and the 20th century. For each, information is given under the same set of headings, which includes class and customs, hazards and dangers etc., and as such is very useful for comparing and contrasting periods of history. Well worth a visit.

Smithsonian Education
www.smithsonianeducation.org/educators/index.html

Select History and Culture. This gives lesson plans that can be downloaded and has a search facility to access 2000 resources. Bear in mind that it is an American site.

Specific topics

The websites listed above are fantastic and probably all you need, but it seemed a shame not to include these excellent sites covering specific history topics.

Britons at War

www.nationalmediamuseum.org.uk/nmem/britonsatwar/home.asp
Teaching resources for KS2 featuring archive photographs and film of World War 2.

Empires

www.pbs.org/empires/index.html
This provides information on some of the great empires: the Greek, the Napoleonic, Queen Victoria's Empire and the Roman Empire to name but a few.

Essential Norman Conquest

http://essentialnormanconquest.com
A really interesting site that has lots to look at, including a day-by-day timeline and an A–Z encyclopedia of the Norman invasion of England and Wales.

History of the Monarchy (Kings and Queens)

www.royal.gov.uk/HistoryoftheMonarchy/HistoryoftheMonarchy.aspx

The Plague

www.channel4.com/history/microsites/H/history/plague/index.html
Everything you need to know about the 1665 plague in England.

Try also:

Civil War in England

www.channel4.com/history/microsites/H/history/war/index.html

Tudorhistory.org

www.tudorhistory.org
This has a huge amount of well organized information, documents and images. Well worth a visit.

ICT

See also: **Part 3 – E-safety; Part 4, Section 1 – Computer Games (for fun)**

Typical questions

- What is a spreadsheet?
- How do I set up an e-mail?
- How do I have a Facebook page?
- Have you a book on creating a Power Point?
- What is a learning platform?

Considerations

In reality, most children will have more knowledge about ICT than you or I do! Most queries related to this are in fact to do with using ICT in the library or school environment and are more to do with 'glitches'. Parents often have concerns about safety relating to their child's use of the internet. These issues are looked at in **Part 3 – E-safety**. However, for those children, parents, librarians and teachers amongst us who need to check the difference between e-mail and Facebook, some of the following resources may be very useful. For more detailed enquiries on individual bits of software, hardware or ICT projects the library shelves will probably be littered with texts. The main problem is keeping up with developments.

Programme of study

To find out exactly what is studied at each level use the **programme of study** within the curriculum. These are slightly different for each of the four countries of the United Kingdom. However, there are excellent guidelines given on the web pages listed below and are well worth consulting to understand exactly what your child will be doing in class.

England
> **http://curriculum.qcda.gov.uk/key-stages-1-and-2/subjects/index.aspx**
> **http://curriculum.qcda.gov.uk/key-stages-3-and-4/subjects/index.aspx**

Wales
> **http://wales.gov.uk/topics/educationandskills/schoolshome/ curriculuminwales/arevisedcurriculumforwales/nationalcurriculum/ ?lang=en**

Scotland
> **www.ltscotland.org.uk/understandingthecurriculum/ howisthecurriculumstructured/curriculumareas/index.asp**

Northern Ireland
www.nicurriculum.org.uk/foundation_stage
www.nicurriculum.org.uk/key_stages_1_and_2
www.nicurriculum.org.uk/key_stage_3
www.nicurriculum.org.uk/key_stage_4

Subject specifications

For **subject specifications and past papers** at GCSE and other levels it is essential to use the correct examination board specifications. It is important for pupils to check this with their teachers and make a note. How to access specifications and past papers for this subject can be found in **Part 3 – Examinations, Assessments and Revision**. Using past papers is an important part of revision so it is worth encouraging pupils to use this valuable resource.

Where to look

Hoole, G. and Smith, C. (2011) *The Really Really Really Easy Step-by-step Computer Book: for absolute beginners of all ages*, **Struik Lifestyle**

Oxford Illustrated Computer Dictionary, Oxford University Press, 2006

*Rooney, A. (2009) *The Great Big Book of Computing*, QED Publishing
Clearly presented, getting started with computers for children.

Try also:

Rooney, A. *Spreadsheets, Graphs and Charts*, **QED Publishing**

Rooney, A. *Emails and Multimedia Messages*, **QED Publishing**

Rooney, A. *Writing Programs*, **QED Publishing**

Rooney, A. *Finding and Sorting Information*, **QED Publishing**

All the above are aimed at KS2 (age 7–11) children.

Websites

General

CLEO (Cumbria and Lancashire Education Online)
www.cleo.net.uk
This provides online resources for use in school and at home as well as giving support to teachers. It has a wide range of resources, but quality-wise they are a mixed bag. However, some are excellent, so it is worth trying. Select ICT, then the relevant Key Stage.

Do I.T.

http://doit.ort.org

An outline course that covers the basics of ICT, including software, hardware, computer languages, information systems, networks and the internet. A very good starting-point.

Primary School Teaching Ideas

www.teachingideas.co.uk

Select ICT for loads of activities and lesson plans. Excellent.

Software

Powerpoint in the Classroom

www.actden.com/pp

A great step-by-step guide to creating a Power Point presentation, with all the features.

Try also: **www.actden.com** for other online learning resources. The home page provides a list of software tutorials and online courses.

Teach with ICT

www.teachict.co.uk

This has resources that encourage pupils to use ICT skills to word process, create posters, websites and databases and lots more. To get the full set of resources you need to register, but to be honest, there is enough without doing that.

Internet

GetNetWise

www.getnetwise.org

Packed with information on using the internet safely. It is useful for families and schools. It covers internet safety, child-safe search engines, online chat and much more.

Think U Know

www.thinkuknow.co.uk

An excellent site dealing with internet safety. It is divided by age group, which means the information is age appropriate. The design is excellent and the information comes from the Child Exploitation and Online Protection Centre, 33 Vauxhall Bridge Road, London, SW1V 2WG, tel: 0870 000 3344. There are fantastic teacher/trainer and parent/carer areas, which should tell you all you need to know and more. Highly recommended.

WebWise

www.bbc.co.uk/webwise

This is a beginners' guide to using the internet, covering using the web, e-mail, music, photos, webcams and much more. Excellent.

Graphics and images

Discovery Education Clip Art

http://schooldiscovery.com/clipart/index.html

This has over 3000 clip-art images, organized into categories. It also has information on how to use clip art in documents.

Dorling Kindersley Clip Art

www.clipart.dk.co.uk

Provides thousands of images from the Dorling Kindersley picture library. It enables you to browse by A–Z images or by school subject. It also provides help on how to use clip art in school projects. Excellent.

Freefoto

www.freefoto.com/index.jsp

If you need a photo to enhance a piece of school work or anything else that is non-commercial, then this collection of 132,000 free photos is for you. The photos are organized into over 3600 categories. Very useful.

MATHEMATICS (NUMERACY)

Typical questions

- How do I calculate percentage change?
- What does my child need to know for KS2?
- Can I get a copy of the times tables?
- My child needs help with algebra – what could I use?
- What is the GCSE maths syllabus?

Considerations

Maths is one of those subjects that many adults dread and they often feel at a loss as to how to help their child, especially since teaching techniques have changed or have been developed and adapted since many parents went to school. However, it can also be an unpopular subject with children too, which means that enquiries for help have to be handled with great a deal of sensitivity. Maths textbooks can be difficult to use if you are not numerically minded and are already struggling. For this reason, if you are suggesting the use of some maths books, choose ones that are clear and concise.

Some of the resources suggested below are useful to have or recommend.

A very useful tool for parents is the downloadable version of the **KS3 Mathematics Framework**, which can be found at **www.counton.org**. It enables parents to know what their child should be doing and achieving.

Programme of study

To find out exactly what is studied at each level use the **programme of study** within the curriculum. These are slightly different for each of the four countries of the United Kingdom. However, there are excellent guidelines given on the web pages listed below and they are well worth consulting to understand exactly what your child will be doing in class.

England
> http://curriculum.qcda.gov.uk/key-stages-1-and-2/subjects/index.aspx
> http://curriculum.qcda.gov.uk/key-stages-3-and-4/subjects/index.aspx

Wales
> http://wales.gov.uk/topics/educationandskills/schoolshome/
> curriculuminwales/arevisedcurriculumforwales/nationalcurriculum/
> ?lang=en

Scotland
www.ltscotland.org.uk/understandingthecurriculum/
howisthecurriculumstructured/curriculumareas/index.asp

Northern Ireland
www.nicurriculum.org.uk/foundation_stage
www.nicurriculum.org.uk/key_stages_1_and_2
www.nicurriculum.org.uk/key_stage_3
www.nicurriculum.org.uk/key_stage_4

Subject specifications

For **subject specifications and past papers** at GCSE and other levels it is essential to use the correct examination board specifications. It is important for pupils to check this with their teachers and make a note. How to access specifications and past papers for this subject can be found in **Part 3 – Examinations, Assessments and Revision.** Using past papers is an important part of revision so it is worth encouraging pupils to use this valuable resource.

Where to look

Ball, J. (2009) *Mathsmagicians*, **Dorling Kindersley**
A fun book to put maths in the context of everyday things.

Brodie, A. (2010) *Parent's Survival Guide to Maths Homework: make sense of your kid's maths*, **A&C Black**

Carol Vorderman's Maths Made Easy series for KS1 and KS2, **Dorling Kindersley**
Full details from **www.dorlingkindersley-uk.co.uk**

Montague-Smith, A. *Great Big Book of Maths: first steps*, **QED Publishing**
Especially for 3- to 5-year-olds.

Montague-Smith, A. *Great Big Book of Maths: on your way*, **QED Publishing**
Especially for 5- to 7-year-olds, using simple games and challenges for adding, subtracting, dividing and multiplying.

Poskitt, K. (2010) *Murderous Maths of Everything*, **Scholastic**
and other titles from the **Murderous Maths series,**
www.murderousmaths.co.uk
Books to prove maths can be fun and really interesting.

Rogers, K. and Large, T. *Usborne Illustrated Maths Dictionary*, **Usborne**

Thielbar, M. (2010) *The Kung Fu Puzzle: a mystery with time and temperature*, Manga Maths Mysteries series, Lerner Books

Thielbar, M. (2010) *The Lost Key: a mystery with whole numbers*, Manga Maths Mysteries series, Lerner Books

Thielbar, M. (2010) *The Secret Ghost: a mystery with distance and measurement*, Manga Maths Mysteries series, Lerner Books

Vorderman, C. (2009) *Carol Vorderman's Maths Dictionary*, Dorling Kindersley

Websites

General

CLEO (Cumbria and Lancashire Education Online)

www.cleo.net.uk

This provides online resources for use in school and at home as well as giving support to teachers. It has a wide range of resources, but quality-wise they are a mixed bag. However, some are excellent, so it is worth trying. Select Maths, then the relevant Key Stage.

Fact Monster

www.factmonster.com

Click on Maths and Money for money, measurement and times tables.

$Official Murderous Maths Website

www.murderousmaths.co.uk

Select Teacher Resources for fun maths tricks. Not just for teachers! Or click on Try Some Tricks and Games, which is secretly hidden under one of the pictures – try the one with the pink pig.

Primary School Teaching Ideas

www.teachingideas.co.uk

Select Maths for loads of activities and lesson plans. Also select Early Years, then Maths, for younger children. Excellent.

KS1

KS1 Bitesize Maths

www.bbc.co.uk/schools/ks1bitesize/

Fun, animated games for KS1. Excellent.

KS1 Maths Resource

http://cleo.skoool.co.uk/PRIMARY_MATHS.ASPX

This has interactive maths lessons covering measurement and data, numbers and shape and size. Excellent.

KS2

Carol Vorderman's Maths Homework Help

www.dorlingkindersley-uk.co.uk/static/html/features/made_easy/maths.html

This has printable worksheets on KS2 maths topics such as adding, times tables, shapes and fractions. It also has online quizzes and a maths glossary.

$KS2 Bitesize Maths

www.bbc.co.uk/schools/ks2bitesize/maths/number

This has fun, animated sections on number, shape, space and measures, handling data. Click also on For Teachers Bitesize Maths for lesson plans, worksheets and activities.

KS2 Maths Resource

http://cleo.skoool.co.uk/PRIMARY_MATHS.ASPX

This has interactive maths lessons covering measurement and data, numbers and shape and size. Excellent.

KS3

KS3 Bitesize Maths

www.bbc.co.uk/schools/ks3bitesize/maths

Excellent site covering all maths topics: algebra, measures, handling data etc. It provides revision notes, an activity and test for specific topics.

KS3 Maths Resources

http://cleo.skoool.co.uk/keystage3.aspx?id=65

Covers polygons, graphs, angles and lines, Pythagoras, trigonometry, decimals, algebra and simultaneous equations.

Maths for KS3 and KS4

http://lgfl.skoool.co.uk/index.aspx

Select KS3 or KS4, then Maths, then select specific topics.

MathsZone

www.channel4.com/learning/microsites/M/mathszone/index.shtml

This is an interactive role-play adventure game that uses maths concepts from the curriculum framework for KS3.

KS4

KS4 Maths Resources

http://cleo.skoool.co.uk/keystage4.aspx?id=317

Covers algebra, shape, space and measure.

Maths games and puzzles

$Count On

www.counton.org

This has loads of numeracy games and activities aimed at Year 7 to Year 9.

Maths Booster

www.bgfl.org/mathsbooster

Games on all maths topics.

Nrich

www.nrich.maths.org

Nrich are specialists in mathematics and this site offers a host of challenging and interesting mathematical problems. Not for the faint-hearted!

Specific topics

3-D Shapes

www.liv.ac.uk/~spmr02/atm/poster.html

Don't be put off! If you're looking for the properties of 3D shapes this is great. There is a name index, which may be easier to use than the picture index.

Skill in Arithmetic

www.themathpage.com

Maybe not the best, as it is a bit too wordy, but for some this may be a good way to understand maths techniques.

Times Tables

www.multiplication.com/students.htm

Lots of games, worksheets and activities to learn and test children's knowledge of times tables. Useful both at home and in the classroom.

Virtual Tangram

www.amblesideprimary.com/ambleweb/mentalmaths/tangram.html

Play with the shapes to create new ones and pictures. Includes ideas for activities.

Visual Fractions

www.visualfractions.com

Practical help to identify, rename, compare, add, subtract, multiply and divide fractions. Simple exercises to follow.

MODERN FOREIGN LANGUAGES (MFL)

See also: **Part 2 – Welsh and Gaelic**

Typical questions

- Have you got a French dictionary?
- I need to construct some German conversations for my oral exam.
- How do you say . . . ?
- What is Spanish for. . . ?

Considerations

The most popular modern foreign languages studied in schools are French, Spanish and German, and in some cases, Italian. Most pupils take at least one foreign language for GCSE. When dealing with enquiries try to select resources sympathetically. Pupils struggling with a language need clear, step-by-step information. With this in mind, it would be advisable to bookmark some of the sites below and to have a few good language dictionaries and grammar guides available. It is worth finding out which languages your local schools teach. Not all schools in the same area do the same, as I discovered recently on a French/Spanish schools partnership project I was involved in. If you are keen to help local schools to further enhance pupils' language skills, think about providing story books in other languages – not to be confused with bilingual texts. At Bradford we now have story books from **European Schoolbooks, www.eurobooks. co.uk,** from the KS2 Schemes of Work by Catherine Cheater and Steve Haworth. It is amazing how children enjoy picking up books they recognize (from English) in another language and trying to work out the words, e.g. *Je veux mon p'tipot!* by Tony Ross.

Programme of study

To find out exactly what is studied at each level use the **programme of study** within the curriculum. These are slightly different for each of the four countries of the United Kingdom. However, there are excellent guidelines given on the web pages listed below and they are well worth consulting to understand exactly what your child will be doing in class.

England
> **http://curriculum.qcda.gov.uk/key-stages-1-and-2/subjects/index.aspx**
> **http://curriculum.qcda.gov.uk/key-stages-3-and-4/subjects/index.aspx**

Wales

http://wales.gov.uk/topics/educationandskills/schoolshome/
curriculuminwales/arevisedcurriculumforwales/nationalcurriculum/
?lang=en

Scotland

www.ltscotland.org.uk/understandingthecurriculum/
howisthecurriculumstructured/curriculumareas/index.asp

Northern Ireland

www.nicurriculum.org.uk/foundation_stage
www.nicurriculum.org.uk/key_stages_1_and_2
www.nicurriculum.org.uk/key_stage_3
www.nicurriculum.org.uk/key_stage_4

Subject specifications

For **subject specifications and past papers** at GCSE and other levels it is essential to use the correct examination board specifications. It is important for pupils to check this with their teachers and make a note. How to access specifications and past papers for this subject can be found in **Part 3 – Examinations, Assessments and Revision.** Using past papers is an important part of revision, so it is worth encouraging pupils to use this valuable resource.

Where to look

General

First German Words, **Oxford University Press, 2007**

Covers 400 first words for younger children or to get older children off to a good start when learning a new language. Also available in French and Spanish.

Usborne Easy Spanish, **Usborne**

Also available for French and German.

Websites

BBC GCSE French: Bitesize

www.bbc.co.uk/schools/gcsebitesize/french

Revise listening, reading, speaking, writing and grammar. Very worthwhile, allowing you to test what you know.

BBC GCSE German: Bitesize

www.bbc.co.uk/schools/gcsebitesize/german

Revise listening, reading, speaking, writing and grammar. Very worthwhile, allowing you to test what you know.

BiLingual Resources
http://oxforddictionaries.com/page/bilingualresources
Select from French, German or Spanish resources. Excellent set of worksheets for all. Highly recommended for classroom or home use.

CLEO (Cumbria and Lancashire Education Online)
www.cleo.net.uk
This provides online resources for use in school and at home as well as giving support to teachers. It has a wide range of resources, but quality-wise they are a mixed bag. However, some are excellent, so it is worth trying. Select MFL, then the relevant Key Stage.

Homework High
www.channel4.com/learning/microsites/H/homeworkhigh
Select Languages. You can search for specific answers by typing in your question. It has lots of categories for previously asked questions for French, German and Spanish. Very useful.

Primary School Teaching Ideas
www.teachingideas.co.uk
Select Modern Foreign Languages for loads of activities and lesson plans. Excellent.

Student Resources from Ashcombe School
www.ashcombe.surrey.sch.uk
Select Student resources, then Languages, choose from French, German, Spanish or Italian.

WordReference.com
www.wordreference.com
Type in an English word and select the language you want to translate to. It can also translate the other way round. Uses reputable dictionaries such at the Oxford dictionaries.

French

Bourdais, D. and Finnie, S. (2006) *Au parc*, Franklin Watts, French Words I Use series
Introduces children learning French to some key words for talking about the world around them. Other titles in the series include *En ville, Á l'école, Á la maison*.

Davies, H. and Holmes, F. *Usbourne French Dictionary for Beginners,* **Usbourne**

The Usbourne quick-links facility **www.usbourne-quicklinks.com** offers pronunciation of words by a native French speaker. Over 2000 words are included in this volume.

Websites

Asterix

www.asterix.tm.fr

French search engine.

www.google.fr

http://fr.yahoo.com

French search engine.

French Revision

www.frenchrevision.co.uk

French Teacher

www.frenchteacher.net

A vast amount of resources available. Select Resources, then year group for secondary school, or select Primary School Resources.

Fusee

www.fusee.co.uk

This is to support Hodder and Stoughton's KS3 French course but has some useful activities.

Online French Course

www.jump-gate.com/languages/french

This has nine lessons covering the basics.

Wild French

www.wildfrench.co.uk

Offers a range of online resources to both teachers and learners.

Zut!

www.zut.org.uk/index.html

Interactive activities for French. Select either Beginner Year 7–9; Intermediate Year 10–11; Advanced Year 12–13. If you use the site between 9am and 4pm weekdays there is a subscription, the rest of the time it is free!

German
Collins German Dictionary and Grammar, Collins, **2010, 6th edition**

Websites
www.google.de
German search engine.

http://de.yahoo.com
German search engine.

Gut!
http://gut.languageskills.co.uk/index.html
Interactive activities for German. Select either Beginner Year 7–9; Intermediate Year 10–11; Advanced Year 12–13. If you use the site between 9am and 4pm weekdays there is a subscription, the rest of the time it is free!

Web German
http://webgerman.com
This has some good bits, mainly the German language practice.

Spanish
Oxford Learner's Spanish Dictionary, **Oxford University Press**
For children 11 years and over.

Websites
www.google.es
Spanish search engine.

http://es.yahoo.com
Spanish search engine.

Español Extra
www.espanol-extra.co.uk
This has some free online Spanish resources for teachers and learners. Click on GCSE vocabulary revision.

Oye!
http://oye.languageskills.co.uk/index.html
Interactive activities for Spanish. Select either Beginner Year 7–9; Intermediate Year 10–11; Advanced Year 12–13. If you use the site between 9am and 4pm weekdays there is a subscription, the rest of the time it is free!

Tips and pitfalls

For those who are really struggling, suggest a tutor. See **Part 3 – Home Education (includes home tutors)**.

MUSIC

See also: **Part 4, Section 1 – Music – Enjoying and Playing Musical Instruments**

Typical questions

- Do you have a contact for a piano teacher?
- What does my child do for her Grade 1 flute exam?
- I'm doing a project on Bach – have you any information?
- What does my child do for GCSE music?

Considerations

Music is a specialist subject and, as such, children studying music to any examination level will probably know more than you – unless, of course, you are a musician too. Enquiries can be varied, ranging from the meaning of terminology, to how to play an instrument or reading music. Children's libraries will probably only have general books on music and for more specialist books you will need to venture into the general non-fiction collection. Even then, for some queries a more specialist collection may be needed. If you are in an area that has a music college or equivalent it may be worth finding out if GCSE pupils can use its resources. If so, keep contact details, opening hours and conditions of use up to date and accessible. For terminology queries try:

Online Music Encyclopaedia
http://library.thinkquest.org/10400/html/index.html
Although the back-drop is poor, the layout and information make up for it. Very useful.

You could also try **Music Glossary, www.naxos.com/education/glossary.asp**. This has an alphabetical list of hundreds of musical terms.

Music teachers

Find a Music Teacher
www.musicteachers.co.uk
Select by either county or area. Gives contact details, experience, instruments and levels taught.

Incorporated Society of Musicians
www.ism.org
Click on Find a Teacher or Musician, enter instrument from drop-down menu, enter postcode.

Programme of study

To find out exactly what is studied at each level use the **programme of study** within the curriculum. These are slightly different for each of the four countries of the United Kingdom. However, there are excellent guidelines given on the web pages listed below and these are well worth consulting to understand exactly what your child will be doing in class.

England

http://curriculum.qcda.gov.uk/key-stages-1-and-2/subjects/index.aspx
http://curriculum.qcda.gov.uk/key-stages-3-and-4/subjects/index.aspx

Wales

http://wales.gov.uk/topics/educationandskills/schoolshome/
curriculuminwales/arevisedcurriculumforwales/nationalcurriculum/
?lang=en

Scotland

www.ltscotland.org.uk/understandingthecurriculum/
howisthecurriculumstructured/curriculumareas/index.asp

Northern Ireland

www.nicurriculum.org.uk/foundation_stage
www.nicurriculum.org.uk/key_stages_1_and_2
www.nicurriculum.org.uk/key_stage_3
www.nicurriculum.org.uk/key_stage_4

You may also be interested in *Music education in England – a review by Darren Henley for the Department for Education and the Department of Culture, Media and Sport*, available from www.education.gov.uk/publications. Select Schools, then Subjects. This review of music education in the English school system lays down recommendations for minimum expectations of what any child going through the system should receive in terms of an education in music. It also outlines a national plan, which lays down the expectations for how Music Education should develop over the coming years.

Subject specifications

For **subject specifications and past papers** at GCSE and other levels it is essential to use the correct examination board specifications. It is important for pupils to check this with their teachers and make a note. How to access specifications and past papers for this subject can be found in **Part 3 – Examinations, Assessments and Revision.** Using past papers is an important part of revision, so it is worth encouraging pupils to use this valuable resource.

Where to look

Chambers Dictionary of Music, Chambers, 2006

Children's Book of Music: an introduction to the world's most amazing music and its creators (includes a CD of musical highlights), Dorling Kindersley, 2010
This explores music and musicians from earliest times to the present, covering the diverse range of musical styles and instruments.

Helsby, G. and Chapman, J. (2009) *My First Classical Music Book*, Naxos Books

Larkin, C. (ed.) (2007) *Encyclopaedia of Popular Music*, 5th edition, Omnibus Press in association with Muze
Covers rock, pop and jazz, with over 3000 entries.

Latham, A. (ed.) (2004) *The Oxford Dictionary of Musical Terms*, Oxford University Press

Rough Guide to Classical Music, Rough Guides, 2005

Websites

BBC GCSE Music: Bitesize
www.bbc.co.uk/schools/gcsebitesize/music
This covers elements of music; music in the 20th century; music for dance; performing; popular music; western classical tradition and world music. It provides revision and tests.

CLEO (Cumbria and Lancashire Education Online)
www.cleo.net.uk
This provides online resources for use in school and at home as well as giving support to teachers. It has a wide range of resources, but quality-wise they are a mixed bag. However, some are excellent, so it is worth trying. Select Music, then the relevant Key Stage.

Creating Music
www.creatingmusic.com
An online creative music tool for children of all ages.

DSO Kids Listen and Learn
www.dsokids.com
Select the Listen and Learn feature to hear music by composers or by instrument. There is also information on music theory as well as some games and activities to do at home.

Music

www.enchantedlearning.com/music

Information and print-outs on notes, notation and scales. Suitable for younger children, with lots of activities to do.

Music at School

www.musicatschool.co.uk

This has worksheets, schemes of work, online lessons and quizzes all aimed at Year 7 to GCSE. It also has the GCSE syllabus. It is a well presented, easy-to-use site. Well worth a visit.

Music by Arrangement

www.musicbyarrangement.co.uk

Select Free Stuff for a small selection of free downloads – on starting a music group at school and easy sheet music for orchestra, recorders and brass ensemble.

Music for Youth

www.mfy.org.uk

This is a national music education charity providing young people with free access to performances and giving young musicians opportunities to perform.

The MusicLand

www.themusicland.co.uk

Free to use, but you need to register first. Lots of music resources available.

Music Mysteries

www.bbc.co.uk/northernireland/schools/4_11/music/mm

This has lots of games to help children to understand basic musical concepts: sound; rhythm and mood as well as the orchestra. The site is designed to support the Northern Ireland music curriculum for KS1 and KS2 but would be equally useful outside of Northern Ireland. There is also a Teachers' Guide, which includes lesson plans.

Music Notes

http://library.thinkquest.org/15413

This offers a fantastic amount of information on music theory, history, styles and instruments.

Music Scores

www.music-scores.com

This is for classical sheet music. Although a members' site, it does allow non-members to download some of its sheet music. Arranged by composers, instruments and categories.

Music Sense
www.bbc.co.uk/music/parents/activities/musicsense/index.shtml
This is an interactive guide that helps you to understand key terms in music by bringing them to life with sound and moving images. Well worth a visit.

Music Teacher's Resource Site
www.mtrs.co.uk
This has free resources and schemes of work for teachers of KS3 and KS4 music, as well as worksheets for pupils.

Primary School Teaching Ideas
www.teachingideas.co.uk
Select Music for loads of activities and lesson plans. Excellent.

Composers and musicians

Ziegler, R. (2008) *Great Musicians*, Dorling Kindersley, Eyewitness Guides series

Websites

Ariama
www.ariama.com
Great for information on composers, conductors, performers and orchestras.

Composers
www.boosey.com/pages/cr
Boosey and Hawkes provides a list of composers and their works.

Music Encyclopaedia
http://library.thinkquest.org/10400
Information on composers and types of music.

The orchestra

Helsby, G. and Glennie, E. (2007) *Meet the Instruments of the Orchestra*, Naxos Books

Websites

The Orchestra
www.playmusic.org/stage.html
A lovely, colourful orchestra, for children to click around and discover the instruments. Suitable for KS2 and above. Excellent.

Theory

Elliot, K. (2004) *The Complete Theory Fun Factory*, Boosey and Hawkes

Websites

Music Notes

http://library.thinkquest.org/15413

This offers a fantastic amount of information on music theory, history, styles and instruments.

Music Sense

www.bbc.co.uk/music/parents/activities/musicsense/index.shtml

This is an interactive guide that helps you understand key terms in music by bringing them to life with sound and moving images. Well worth a visit.

Reading Music

www.datadragon.com/education/reading

This takes you through the basics of reading music, from clefs to counting. Useful for KS3 onwards.

Ricci Adams' musictheory.net

www.musictheory.net

A great set of lessons for music theory, with tests and tools, covering from beginners to advanced.

Tips and pitfalls

There are a lot of resources mentioned in **Part 4, Section 1 – Music – Enjoying and Playing Musical Instruments,** which are equally useful, especially for queries on instruments, bands and songs.

P.E. (PHYSICAL EDUCATION)

See also: **Part 2 – Science (Biology); Part 3 – Food and Healthy – Eating; Part 3 – Drugs and Smoking; Part 4, Section 2 – Sports**

Typical questions

- Have you any books on sports fitness?
- How does healthy eating help physical fitness?
- Have you got anything on coaching skills?

Considerations

P.E. can be studied for GCSE. Pupils studying P.E. require a wider knowledge of the subject relating to physical fitness, healthy eating, diet and lifestyle, as well as basic knowledge of how the body works. For those not studying GCSE many queries will relate to specific sports. Many of these can be answered by referring to the suggestions in **Part 4, Section 2 – Sports**. Younger children may ask how to play a specific sport or how to develop skills. They too are increasingly involved in looking at the link between physical fitness and healthy eating and lifestyle. Many of the resources mentioned in **Part 2 – PSHE** will also be useful.

Programme of study

To find out exactly what is studied at each level use the **programme of study** within the curriculum. These are slightly different for each of the four countries of the United Kingdom. However, there are excellent guidelines given on the web pages listed below and these are well worth consulting to understand exactly what your child will be doing in class.

England

http://curriculum.qcda.gov.uk/key-stages-1-and-2/subjects/index.aspx
http://curriculum.qcda.gov.uk/key-stages-3-and-4/subjects/index.aspx

Wales

http://wales.gov.uk/topics/educationandskills/schoolshome/
curriculuminwales/arevisedcurriculumforwales/nationalcurriculum/
?lang=en

Scotland

www.ltscotland.org.uk/understandingthecurriculum/
howisthecurriculumstructured/curriculumareas/index.asp

Northern Ireland
  www.nicurriculum.org.uk/foundation_stage
  www.nicurriculum.org.uk/key_stages_1_and_2
  www.nicurriculum.org.uk/key_stage_3
  www.nicurriculum.org.uk/key_stage_4

Subject specifications

For **subject specifications and past papers** at GCSE and other levels it is essential to use the correct examination board specifications. It is important for pupils to check this with their teachers and make a note. How to access specifications and past papers for this subject can be found in **Part 3 – Examinations, Assessments and Revision**. Using past papers is an important part of revision, so it is worth encouraging pupils to use this valuable resource.

Where to look

The **Training for Sport** series has four books that incorporate sports science, nutrition, training programmes and exercise:

Mason, P. (2010) *Improving Strength and Power*, Wayland

Mason, P. (2010) *Improving Speed*, Wayland

Mason, P. (2010) *Improving Flexibility*, Wayland

Mason, P. (2010) *Improving Endurance*, Wayland

or:

The **Aspects of P.E.** series has six titles that together cover the world of sport and P.E. in Britain today, covering many of the issues too. The series is out of print but appears to be available through Amazon:

Mullan, N. and Bizley, K. (2007) *Health-related Fitness*, Heinemann

Mullan, N. and Bizley, K. (2007) *How Sport is Organized*, Heinemann

Mullan, N. and Bizley, K. (2007) *Performance in Sport*, Heinemann

Mullan, N. and Bizley, K. (2007) *Sport in Society*, Heinemann

Mullan, N. and Bizley, K. (2007) *Taking Part in Sports*, Heinemann

Mullan, N. and Bizley, K. (2007) *The Working Body*, Heinemann

Try also:

Beashel, P. (2001) *The World of Sport Examined,* **2nd edition, Nelson Thornes**

This is a book for GCSE. It has clear text with colourful illustrations, linking theory to practical work. It also has exam-style questions to test knowledge.

Goodman, P. (2007) *Exercise and Your Body,* **Wayland**

Sheen, B. (2008) *The Real Deal: keeping fit,* **Heinemann**

Solway, A. (2010) *Sport Science,* **Raintree**

Websites

Association of the British Pharmaceutical Industry

http://abpischools.org.uk/page/resource/age/subject.cfm

This provides a huge amount of resources for schools and children. Select P.E. 14–16. This covers topics such as a balanced diet; digestion; heart and circulation; drugs of abuse; and breathing and asthma. For teachers there is a vast amount of material, including Curriculum Links which actually link by country, i.e. England, Wales, Scotland and Northern Ireland, and within these by Key Stages. Excellent.

BBC GCSE P.E.: Bitesize

www.bbc.co.uk/schools/gcsebitesize/pe

This covers revision for sports training videos; analysis of performance, applied anatomy and physiology; exercises and training; factors affecting performance (nutrition, drugs, hygiene, age, motivation and technology; or for AQA pupils school, social grouping, leisure time, sports facilities, sponsorship and media); safety and risk.

Children's British Heart Foundation

www.bhf.org.uk/cbhf

Designed for 7- to 11-year-olds with games, activities and information about keeping your heart healthy.

CLEO (Cumbria and Lancashire Education Online)

www.cleo.net.uk

This provides online resources for use in school and at home as well as giving support to teachers. It has a wide range of resources, but quality-wise they are a mixed bag. However, some are excellent, so it is worth trying. Select P.E., then the relevant Key Stage.

Kidnetic
www.kidnetic.com
An American site from the International Information Council Foundation that deals with healthy eating for energy and stamina.

Primary School Teaching Ideas
www.teachingideas.co.uk
Select P.E. for loads of activities and lesson plans. Excellent.

Sports Coach
www.brianmac.co.uk
Training regimes from a top sports coach.

Sport England
www.sportengland.org

Sport Fitness Adviser
www.sport-fitness-advisor.com
This gives sport-specific training.

Sport Injuries
www.sportsinjuryclinic.net
This is a virtual sports injury clinic. Each type of sports injury has further specific information, with types of treatment. Useful for sports students because it relates types of sports injuries to specific sports and why they might happen.

YHeart
www.yheart.net
A site from the British Heart Foundation for the over-11s.

Yoobot
www.yoobot.co.uk
This is a game and learning tool developed by the British Heart Foundation to help children think about the physical exercise they do and eating habits, in order to take more responsibility for their own health.

Youth Sport Trust
www.youthsporttrust.org
The aim of this site is to encourage all children, regardless of ability and age, to take part in P.E. and sport, both in and out of school time. Packed with information and activities to be involved in.

Tips and pitfalls

For finding out how the body works and the importance of the heart, use **Part 2
– Science**.

PSHE (PERSONAL, SOCIAL AND HEALTH EDUCATION)

See also: **Part 3 – Bullying; Part 3 – Drugs and Smoking; Part 3 – Alcohol; Part 3 – Relationships, Sex and Sexual Health and Puberty; Part 2 – Citizenship.**

Typical questions

- How do I open a bank account?
- What effects does smoking have on my body?
- Where do I find five healthy foods to eat?
- What is bullying?

Considerations

PSHE deals with the emotional, social and personal development of children and young people, in essence offering the skills to take them through life. There is a certain cross-over with Citizenship and some schools teach both together. It is a huge subject, as is highlighted by the number of 'see also' references. The number of questions that you could be asked is endless. However, hopefully, some of them will be covered in the sections listed above. The secret is to deal with each question sensitively: these enquiries are not easy to make. I would also suggest that libraries think ahead and provide good resources that are current and reliable. It is often an area where young people find the information for themselves, rather than asking for it. Libraries need to feel confident that they have the right materials available, that will give good information and advice.

Programme of study

To find out exactly what is studied at each level use the **programme of study** within the curriculum. These are slightly different for each of the four countries of the United Kingdom. However, there are excellent guidelines given on the webpages listed below and these are well worth consulting to understand exactly what your child will be doing in class.

England

> http://curriculum.qcda.gov.uk/key-stages-1-and-2/subjects/index.aspx
> http://curriculum.qcda.gov.uk/key-stages-3-and-4/subjects/index.aspx

Wales

> http://wales.gov.uk/topics/educationandskills/schoolshome/
> curriculuminwales/arevisedcurriculumforwales/nationalcurriculum/
> ?lang=en

Scotland
www.ltscotland.org.uk/understandingthecurriculum/
howisthecurriculumstructured/curriculumareas/index.asp

Northern Ireland
www.nicurriculum.org.uk/foundation_stage
www.nicurriculum.org.uk/key_stages_1_and_2
www.nicurriculum.org.uk/key_stage_3
www.nicurriculum.org.uk/key_stage_4

Subject specifications

For **subject specifications and past papers** at GCSE and other levels it is essential to use the correct examination board specifications. It is important for pupils to check this with their teachers and make a note. How to access specifications and past papers for this subject can be found in **Part 3 – Examinations, Assessments and Revision**. Using past papers is an important part of revision, so it is worth encouraging pupils to use this valuable resource.

Where to look

QED Publishing, www.qed-publishing.co.uk has a wide range of books to help Early Years and KS1 children understand the world around them and to support the PSHE curriculum.

Websites

Childline
Helpline: 0800 1111
www.childline.org.uk
This service is provided by NSPCC, Weston House, 42 Curtain Road, London, EC2A 3NH. The helpline service provides confidential advice and someone to talk to. The website covers bullying, exam anxiety, drugs, sex, abuse, racism, computer/online safety, smoking, eating problems, alcohol and disability.

Child and Youth Health
www.cyh.com
Select Kids Health for 6–12 and Teen Health for 12–17. Kids Health covers 'everything about being a kid', covering family, body, food, health, school, feelings, safety and growing up. Within each of these subjects there are loads of topics, which are dealt with in a very balanced way, looking at the pros and cons, good and bad. Teen Health covers healthy body, healthy

mind, relationships, society and you, and drugs and alcohol. Bear in mind that this is an Australian site. Well worth a visit.

CLEO (Cumbria and Lancashire Education Online)
www.cleo.net.uk

This provides online resources for use in school and at home as well as giving support to teachers. It has a wide range of resources, but quality-wise they are a mixed bag. However, some are excellent, so it is worth trying. Select PSHE, then the relevant Key Stage.

Primary School Teaching Ideas
www.teachingideas.co.uk

Select PSHE for loads of activities and lesson plans. Excellent.

Radio 1 Advice
www.bbc.co.uk/radio1/advice

Provides advice on a wide range of issues and concerns, including sex and relationships; drink and drugs; bullying; study and work; your body; health and well-being; money, law and the world. For each there are further sub-headings of information and contacts for further help. However, a word of caution: the strong content of some of the material on some issues means that it is suitable for KS4 children – and for younger children only with adult guidance.

Spolem
www.spolem.co.uk

Excellent for links to all the topics covered by the PSHE curriculum.

Bullying

Anti-Bullying Network
www.antibullying.net

This provides information on all forms of bullying and has information sheets available for parents, teachers and young people that cover types of bullying, how to prevent bullying, the law and bullying, and lots more.

Bullying UK
www.bullying.co.uk

This has three sections: Young People Advice; Parents; and Schools. It covers all forms of bullying, giving information, advice and tips to combat bullying. It provides contacts for lots of organizations that deal with bullying and there is a free helpline, tel: 0808 800 222.

Drugs, alcohol and smoking

Action on Smoking and Health (ASH)

www.ash.org.uk

Loads of information on smoking, the risks to health and the tobacco industry. The section on Youth Smoking is particularly interesting.

FRANK

www.talktofrank.com

This is designed for young people and has a comprehensive A–Z list of drugs. For each it gives an explanation of what the drug is, slang or street names, the effects, the chances of getting hooked, the law, the appearance and use, the cost, purity and the risks. It is very informative, addressing young people about making informed choices. It also provides a number of options for finding help or to just talk. Highly recommended.

Youthhealthtalk

www.youthhealthtalk.org/young_people_drugs_and_alcohol

This has interviews with 33 young people about their experiences of and opinions on recreational drugs and alcohol. It looks at the issues surrounding why young people use alcohol and drugs and examines British culture and society. This is very useful for discussions and also for making informed choices. There is a list of websites and organizations to use for further help and information.

Health

Hewitt, S. *Keeping Healthy*, QED Publishing

Aimed at 5- to 7-year-olds.

Firth, A. and Leschnikoff, N. (2006) *What's Happening To Me?* (boys edition), Usbourne

Meredith, S. and Leschnikoff, N. (2006) *What's Happening To Me?* (girls edition), Usbourne

Deals with puberty for both boys and girls and their parents, tackling both physical and emotional changes. Suitable for KS2 and KS3.

Websites

Boots Learning Store

www.bootslearningstore.com

This is an interactive educational resource for pupils from 4 to post-16, dealing with issues of health and well-being. It has a Teachers' area for curriculum information and worksheets, as well as a Parents' area.

KidsHealth
http://kidshealth.org
This is a great site, divided by kids, teens and parents, giving information and help on a wide range of issues – health, food, drugs, school and more. There is even a kids' dictionary of medical words.

TeenageHealth
www.teenagehealthfreak.org
Covers alcohol, the body, sex, smoking, weight and much more. Fantastic, and well presented too.

Youthhealthtalk
www.youthhealthtalk.org
Young people talk about their real-life experiences of health and lifestyle. The site covers an extensive list of A–Z subjects. It also has an extensive list of resources and where to get further information, with full contact details for all organizations mentioned. Excellent.

Money

Hollander, B. (2009) *Managing Money*, Pearson Educational
Includes how banks work and the principles of budgeting.

Llewellyn, C. and Gordon, M. (2010) *My Money Choices*, Wayland
Aimed at younger children, KS1 and lower KS2. It includes activities that parents and teachers can do to complement the book.

Llewellyn, C. and Gordon, M. (2010) *Saving My Money*, Wayland

My Money Week 2010: primary activity pack
The pack contains flexible activity ideas to help teach personal finance across the curriculum in My Money Week and beyond. Available to download from **www.education.gov.uk/publications**. Select Youth and Adolescence, then Information, Advice and Guidance. Also *My Money Week 2010: secondary activity pack*.

My Money: primary parents' guide
This is a guide for parents and carers of primary school children. It outlines the importance of children learning about money and describes ways in which parents and carers can help their children to understand the issues. Available to download from **www.education.gov.uk/publications**. Select Youth and Adolescence, then Information, Advice and Guidance. Also *My Money: secondary parents' guide*.

My Money: PSHE education teacher handbook

This handbook is for teachers of PSHE to help them build personal finance education into schemes of work with Key Stages 3 and 4 learners. It aims to give teachers practical help in equipping pupils with a solid understanding of money and all that is associated with it. Available from **www.education.gov.uk/publications**. Select Youth and Adolescence, then Information, Advice and Guidance.

Websites

DebtCred

www.debtcred.org.uk

This is an excellent resources site to support teachers, educators and parents in delivering economic and financial capability to KS3 and KS4 pupils. Packed with online materials and resources. Well worth a visit.

Financial Capability

www.pfeg.org

This comes from the Personal Finance Education Group to teach and provide resources for developing money sense in children and young people. Excellent.

Money Makes the World Go Around

www.museumoflondon.org.uk/Schools/Resources/citi.htm

The *Money Makes the World Go Around* presentation and quiz are available free to download. These are resources produced to support KS4 teaching of Citizenship/PSHE.

MyMoneyWeek

www.mymoneyonline.org

Packed with information for schools and parents.

Tips and pitfalls

Remember to refer to the resources mentioned in the sections listed under 'see also'.

RE (RELIGIOUS EDUCATION)

Typical questions

- Who were Jesus's disciples?
- I need to know the five Ks for Sikhism.
- When is Ramadan?
- Have you got a picture of a synagogue?
- How do religions worship?

Considerations

Religion taught in the UK looks at religions from around the world, concentrating on the six main world religions – Buddhism, Christianity, Hinduism, Islam, Judaism and Sikhism. Most enquiries should be fairly straightforward to answer, with most libraries having a range of books on the various religions. As pupils progress to KS3 and GCSE levels, Philosophy and Ethics are introduced. For these not only are some of the resources in **Part 2 – Citizenship** useful, but also the general non-fiction collection within your library will be useful. There are also some excellent websites, listed below.

Programme of study

To find out exactly what is studied at each level use the **programme of study** within the curriculum. These are slightly different for each of the four countries of the United Kingdom. However, there are excellent guidelines given on the web pages listed below and these are well worth consulting to understand exactly what your child will be doing in class.

England

http://curriculum.qcda.gov.uk/key-stages-1-and-2/subjects/index.aspx
http://curriculum.qcda.gov.uk/key-stages-3-and-4/subjects/index.aspx

Wales

http://wales.gov.uk/topics/educationandskills/schoolshome/
curriculuminwales/arevisedcurriculumforwales/nationalcurriculum/
?lang=en

Scotland

www.ltscotland.org.uk/understandingthecurriculum/
howisthecurriculumstructured/curriculumareas/index.asp

Northern Ireland

www.nicurriculum.org.uk/foundation_stage

www.nicurriculum.org.uk/key_stages_1_and_2

www.nicurriculum.org.uk/key_stage_3

www.nicurriculum.org.uk/key_stage_4

You may also be interested in ***Religious Education Guidance in English Schools: non-statutory guidance 2010***, available from **www.education.gov.uk/publications**. Select Schools, then Subjects. This publication is aimed at local authorities, schools and education professionals. It aims to support the provision of high-quality religious education (RE) in maintained schools in England. It provides clear, non-statutory guidance about RE in the curriculum and the roles of those who have a responsibility for, involvement with or interest in the subject.

Subject specifications

For **subject specifications and past papers** at GCSE and other levels it is essential to use the correct examination board specifications. It is important for pupils to check this with their teachers and make a note. How to access specifications and past papers for this subject can be found in **Part 3 – Examinations, Assessments and Revision**. Using past papers is an important part of revision so it is worth encouraging pupils to use this valuable resource.

Where to look

*Self, D. (2008) *Lion Encyclopaedia of World Religions*, Lion Hudson
Provides information on world faiths through their origins, festivals, beliefs and the daily life of their followers. It covers the six major religions (Judaism, Christianity, Islam, Hinduism, Buddhism, Sikhism) as well as East Asian and modern religions.

Usborne Book of World Religions, **Usborne, 2005**

Usborne Encyclopaedia of World Religions*, **Usborne, 2010
Covers the beliefs, history and customs of the world's major religions as well as lesser-known faiths. It is internet linked.

Websites

General

BBC Schools Religion
www.bbc.co.uk/schools/religion
This covers the six main religions – Buddhism, Christianity, Hinduism,

Islam, Judaism and Sikhism – providing facts, links, worksheets and the dates of the main festivals. Excellent.

CLEO (Cumbria and Lancashire Education Online)
www.cleo.net.uk

This provides online resources for use in school and at home as well as giving support to teachers. It has a wide range of resources, but quality-wise they are a mixed bag. However, some are excellent, so it is worth trying. Select RE, then the relevant Key Stage.

People of Faith
http://pof.reonline.org.uk

This explores Buddhism, Christianity, Hinduism, Islam, Judaism and Sikhism from the viewpoint of individual believers.

Primary School Teaching Ideas
www.teachingideas.co.uk

Select RE for loads of activities and lesson plans. Excellent.

RE Online
http://ks3.reonline.org.uk

A fantastic site for KS3, packed with resources. Choose the religion and the theme you are studying from the drop-down lists or search by keyword. Excellent.

Religion Curriculum Resources
www.cleo.net.uk

Select Key Stage, then RE. This has some fantastic online resources for all aspects of the six main religions, designed to be Key Stage-appropriate. Well worth a visit.

Religion for Schools
www.world-faiths.com

Aimed at KS3 and KS4 pupils and covers the six main religions as well as Philosophy and Ethics. It has teachers' resources and projects for Years 8 and 9 as well as a short course for GCSE students to test their knowledge and understanding of what they are expected to know for GCSE. Excellent.

Sacred Texts
www.bl.uk/learning/citizenship/sacred/sacredintro.html

An interactive site to promote the understanding of 12 stories from six different religions. Each has been animated using images from the British Library's collection.

The websites above are excellent, and between them cover practically all you need for the RE curriculum, but some of the websites provided by individual religions may offer some further information and sources to consider.

Buddhism

Questions and Answers on Buddhism
www.buddhanet.net
This covers the Buddhist scriptures, rebirth, vegetarianism, meditation etc.

Tour of a Buddhist Monastery
www.thegrid.org.uk/learning/re/virtual/buddhisttrail/index.shtml
A set of photos showing a Buddhist monastery.

Christianity

Educhurch
www.educhurch.org.uk
This compares three different Christian churches and is a resource for schools.

Online Bible
www.biblegateway.com/passage/?search
This enables searching of the whole Bible by chapter, passage, keyword or topic. Also has different versions of the text to choose from.

Re:Quest
www.request.org.uk
This is described as a toolkit for teaching about Christianity in RE; however, it is equally useful to pupils for homework and projects. It has materials for KS1 to KS4, including video and whiteboard presentations. The teachers' resources include a photo resource centre, which is great for projects.

Hinduism

Hinduism for Schools
www.hinduism.fsnet.co.uk
This is well presented, with sections for KS1 and for KS2–3 which are further divided, making this a great site for school projects and learning. There are also a glossary, dates of festivals and prayers.

Islam

Islam Newsround Special
http://news.bbc.co.uk/cbbcnews/hi/specials/2005/islam

A guide to Islam, covering faith, being a Muslim, reports, discussions and interviews with Muslim children. Excellent.

Pilgrimage to Mecca – Hajj

www.channel4.com/life/microsites/H/hajj

Watch the episodes of *Hajj: The Greatest Trip on Earth.*

Judaism

The Jewish Connection

www.spirit-staffs.co.uk/synagogue/index1.htm

Questions on the Jewish faith are answered by four Jewish people at a synagogue. This is useful, to hear real people talking about their religion.

Jewish Festivals

www.ort.org/ort/edu/festivals/index.html

This gives a list of Jewish festivals, and information and some pictures for each.

Sikhism

Sikh Ceremonies and Festivals

www.sikhs.org/fest.htm

Sikhism for Children

www.atschool.eduweb.co.uk/carolrb/sikhism/sikhism1.html

Provides information on Sikhism divided by themes such as history, the five Ks, family life, symbols etc., all aimed at primary schools.

Sikh Temple Photos

www.thegrid.org.uk/learning/re/virtual/sikh/index.shtml

SCIENCE

See also: **Part 1, Section 3 – Space, Astronomy and the Solar System**

Typical questions

- Have you got a book of science experiments?
- What is the symbol for …?
- How does the heart work?
- I need a diagram of a nerve cell.

Considerations

Science for KS3 and GCSE covers Physics, Chemistry and Biology. For younger children, i.e. those in KS1 and KS2, the generic term 'science' is used to explore all of the above. All pupils will take Science for GCSE, with some pupils opting to do Extra Science as a separate GCSE. Science in itself is a huge subject, but fortunately it is well covered through both books and websites. It is certainly worth making sure that you understand what the enquirer needs and the level required.

Programme of study

To find out exactly what is studied at each level use the **programme of study** within the curriculum. These are slightly different for each of the four countries of the United Kingdom. However, there are excellent guidelines given on the web pages listed below and these are well worth consulting to understand exactly what your child will be doing in class.

England

http://curriculum.qcda.gov.uk/key-stages-1-and-2/subjects/index.aspx
http://curriculum.qcda.gov.uk/key-stages-3-and-4/subjects/index.aspx

Wales

http://wales.gov.uk/topics/educationandskills/schoolshome/
curriculuminwales/arevisedcurriculumforwales/nationalcurriculum/
?lang=en

Scotland

www.ltscotland.org.uk/understandingthecurriculum/
howisthecurriculumstructured/curriculumareas/index.asp

Northern Ireland

www.nicurriculum.org.uk/foundation_stage
www.nicurriculum.org.uk/key_stages_1_and_2
www.nicurriculum.org.uk/key_stage_3
www.nicurriculum.org.uk/key_stage_4

Subject specifications

For **subject specifications and past papers** at GCSE and other levels it is essential to use the correct examination board specifications. It is important for pupils to check this with their teachers and make a note. How to access specifications and past papers for this subject can be found in **Part 3 – Examinations, Assessments and Revision**. Using past papers is an important part of revision, so it is worth encouraging pupils to use this valuable resource.

Where to look

General

*The Kingfisher Science Encyclopaedia, 2 vols, **Kingfisher Books, 2011**
   Arranged by themes: planet Earth; living things; human biology; chemistry and the elements; materials and technology; light and energy; forces and movement; electricity and electronics; space and time; and conservation and the environment. The text is complemented by the illustrations and photographs.

*Rogers, K. et al. (2009) *The Usborne Science Encyclopaedia*, **Usborne**
   Covers Physics, Chemistry, Biology as well as new fields such as Genetics. It has revision questions; units of measurement including measuring nature; science laws and symbols; Earth and space facts; a list of scientists and inventors and an extensive A–Z of scientific terms. Highly recommended.

*The Usborne Illustrated Dictionary of Biology, **Usborne**

*The Usborne Illustrated Dictionary of Physics, **Usborne**

*The Usborne Illustrated Dictionary of Chemistry, **Usborne**

*The Usborne Illustrated Dictionary of Science, **Usborne**
   Well presented, clear information, ideal for revision and understanding the subject.

Watts, C. (2009) *The Most Explosive Science Book in the Universe by the Brainwaves*, **Dorling Kindersley**
   Have lots of fun with the Brainwave characters discovering what science is all about.

Try also:

*Horrible Science series by Nick Arnold, Scholastic
Described as 'real science with the squishy bits left in'. They are lots of fun, with real facts. Titles include *Really Rotten Experiments, The Horrible Science of You, Bulging Brains* and *Sick! From measley medicine to savage surgery.* **www.horrible-science.co.uk**

For a colourful and clear introduction to science use:

Green, D. et al. (2008) *Biology: life as we know it*, Kingfisher

Green, D. and Basher, S. (2010) *Chemistry: getting a big reaction*, Kingfisher

Green, D. and Basher, S. (2008) *Physics: why matter matters*, Kingfisher

Science experiments

There are lots of books on doing science experiments at home. It is worth looking to see what is available in the library. Try:

Arnold, N. (2007) *Freaky Food Experiments*, Scholastic

Bingham, J. (2006) *The Usborne Book of Science Experiments*, Usborne

***Robert Winston's Science Experiments*, Dorling Kindersley, 2011**

Websites

BBC GCSE Science: Bitesize
www.bbc.co.uk/schools/gcsebitesize/science
The topics are arranged by examination board, so it is essential that you know which course and exam you are following. Also covers Additional Science, and available for Scottish Standard Grade.

BBC KS2 Science: Bitesize
www.bbc.co.uk/schools/ks2bitesize/science
Covers living things and materials.

BBC KS3 Science: Bitesize
www.bbc.co.uk/schools/ks3bitesize/science
This covers organisms; behaviour and health; chemical and material behaviour; energy; electricity and forces; the environment; the Earth and the universe. For each there are revision notes, and activity and a test.

CLEO (Cumbria and Lancashire Education Online)
www.cleo.net.uk

This provides online resources for use in school and at home as well as giving support to teachers. It has a wide range of resources, but quality-wise they are a mixed bag. However, some are excellent, so it is worth trying. Select Science, then the relevant Key Stage.

Fact Monster
www.factmonster.com

Click on Science for Biology, Chemistry and Physics.

Homework High: Science
www.channel4learning.com/apps/homeworkhigh/science/index.jsp

Enables children to ask questions by keyword or specific queries. It has heaps of previously answered questions to view on a vast number of science topics.

National Maritime Museum
www.nmm.ac.uk

This has a fantastic set of interactive resources searchable by Key Stage (starting from early years up to and beyond KS4), curriculum subject, e.g. science, and by theme. Excellent.

People and Discoveries
www.pbs.org/wgbh/aso/databank/bioindex.html

This gives a list of scientists from the last century. Click on the scientist's name for information about them and to find further activities linked to their work and discoveries. Well worth a visit.

Planet Science
www.planet-science.com

This has sections for Under 11s, Over 11s and Parents/Teachers. The presentation is amazingly visual and provides information on different science subjects, with videos to support. Planet Science supports the curriculum, pupils and teachers, not by going over the same ground, but by its mission to 'tickle your curiosity, excite your interest and unleash your passion for science'. I think it will succeed!

Primary School Teaching Ideas
www.teachingideas.co.uk

Select Science for loads of activities and lesson plans. Excellent.

School Science
www.schoolscience.co.uk

This has over 700 science online learning resources, divided by age group. It is packed with activities and free downloads both for school and for home use. Further links can be found using Science Link. Excellent.

Science for KS1 and KS2
http://lgfl.skoool.co.uk/primary_science.aspx
These are excellent interactive science lessons covering energy and forces; environmental awareness and care; living things and materials.

Science Links
www.moorlandschool.co.uk/earth/link.htm
Select links for science websites, divided by Physics, Biology and Chemistry.

Science Museum
www.sciencemuseum.org.uk/educators/classroom_and_homework_resources
This has some classroom resources by Key Stages covering climate science, electricity and magnetism, materials, light and genetics, amongst others.

SciNet
www.nelsonthornes.com/secondary/science/scinet/scinet/index.htm
This is a great site for basic information on science topics such as reactions, elements, electricity, light, plants and the body. Well organized and presented. Suitable for KS3.

Smithsonian Education
www.smithsonianeducation.org/educators/index.html
Select Science and Technology. This gives lesson plans that can be downloaded and has a search facility to access 2000 resources. Bear in mind that it is an American site.

Biology/Life sciences

ARKive
www.arkive.org
Films and photographs on wildlife and endangered species from around the world. This is a vast website promoting an understanding of the world's biodiversity.

BBC Human Body
www.bbc.co.uk/science/humanbody
Resources and games covering the human body, such as muscles, skeleton, the nervous system etc.

Biology for KS3 and KS4
http://lgfl.skoool.co.uk/index.aspx
Select KS3 or KS4, then Biology, choose from Cells and cell functions; Humans as organisms; Green plants as organisms; Living things in the environment, then select specific topics within these categories. This provides excellent animated online lessons.

Brain Exploration
www.pbs.org/wgbh/aso/tryit/brain
An exploration of the brain; activity based on Wilder Penfield's mapping of the brain's motor cortex.

DNA Workshop
www.pbs.org/wgbh/aso/tryit/dna
An activity that allows you to have a go at DNA replication and protein synthesis.

Education Index
www.educationindex.com/biology
A gateway to loads of Biology/Life sciences sites, selected for their educational resources for children and young people.

How the Body Works: Movies
http://kidshealth.org/kid/htbw/htbw_main_page.html
These are animated films to show how the body works. They range from the heart and circulatory system to the urinary system. The site also includes quizzes, articles and activities. Well worth a visit.

Inner Body
www.innerbody.com/htm/body.html
This is Human Anatomy Online. Click on one of the anatomy figures to find anatomical information from the skeletal to cardiovascular. Suitable for GCSE level.

Natural History Museum
www.nhm.ac.uk
Packed with information using Nature Online as well as resources from Education. Select Teachers' Resource and search by topic.

Radar's Biology4Kids
www.biology4kids.com
A fantastic site offering information, diagrams and images on cells, micro-organisms, plants, invertebrates, vertebrates and animal systems.

Spolem

www.spolem.co.uk

Although this site covers the three science disciplines, its strength lies with biology. Click on KS2 to view a list of headings Biology – Ecology and Environment; Biology – Human Body; Biology – Life Cycles; Biology – Plants. The subjects for KS3 are biology, cells, heart and circulation, microbiology, nutrition and the skeleton and more. For each it has a list of websites that cover the subject. Well worth a visit.

WWF

www.panda.org

Useful for topics such as natural habitats and biodiversity.

Chemistry

Association of the British Pharmaceutical Industry

http://abpischools.org.uk/page/resource/age/subject.cfm

This provides a huge number of resources for schools and children. The list of topics is extensive, and age suitability is indicated alongside each subject. For teachers there is a vast amount of material, including Curriculum Links, which actually link by country, i.e. England, Wales, Scotland and Northern Ireland, and within these by Key Stages. Excellent.

Atom Builder

www.pbs.org/wgbh/aso/tryit/dna

An activity to have a go at constructing a carbon atom.

Creative Chemistry

www.creative-chemistry.org.uk

Suitable for pupils and schools. It is packed with worksheets, teaching notes and fun activities as well as GCSE information and questions. There are some great chemistry crosswords and puzzles. Excellent.

Chemistry for KS3 and KS4

http://lgfl.skoool.co.uk/index.aspx

Select KS3 or KS4, then Chemistry, choose from Classifying Materials or Patterns of Behaviour, then select specific topics within these categories.

Radar's Chem4Kids!

www.chem4kids.com

A fantastic site offering information, diagrams and images on matter, atoms, elements, reactions and biochemistry. It also has under Et Cetera information on symbols, constants and units. Excellent.

Royal Society of Chemistry
www.rsc.org

Click on Education, then Primary School Resources. Includes free downloads of selected sections of the book *That's Chemistry!* For further resources click on Teaching Resources, then Online Chemistry Resources for Year 7 onwards. It includes the Periodic Table and Spectroscopy in a Suitcase.

Periodic table

For a free copy of a folder-size periodic table produced in association with ABPI contact the Royal Society of Chemistry, Education Department, Thomas Graham House, Science Park, Milton Road, Cambridge, CB4 0WF, Tel: 01223 432221; or download it from **www.rsc.org/Education/Teachers/Resources/PeriodicTable.asp**

Interactive Periodic Table
www.factmonster.com

Click on Science, then Interactive Periodic Table.

WebElements: the periodic table on the web
www.webelements.com

As well as the periodic table, this gives information on the chemical elements. Click on an element for everything you need to know about it. Excellent.

Physics

Davies, K. *What's Physics All About?*, Usborne

A compact book to understand the various topics of physics, force, energy, electricity and space.

Websites

British Gas Generation Green
www.generationgreen.co.uk/school/british-gas-school

Provides a vast number of lesson plans, organized by age groups. They include electricity, alternative energy, the power of the sun, wind and global warming. Also has suggestions for activities.

Building Big
www.pbs.org/wgbh/buildingbig/lab/forces.html

Explore the physics behind large structures. The interactive labs demonstrate the science behind forces, materials, loads and shapes. Also find out detailed information on some big structures: bridges, domes, skyscrapers, dams and tunnels. Well worth a visit.

Electricity

www.thetech.org/exhibits/online/topics/topics.html

Covers heat, light and motion; circuits; conductors and insulators.

Electricity and Magnetism

http://ippex.pppl.gov/interactive/electricity

Energy Resources

www.darvill.clara.net/altenerg/index.htm

Covers fossil fuels, nuclear power, solar power, wind, tidal and hydroelectric power, amongst others. It includes quizzes, worksheets and exam-style questions, listed under Stuff To Do.

Fear of Physics

www.fearofphysics.com

Provides some useful information to explain Physics.

NASA

www.nasa.gov/audience/forstudents

Select an age group from For Students. This has a vast amount of information on aeronautics and space and climate change, to name but a few. Also has a similar For Educators section.

Physics Central

www.physicscentral.com

Physics in Action gives detailed information by topics that include electricity and magnetism and light and optics, amongst others. It also has a fascinating gallery of physics in pictures.

Physics Classroom

www.physicsclassroom.com

Packed with information via the Physics Classroom Topics. Also has Teacher Tools.

Physics for KS3 and KS4

http://lgfl.skoool.co.uk/index.aspx

Select KS3 or KS4, then Physics, choose from Electricity and Magnetism; Forces and Motion; Light and Sound; The Earth and beyond, then select specific topics within these categories.

Physics 2000

www.colorado.edu/physics/2000/index.pl

This is an interactive journey through modern physics.

Zephyrus Physics

www.zephyrus.co.uk/welcometophysics.html

Covers magnetism, electricity, light, sound, energy, forces, matter and the solar system. This has very basic information but the worksheets and revision exercises make it a useful test of knowledge.

Science fun and games

Many of the websites above also include games that relate to science.

Science Puzzles

http://puzzling.caret.cam.ac.uk

WELSH AND GAELIC

Typical questions

- What is the Welsh for . . . ?
- What is the Gaelic for . . . ?

Considerations

These are subjects that libraries in Wales and Northern Ireland may find themselves answering. If you are not a Welsh or Gaelic speaker this may be difficult, but no more so than any enquiry dealing with a foreign language. It would be sensible to find out how many schools in your area teach Welsh or Irish and to discuss with them the type of resources your library could provide to complement their teaching. At the very least a set of good dictionaries and grammar texts would be useful. As mentioned in **Part 2 – Modern Foreign Languages (MFL)**, it may be useful to have story books in Welsh and Irish to further support the use of Welsh and Irish in the home and thus keep both languages vital in their communities and countries.

Programme of study

To find out exactly what is studied at each level use the **programme of study** within the curriculum. These are slightly different for each of the four countries of the United Kingdom. However, there are excellent guidelines given on the web pages listed below and these are well worth consulting to understand exactly what your child will be doing in class.

Wales
> http://wales.gov.uk/topics/educationandskills/schoolshome/
> curriculuminwales/arevisedcurriculumforwales/nationalcurriculum/
> ?lang=en

Scotland
> www.ltscotland.org.uk/understandingthecurriculum/
> howisthecurriculumstructured/curriculumareas/index.asp

Northern Ireland
> www.nicurriculum.org.uk/foundation_stage
> www.nicurriculum.org.uk/key_stages_1_and_2
> www.nicurriculum.org.uk/key_stage_3
> www.nicurriculum.org.uk/key_stage_4

Subject specifications

For **subject specifications and past papers** at GCSE and other levels it is essential to use the correct examination board specifications. It is important for pupils to check this with their teachers and make a note. How to access specifications and past papers for this subject can be found in **Part 3 – Examinations, Assessments and Revision**. Using past papers is an important part of revision, so it is worth encouraging pupils to use this valuable resource.

Where to look

Dictionaries

Irish

Buntús Foclóra: a children's Irish picture dictionary, Gill and Macmillan, 2004

Collins Gem Irish School Dictionary, 2004, Collins

Collins Very First Irish Dictionary, 2010, Collins

Welsh

Convery, A. (2006) *Collins Welsh Dictionary*, Collins

Online Welsh Dictionary
www.geiriadur.net
From the University of Wales, Trinity Saint David.

Welsh Dictionary
www.bbc.co.uk/cgi-bin/wales/learnwelsh/welsh_dictionary.pl

Learning and revision

Irish

BBC GCSE Irish: Bitesize
www.bbc.co.uk/schools/gcsebitesize/irish
Revise listening, reading, speaking and writing. Very worthwhile, allowing you to test what you know.

Gaelic Learners
www.ltscotland.org.uk/learningteachingandassessment/
curriculumareas/languages/gaelic/index.asp

Gaelic Resource Bank
http://gaidhlig.ltscotland.org.uk

Irish Curriculum
www.nicurriculum.org.uk/irish_medium/useful_links

Wilkes, A. and Shacknell, J. (2001) *Irish for Beginners*, Usborne Publishing

Welsh

BBC GCSE Welsh: Bitesize
www.bbc.co.uk/schools/gcsebitesize/welshsecondlanguage
Revise conversation. Very worthwhile, allowing you to test what you know.

Learn Welsh
www.bbc.co.uk/wales/learning/learnwelsh

Sut!
http://sut.languageskills.co.uk/index.html
Interactive activities for Welsh. Select either Beginner Year 7–9; Intermediate Year 10–11; Advanced Year 12–13. If you use the site between 9am and 4pm weekdays there is a subscription. The rest of the time it is free!

Wilkes, A. and Shacknell, J. (2001) *Welsh for Beginners*, 2nd revised edition, Usborne Publishing

Part 3

School and Home Life: Issues and Concerns

ALCOHOL AND ALCOHOLISM

See also: **Part 2 – PSHE**

Typical questions
- How many young people drink in the UK?
- What effects does alcohol have on the body?
- What are 'alcopops'?
- What is the legal age to drink alcohol?

Considerations
This can be an emotive issue, so tread carefully when dealing with enquiries. Many will be for school topics, but occasionally the enquiry could be from a concerned parent. Some excellent websites are given below and most libraries will have a fairly good collection of books on the subject. As with many subjects that affect teenage health and lifestyle, you may find that you need to venture out of the children's library and into the general non-fiction collection. Also look at the suggestions in **Part 2 – PSHE**.

Where to look
Bremner, P. et al. (June 2011) *Young People, Alcohol and Influences*, report from the Joseph Rowntree Foundation
Available to download either as a summary or as a full report, **www.jrf.org.uk/publications/young-people-alcohol-and-influences**

Other related reports are available too, including:

Percy, A. et al. (2011) *Teenage Drinking Cultures* and Eadie, D. et al. (2010) *Pre-teens Learning about Alcohol: drinking and family contexts*

Lynett, R. (2009) *Alcohol*, Heinemann, The Real Deal series

Ridley, S. (2010) *Alcohol*, Franklin Watts, How Can I Be Healthy series

Your Kids and Alcohol
This offers parents facts and advice on the best ways to approach their children on the subject of alcohol and alcohol consumption. It outlines government guidelines and provides useful contacts for parents who believe that their child may have problems resulting from alcohol abuse. Available to download from **www.education.gov.uk/publications**, Select Children and Families, then Health and Disabilities.

Websites

Alcoholics Anonymous
PO Box 1
10 Toft Green
York Y01 7ND
Helpline: 0845 769 7555
www.alcoholics-anonymous.org.uk
Click on Message for Young People.

Child and Youth Health
www.cyh.com
Select Teen Health for 12–17, then Drugs and alcohol. Bear in mind that this is an Australian site. Well worth a visit.

Drinkaware
www.drinkaware.co.uk
Click on Talking to under 18s from the top menu. Select either Professionals or Parents. Under Professionals you will find factsheets for under-18s available to download and research reports. Under Parents you will find information on the law on alcohol, talking to your child about alcohol, advice and much more. Well worth a visit.

National Association for Children of Alcoholics
Helpline: 0800 358 3456
www.nacoa.org.uk
Provides information, advice and support for children affected by their parents' drinking.

Portman Group
www.portman-group.org.uk
The Portman group works with alcohol producers to raise standards of alcohol marketing and to challenge companies to be socially responsible. Click on Alcohol Information for some excellent factsheets, especially Alcohol and Young People.

Youthhealthtalk
www.youthhealthtalk.org/young_people_drugs_and_alcohol
This has interviews with 33 young people about their experiences of and opinions on recreational drugs and alcohol. It looks at the issues surrounding why young people use alcohol and drugs and examines British culture and society. This is very useful for discussions and also for making informed choices. There is a list of websites and organizations to use for further help and information.

BEREAVEMENT

Typical questions

- Have you got any books on coping with death?
- Are there any organizations that give support to children who have suffered bereavement?

Considerations

This is a probably the most painful of all subjects for children and parents to address but it is certainly a subject that should be talked about. Even if you don't find that you get many queries on dealing with bereavement, it is certainly an area where our library shelves should reflect the importance of helping children to cope emotionally with death and dying. For this reason I would advocate all libraries looking at the reading lists offered by **Winston's Wish, www. winstonswish.org.uk** and checking that they have some if not all of the titles in stock. The list includes story, picture and information books such as **Michael Rosen's** *The Sad Book* (2004) **Walker Books**.

Also worth looking at are:

Good Books for Tough Times: books for children aged 5–8 (2011) **Partnership for Children**

Good Books for Tough Times: books for children aged 9–12 (2011) **Partnership for Children**

These are excellent publications with a foreword from Michael Morpurgo, who suggests during difficult times that 'reading is probably the best therapy there is, other than talking to mum or dad'. They give suggestions of young fiction to read that covers different situations, including bereavement. I would suggest that many of the titles are suitable beyond age 12. Highly recommended, and available to download from **www.partnershipforchildren.org.uk**.

Where to look

Krasny Brown, L. (1998) *When Dinosaurs Die: a guide to understanding death*, **LB-Kids**
Explains in simple language the feelings people may have when someone dies.

Out of the Blue: making memories last when someone has died
Written and designed to support teenagers through bereavement, using a range of activities. Available from **www.winstonswish.org.uk**.

Winston's Wish and Crossley, D. (2010) *Muddles, Puddles and Sunshine: your activity book to help when someone has died,* **Hawthorn Press**
This has practical and sensitive support for bereaved children. It includes guidelines for adults.

CBBC Newsround – Gone: children coping with death
http://news.bbc.co.uk/newsround/14394831

When a pet dies try:

Edwards, N. (2005) *Saying Goodbye to a Pet,* **Chrysalis Children's Books**

Websites and organizations

Bereavment
www.partnershipforchildren.org.uk/resources.html
Select Bereavement for information, advice and links.

Childhood Bereavement Network
www.childhoodbereavementnetwork.org.uk
To find local organizations dealing with bereavement.

Winston's Wish
4th floor
St James House
St James Square
Cheltenham
Glouestershire
GL50 3PR
Helpline: 08452 03 04 05
www.winstonswish.org.uk
A charity for bereaved children, young people and their families in the UK. It provides information and downloadable lesson plans for schools on how to deal with bereaved children. For parents it has information and downloads on every aspect of bereavement. It has an excellent suggested reading list, which I would recommend to anyone having to deal with a bereaved child – select from the menu. There is also another useful reading list in the parents section. Links to other organizations are available.

BULLYING

See also: **Part 2 – PSHE**

Typical questions

- How can I stop my child being bullied?
- What is bullying?

Considerations

Bullying is a major and growing problem, particularly in schools. Bullying affects children in both primary and secondary schools. It is usually peer led, with the victim being either physically or mentally hurt repeatedly over a long period of time. For this reason, this is a particularly sensitive issue to deal with. It is useful to have details of local organizations that could talk to either the victim or the parents of the victim. Some of the online websites offer advice and suggestions for further help. The **Department for Education, www.education.gov.uk/ popularquestions/schools/Attendanceanddiscipline/bullying** recommends Childline (see below) and also answers other recurring questions about bullying. There are also numerous books on the subject similar to the ones suggested below. Victims of bullying, probably more than anything, want someone to help them stop the problem. However, on this occasion, it can't be you, but hopefully, you can give them reassurance that there are people who can and will help them.

Bullying is also one of the issues covered by the PSHE curriculum, so you may get queries about it as an anti-social behaviour activity. Again, the websites below should be sufficient.

Where to look

Amos, J. (2006) *Bully*, Evans Publishing, Good Bad series
This title consists of three stories, through which children will be able to identify with the characters. It tells the stories of Michael, Sharon and Li as each child experiences what it is like to be a bully. This series supports the curriculum for PSHE.

Edwards, N. (2005) *Talking about Bullying*, Chrysalis Children's Books
Aimed at younger children, using simple language to give information and support.

Sullivan, K. (2000) *The Anti-bullying Handbook*, Oxford University Press

Fiction for older children:

Brooks, Kevin (2005) *Kissing the Rain*, Chicken House Publishing

Also worth looking at are:

***Good Books for Tough Times: books for children aged 5–8* (2011) Partnership for Children**

***Good Books for Tough Times: books for children aged 9–12* (2011) Partnership for Children**
These are excellent publications with a foreword from Michael Morpurgo, who suggests during difficult times that 'reading is probably the best therapy there is, other than talking to mum or dad'. They give suggestions of young fiction to read covering different situations, including bullying. I would suggest many of the titles are suitable beyond age 12. Highly recommended. Available to download from **www.partnershipforchildren.org.uk**.

Websites
Anti-Bullying Network
www.antibullying.net
Provides information on all forms of bullying and has available for parents, teachers and young people information sheets that cover types of bullying, how to prevent bullying, the law and bullying and lots more.

Bully Free Zone
www.bullyfreezone.co.uk

Bullying: a guide for young people
www.autism.org.uk/living-with-autism/education/bullying-guide-for-young-people.aspx
Information for young people with autism or Asperger's Syndrome on how to deal with bullying. It explains what bullying is, what to do if you are bullied and how to get support.

Bullying
www.bbc.co.uk/schools/studentlife/schoolissues
Offers guidance on dealing with bullying.

Bullying
www.partnershipforchildren.org.uk/resources.html
Select Bullying for information, advice and links.

Bullying UK

www.bullying.co.uk

This has three sections: Young People's Advice; Advice for Parents; and Guidance for Schools. It covers all forms of bullying, giving information, advice and tips to combat bullying. It provides contacts for lots of organizations that deal with bullying and there is a free helpline, tel: 0808 800 222.

Childline

Helpline: 0800 1111

www.childline.org.uk

This service is provided by NSPCC, Weston House, 42 Curtain Road, London, EC2A 3NH. The helpline service provides confidential advice and someone to talk to. The website deals with bullying.

Family Lives

CAN Mezzanine

49-51 East Road

Old Street

London N1 6AH

United Kingdom

Tel: 0808 800 2222

http://www.familylives.org.uk/

Radio 1 Advice

www.bbc.co.uk/radio1/advice

Provides advice on a wide range of issues and concerns, including bullying. There are further subheadings of information and contacts for further help. However, a word of caution: the strong content of some of the material on some issues means that it is suitable for KS4 children – and for younger children only with adult guidance.

Tips and pitfalls

This a very sensitive area, and tempting as it is to offer advice and a shoulder to cry on, it is definitely one for the relevant professionals. Suggest to parents that they initially take the matter up with their child's school to seek ways to resolve the situation together. They can also call the **Family Lives** (formerly Parentline Plus) helpline (see above) for advice and guidance.

If you do find yourself dealing with a distressed child, then tread carefully and offer suggestions for where to get help, including that they should talk to their teacher, parents or older brother or sister.

DRUGS AND SMOKING

See also: **Part 2 – PSHE**

Typical questions

- What are the names of different drugs?
- What are the effects of smoking?
- Do you know how many young people smoke?
- What is 'weed'?

Considerations

This is a topic covered in most schools, especially under the PSHE curriculum. You will probably have a good collection of books on drugs, tobacco and smoking available in your library, most of which have been very well researched and present information for children and young people. There are a few suggestions below, but these are by no means the only ones. You may also find that you are asked for information by parents, either for personal family reasons or for school. Many of the books will be suitable, but you may also suggest some of the websites below, which are aimed at children and young people and their carers.

The publication *Drugs: guidance for schools* provides guidance on 'all matters relating to drug education, the management of drugs within the school community, supporting the needs of pupils with regard to drugs and drug policy developments'. It is free to download from **www.education.gov.uk/publications** and would be useful to parents as well as schools.

In addition, it should also be mentioned that drugs is not only about illegal drugs but also about prescribed drugs (medicines). For those checking a prescribed drug, look at *British National Formulary for Children*, **British Medical Association and Royal Pharmaceutical Society of Great Britain**. This has information on the safe and effective use of medicines to treat childhood disorders, covering from the new-born to adolescents.

Where to look

Drugs

Deboo, A. (2008) *Tough Topics: drugs*, **Heinemann**

Elliot-Wright, S. (2009) *Heroin*, **Wayland**

Emmett, D. and Nice, G. (2007) *Getting Wise to Drugs: a resource for teaching children about drugs, dangerous substances and other risky situations*, **Jessica Kingsley Publishers**
This is for use with children aged from 8 to 12 years.

Emmett, D. and Nice, G. (2005) *Understanding Street Drugs: a handbook of substance misuse for parents, teachers and other professionals*, 2nd edition, Jessica Kingsley Publishers

Rooney, A. (2010) *Dealing with Drugs*, Evans Publishing

Understanding drugs
This is a pack of resources for KS3 teachers. It aims to help promote awareness and understanding of drugs. The pack contains a teacher's guide, a teacher's booklet and a sample copy of the pupil booklet. It is an excellent set of resources that would be useful to parents too. Available to freely download from **www.education.gov.uk/publications**. Select Youth and Adolescence, then Alcohol, drugs and substance abuse.

Vogt, F. (2002) *Addiction's Many Faces: tackling drug dependency amongst young people: causes, effects and prevention*, Hawthorn Press
These are stories from young drug users and their parents that are highly illuminating about why young people use drugs and that offer ways of prevention, coping and treatment.

Fiction for older children:

Burgess, M. (2003) *Junk*, Penguin

Websites

ABPI (Association of the British Pharmaceutical Industry): Resources for Schools
www.abpischools.org.uk
Select age range 5–7, 7–11, 11–14, 14–16, then PSHE. For each age group there are different levels of information. For KS2 the information concentrates on medicines and for KS3 there is more on drugs of abuse.

Child and Youth Health
www.cyh.com
Select Teen Health for 12–17, then drugs and alcohol. Bear in mind that this is an Australian site. Well worth a visit.

Childline
Helpline: 0800 1111
www.childline.org.uk
This service is provided by NSPCC, Weston House, 42 Curtain Road, London, EC2A 3NH. The helpline service provides confidential advice and someone to talk to. The website covers drugs and smoking.

D World

www.drugscope-dworld.org.uk

Excellent site for children, parents and teachers, offering advice, information, the law, reading lists, resources, projects and stories. There is also the DrugScope Information Service (not for counselling), tel: 020 7520 7550.

Drugs

www.direct.gov.uk/en/YoungPeople/HealthAndRelationships/index.htm
Select Drug Problems.

The Drug Education Forum

www.drugeducationforum.org.uk

This is packed with information dealing with drugs education for children and young people. The Forum consists of 31 national organizations concerned with policy and offering the best and most effective research on drug education.

FRANK

www.talktofrank.com

This is designed for young people and has a comprehensive A–Z list of drugs. For each it gives an explanation of what the drug is, slang or street names, the effects, the chances of getting hooked, the law, the appearance and use, the cost, purity and the risks. It is very informative, addressing young people about making informed choices. It also provides a number of options for finding help or just to talk. Highly recommended.

Know Cannabis

www.knowcannabis.org.uk

Know the Score

www.knowthescore.info

An excellent site, packed with information and advice on drugs in Scotland. It has an A–Z list of drugs and a fantastic set of pocket guides on many drugs, available to download freely. Well worth a visit.

Radio 1 Advice

www.bbc.co.uk/radio1/advice

Provides advice on a wide range of issues and concerns, including drink and drugs. For each there are further sub-headings of information and contacts for further help. However, a word of caution: the strong content of some of the material on some issues means that it is suitable for KS4 children – and for younger children only with adult guidance.

Release

www.release.org.uk

Provides a list of drugs, with information on the chemistry, history and risks associated with a drug. Also has a very thorough section on drugs and the law.

Youthhealthtalk

www.youthhealthtalk.org/young_people_drugs_and_alcohol

This has interviews with 33 young people about their experiences of and opinions on recreational drugs and alcohol. It looks at the issues surrounding why young people use alcohol and drugs and examines British culture and society. This is very useful for discussions and also for making informed choices. There is a list of websites and organizations to use for further help and information.

Smoking

Lynette, R. (2009) *Tobacco*, Heinemann, The Real Deal series

Ridley, S. (2010) *Smoking*, Franklin Watts, How Can I Be Healthy series

Websites

Action on Smoking and Health (ASH)

1st Floor

144–145 Shoreditch High St

London E1 6JE

Tel: 0207 739 5902

www.ash.org.uk

This has an excellent set of factsheets available to download. Select Information and Resources. Titles that could be of particular interest include *Smoking Statistics* and *Young people and smoking.*

Kids Against Tobacco Smoke

http://kats.roycastle.org

Designed especially for children, from the Roy Castle Lung Cancer Foundation, The Roy Castle Centre, 4–6 Enterprise Way, Wavetree Technology Park, Liverpool, L13 1FB, tel: 0151 254 7200. Has a section called The Facts which covers smoking statistics; health costs; smoking and the environment; smoking and disease and lots more, all presented in a child-friendly format. It also has a young person's guide to stopping smoking.

Smoking
> **www.direct.gov.uk/en/YoungPeople/HealthAndRelationships/index.htm**
> Select Smoking and Giving Up.

Tips and pitfalls

Always deal with the subject of drugs and smoking seriously and refrain from passing judgement. If it is clear that someone is very distressed about the issue, offer the contact details of one of the organizations above without offering advice yourself. This does not mean that you cannot listen sympathetically for a short amount of time, whilst providing the information a library can offer. You may also have local organizations dealing with these issues, in which case keep contact details up to date and accessible.

ENGLISH AS AN ADDITIONAL LANGUAGE (EAL)

Typical questions

- What does English as an additional language mean?
- How can I help my child with EAL?
- What support is there at school for EAL?

Considerations

This can be a complicated enquiry, not least because English-language skills may be in deficit. However, patience, perseverance and sensitivity should, hopefully, help towards finding information. Your education department should have information and it would be worth finding out who is the contact.

Where to look

Supporting Children Learning English as an Additional Language: guidance for practitioners in the Early Years Foundation Stage 2007
http://nationalstrategies.standards.dcsf.gov.uk/node/84861
Advice and guidance booklet available to download freely.

Websites

English as an additional language
www.education.gov.uk/schools/pupilsupport/inclusionandlearnersupport/eal
The Department for Education has information and links to local authorities that have designed resources to support EAL.

English as an additional language
www.naldic.org.uk
Includes information and documents for Early Years, Primary and Secondary, including subject-specific resources from the National Association for Language Development in the Curriculum, which is the UK subject association for English as an additional language. Very useful.

Guidance for parents of pupils with EAL
www.bbc.co.uk/schools/parents/english_as_additional_language/

E-SAFETY

Typical questions

- How can I safeguard my child on the internet?
- What guidelines are there for the use of the internet in schools?

Considerations

Keeping children safe whilst using the internet is a priority for parents, librarians and teachers. Many of the sites below offer excellent advice and guidance. Our level of understanding of how the internet is used for malicious intent has improved greatly in recent years. To further help parents to know exactly what to look for, the document *Internet Terms and Language: a guide for parents*, www.direct. gov.uk/en/Parents/YourChildshealthandsafety/InternetSafety/DG_182610 will help them to understand the basic terms used when talking about online chatting, potential dangers, scams and viruses. This is an excellent site with further links.

Where to look

Harris, R. H. and Emberley, M. (2010) Helpful – Fun – Creepy – Dangerous: getting information and staying safe on the internet. In *Let's Talk about Sex*, **Walker Books, pp. 83–7.**

Websites

Childline

> **Helpline: 0800 1111**
> **www.childline.org.uk**
> This service is provided by NSPCC, Weston House, 42 Curtain Road, London, EC2A 3NH. The helpline service provides confidential advice and someone to talk to. The website covers computer/online safety.

Childnet International

> **http://childnet-int.org**
> Packed with information. Click on Projects, especially the Know IT All project, which has extensive online resources for parents and schools.

Click Clever Click Safe

> **http://clickcleverclicksafe.direct.gov.uk/index.html**
> This shows the Click Clever Click Safe Code.

E-safety

> **www.ngfl-cymru.org.uk**
> Click on E-safety in Wales from Additional Links.

GetNetWise

www.getnetwise.org

Packed with information on using the internet safely. It is useful for families and schools. It covers internet safety, child-safe search engines, online chat and much more.

Get Safe Online

www.getsafeonline.org.uk

Internet Watch Foundation

www.iwf.org.uk

Safe Surfing for Families

http://uk.docs.yahoo.com/parents_guide

Think U Know

www.thinkuknow.co.uk

An excellent site dealing with internet safety. It is divided by age group, which means that the information is age appropriate. The design is excellent and the information comes from the Child Exploitation and Online Protection Centre, 33 Vauxhall Bridge Road, London, SW1V 2WG, tel: 0870 000 3344. There are fantastic teacher/trainer and parent/carer areas, which should tell you all you need to know and more. Highly recommended.

UK Council for Child Internet Safety (UKCCIS)

www.education.gov.uk/ukccis

This brings together organizations from industry, children's charities and government to work together to make the internet safer for children. Members include Microsoft, BT, Yahoo, CEOP and NSPCC. Go to Frequently Asked Questions (FAQ) for information on child e-safety. Also select the Byron Reviews for the report *Safeguarding Children in a Digital Age* (March 2008) by Dr Tanya Byron and the 2010 progress report *Do We Have Safer Children in a Digital World?*

EXAMINATIONS, ASSESSMENTS AND REVISION

Typical questions

- How do I find past exam papers?
- What syllabus does my course follow?
- Where is the best place to revise?
- How much revision does my child need to do?
- What tests will my child do at primary school?

Considerations

For pupils to know which syllabus they are following it is essential that they know which exam board their school has opted to use. Schools do not necessarily use the same exam board for all subjects, so pupils should not assume that they know. Knowing the syllabus and what needs to be covered within a subject can help with exam stress and anxiety. For pupils who find exams particularly worrying (and who doesn't?), a number of websites offering advice are listed below.

The question of revision guides for exam revision is always an interesting one. They are certainly very popular, especially if the pupil's own notes are somewhat lacking in content, disorganized or non-existent. However, once the revision guides are borrowed they rarely return until after the exam! The question is, how many can you provide?

Where to look

KS2 assessments

National Curriculum Teacher Assessments and Key Stage Tests
www.direct.gov.uk/en/Parents/Schoolslearninganddevelopment/
ExamsTestsAndTheCurriculum/index.html
Select National Curriculum Key Stage Tests.

Examination boards for GCSE

(Use for specifications and past papers)

AQA (Assessment and Qualifications Alliance)
www.aqa.org.uk
For subject specifications, including all changes. It offers past exam papers, and specimen papers when past papers are not available. Select Qualifications, GCSE, then choose from the subject list as follows.

English; ICT; Maths; Science; Business; Arts – Art and Design, Drama, Performing Arts, Music, Dance, Expressive Arts; Technology and HE; P.E.; Languages – Select language; Humanities – Select subject; Citizenship, Geography, History, RE.

CCEA (Council for the Curriculum Examinations and Assessment Northern Ireland)
www.ccea.org.uk

For subject specifications select Qualifications, in the drop-down menu select the type of qualification, then in the second drop-down menu select subject.

Edexcel
www.edexcel.com

On the home page find Qualifications Finder, from the drop-down menu Qualification Family select the qualification e.g. GCSE, then in the second drop-down menu box select subjects. This will give specifications and question papers with mark schemes.

OCR (Oxford Cambridge and RSA Examinations)
www.ocr.org.uk

Select Qualifications; search by type or by subject. Select subject with qualification for specification. For past papers and mark schemes, select View All Documents.

WJEC (Welsh Joint Education Committee)
www.wjec.co.uk

On the home page find Qualifications and Resources. From the drop-down menu By Subject select a subject, from the second drop-down menu By Level select qualification level, e.g. GCSE, then search. This provides specifications and past papers, amongst other related documents.

Revision and exam anxiety

For KS2 revision

BBC: KS2ReviseWise
www.bbc.co.uk/schools/revisewise

Packed full of activities and questions to help prepare for the KS2 national tests in Maths, Science and English.

Revision guides

There are numerous revision guides on the market and a few titles are mentioned below by way of example. They are certainly popular and well worth having on the library shelves; not all children can afford to buy their own. The difficulty is that you can never have enough.

BBC GCSE Bitesize Revision: English, BBC Educational Publishing, 2002

BBC GCSE Bitesize Revision: French, BBC Educational Publishing, 2002

BBC GCSE Bitesize Revision: Geography, BBC Educational Publishing, 2002

BBC GCSE Bitesize Revision: German, BBC Educational Publishing, 1998

BBC GCSE Bitesize Revision: Maths, BBC Educational Publishing, 2002

BBC GCSE Bitesize Revision: Religion, BBC Educational Publishing, 2002

Collins Revision KS3 English, Collins Publishing, 2009

Collins Revision KS3 Maths, Collins Publishing, 2009

Collins Revision KS3 Science, Collins Publishing, 2009

For more titles visit **www.collinseducation.com**.

Letts Revision Guides
www.lettsandlonsdale.com
Visit the website for an extensive range of revision guides and tools, including revision podcasts for use on PCs and MP3 players. If you are considering purchasing revision guides for home, school or library use, it is well worth a visit.

Websites
BBC Bitesize
www.bbc.co.uk/schools/bitesize
Divided into KS1, KS2, KS3 and GCSE. It provides revision, tests and activities in small, 'bitesize' pieces on most subjects covered by the curriculum. It is particularly good for the reluctant reviser. Highly recommended.

Childline
Helpline: 0800 1111
www.childline.org.uk
This service is provided by NSPCC, Weston House, 42 Curtain Road, London, EC2A 3NH. The helpline service provides confidential advice and

someone to talk to. The website provides information on exam anxiety.

Radio 1 Advice
www.bbc.co.uk/radio1/advice
Provides advice on a wide range of issues and concerns including study and work. For each there are further sub-headings of information and contacts for further help. However, a word of caution: the strong content of some of the material on some issues means that it is suitable for KS4 children – and for younger children only with adult guidance.

Tips and pitfalls

Never advise pupils which examination board they may be doing, no matter how much they may pester you. The only advice you should offer is to ask their teacher and for them to keep a note of the name of the exam board. Each exam board has its own specifications and exam papers – therefore it is essential to use the correct ones for revision and course work. It is worth getting to grips with the websites of the various exam boards because this will give you confidence to suggest them to parents and pupils. For parents, knowing the subject specifications can be empowering in their attempts to offer support and help with their child's education.

FOOD AND HEALTHY EATING

See also: **Part 2 – Citizenship; Part 2 – Design and Technology; Part 2 – PSHE; Part 4, Section 1 – Cooking and Baking**

Typical questions

- What is anorexia?
- What age will my child stop having milk at school?
- How do I find out my BMI?

Considerations

Here we are not talking about food in general, but looking at food issues relating to children and young people. This covers queries about school meals, fruit, milk and healthy eating in schools, as well as eating disorders. Many of the programmes for fruit in school, milk to younger children and school meals may be changing; however, to date they remain in place. Some of the websites below should keep parents informed. Queries related to eating disorders, which usually refer to anorexia, bulimia and over-eating, should be handled carefully. The growing interest in obesity and the subsequent possibility of diabetes is another popular topic area. Most of these should also be covered by the PSHE curriculum.

Where to look

Weight and Eating

> **www.teenagehealthfreak.org/topics/weight%20%26%20eating**
> Covers anorexia, bulimia, dieting, healthy eating and more.

Eating disorders

BEAT (Beating Eating Disorders)

> **Helpline: 0845 634 1414**
> **www.b-eat.co.uk**
> Select Publications for information sheets, which are excellent and include titles such as *Puberty and Eating Disorders*. There are reports too. *Something's Got To Change* and *Time To Tell* are worth looking at and all are available to download freely.

Childline

> **Helpline: 0800 1111**
> **www.childline.org.uk**
> This service is provided by NSPCC, Weston House, 42 Curtain Road,

174

London, EC2A 3NH. The helpline service provides confidential advice and someone to talk to. The website covers eating problems.

Radio 1 Advice

www.bbc.co.uk/radio1/advice

Provides advice on a wide range of issues and concerns, including your body and health and well-being. For each there are further sub-headings of information and contacts for further help. However, a word of caution: the strong content of some of the material on some issues means that it is suitable for KS4 children – and for younger children only with adult guidance.

Healthy eating, diet and nutrition

Dicker, K. (2010) *Diet and Nutrition*, **Evans Publishing**

Try:

Body Needs series from Heinemann, which looks at the way our bodies digest and store food and investigates health problems and diseases. Five titles in the series:

Powell, J. (2009) *Fats for a Healthy Body*, **Heinemann**

Powell, J. (2009) *Carbohydrates for a Healthy Body*, **Heinemann**

Powell, J. (2009) *Proteins for a Healthy Body*, **Heinemann**

Powell, J. (2009) *Vitamins and Minerals for a Healthy Body*, **Heinemann**

Powell, J. (2009) *Water and Fibre for a Healthy Body*, **Heinemann**

Websites

Children's Food Campaign

www.sustainweb.org/childrensfoodcampaign

Packed with information for improving young people's health and well-being and on the campaign for school meals. Excellent.

Fiveaday

www.nhs.uk/LiveWell/5ADAY

Includes a portion guide for fruit and vegetables.

Great Grub Club

www.greatgrubclub.com

The healthy eating site for children from the World Cancer Research Fund.

For parents it includes free, downloadable recipe cards and things to do, and for teachers there are KS2 lesson plans and worksheets.

Healthy Eating

www.eatwell.gov.uk

Packed with information on health issues and diet. It has some useful tools for checking BMI.

Nutrition and School Lunches

www.direct.gov.uk/en/Parents/Schoolslearninganddevelopment/ SchoolLife/DG-4016089

Includes information on free school lunches and milk at primary school.

School Food Trust

www.schoolfoodtrust.org.uk

The national charity and specialist adviser to the government on school meals, children's food and related skills. It has loads of information for schools, parents and children on how to eat healthily and provide a healthy diet.

School Fruit and Vegetable Scheme

www.nhs.uk/Livewell/5ADAY/Pages/Schoolscheme.aspx

If your child is aged 4–6 years and attends infant, primary or a special school maintained by the LEA, they are entitled to a free portion of fruit or vegetable each school day.

FURTHER EDUCATION

Typical questions

- Do I have to do a language for GCSE?
- What are the best subjects for a career in nursing?
- Can I drop Maths?
- Where can I study A levels?
- How many GCSEs do I take?
- Is P.E. a GCSE subject?

Considerations

This section is mainly concerned with the choices available for GCSE and equivalent. Choices will be influenced by understanding how GCSE options affect future decisions and courses. The reports mentioned below are useful documents for understanding subject choices. Equally, choices for A level are made during year 11 and these need careful consideration.

Where to look

Department for Education (December 2010) *It's Your Choice 2010–2011*
www.education.gov.uk/publications
Select Youth and Adolescence, then Information, Advice and Guidance. This publication is aimed at Year 10 and 11 students. It provides information about the options available to them, helping them to make decisions relating to their post-16 phase of learning.

Department for Education (December 2010) *Which Way Now? 2010–2011*
www.education.gov.uk/publications
Select Youth and Adolescence, then Information, Advice and Guidance. This publication is aimed at Year 9. It provides information for pupils to assist them with their subject choices and qualifications in Key Stage 4.

Dixon, B. (2009) *Decisions at 15/16+: a guide to all your options*, Lifetime Publishing, Student Helpbook series
Covers all the options for making important choices beyond Year 11.

Vincent, A. (2010) *Choosing Your GCSEs: also includes diplomas, GNVQs, BTECs and other post-14 options*, 11th edition, Trotman

Woodward, G. (2008) *Choosing Your A-levels: and other post-16 options*, 3rd edition, Trotman

Websites

Where are you heading?
http://yp.direct.gov.uk/14-19prospectus
Search for qualifications and courses in your area.

GIFTED AND TALENTED CHILDREN

Typical questions

- How do I know if my child is gifted?
- What does my child do at school if she is gifted and talented?
- Have you got any books to help support my clever child?

Considerations

The main concern for parents is spotting whether they really have got a 'gifted and talented' child and what this means both for the child and for them. To identify gifted children use the checklist from **Mensa** called *Gifted Children: a checklist for parents*, **www.mensa.org.uk** or the more comprehensive factsheets from the **National Association for Gifted Children (NAGC)**, **www.nagcbritain.org.uk** entitled *Is My Young Child Gifted?* and *Characteristics of Gifted Children*. Select both from the NAGC Factsheets menu. Most of the time, queries may be centred on offering more and varied resources for these children. Many of the books in the library are great for giving information beyond that offered in the classroom, as well as offering books on related topics. Equally some of the online resources listed in this book offer further investigation, challenge, revision and information gathering for enquiring minds. Libraries are great places for the gifted and talented!

Where to look

Teare, B. (2007) *Help Your Talented Child: the essential guide for parents*, **Continuum Books**
    This book should be on every parent's bookshelf. For each subject it gives loads of ideas for how to develop and support your gifted child.

Thomson, M. (2006) *Supporting Gifted and Talented Pupils in the Secondary School*, **Paul Chapman Publishing**

Websites

Chemistry for the Gifted and Talented
    www.rsc.org/Education/Teachers/Resources/Books/GiftedandTalented. asp
    There are worksheets to download for the gifted and talented. Select from 11–14 years and 14–16 years.

Try also:

Joliff, T. *Chemistry for the Gifted and Talented,* **Royal Society of Chemistry, 2007.**

Drama – supporting gifted and talented children
www.nationaldrama.org.uk/nd/index.cfm/publications/ps2-drama-supporting-gifted-and-talented-children
Document for teachers supporting gifted and talented children in KS2.

Gifted and Talented
http://webarchive.nationalarchives.gov.uk/20110809091832/
http://teachingandlearningresources.org.uk/whole-school/gifted-and-talented
Provides a huge amount of information taken from the National Strategies website, which closed in March 2011. Following the closure the content has been made available through the UK Government web archive for reference only. The content has been updated to reflect the latest Government policy.

Mensa
www.mensa.org.uk
Select Gifted Children.

National Association for Able Children in Education
The Core Business Centre
Milton Hill
Abingdon
Oxon OX13 6AB
Tel: 01235 828280
www.nace.co.uk
This is an independent educational organization to support teachers in getting the best from their gifted and talented pupils.

National Association for Gifted Children (NAGC)
Suite 1.2
Challenge House
Sherwood Drive
Bletchley
Milton Keynes
Buckinghamshire MK3 6DP
Tel: 01908 646433
www.nagcbritain.org.uk

Membership organization that provides support, help and encouragement for high-ability children. It is excellent for parents, with lots of factsheets, resources, articles and research. There is similar material for schools.

Scottish Network for Able Pupils (SNAP)
www.ablepupils.com

HOME EDUCATION (INCLUDES HOME TUTORS)

Typical questions

- What is home education?
- How do I home-educate my son?
- Are there any local organizations to help with educating at home?
- Have you got a list of home tutors?

Considerations

Many of us do not understand home education or home schooling and many parents believe that it is forbidden by law and that those undertaking home education are flouting the law. So let's clarify that 'education is compulsory, schooling is not', Section 7 of the Education Act 1996, which applies to England and Wales, states:

Compulsory education
7: Duty of parents to secure education of children of compulsory school age
The parent of every child of compulsory school age shall cause him to receive efficient full-time education suitable –

a. to his age, ability and aptitude and

b. to any special educational needs he may have, either by regular attendance at school or otherwise.

Home education is covered under 'education otherwise', Section 7, and ensures that every parent has the right to choose not to send their child into the state schooling system. Taken from Education Otherwise, www.education-otherwise.net. Click on HE and the Law. The legalities of home education (HE) in Scotland and Northern Ireland can be found under HE and the Law, then HE in Scotland or HE in Northern Ireland.

Parents who ask about the options for home education may have personal reasons why they have decided to consider educating at home. For this reason, offer information on where to get help and advice, but without prying into why, unless this information is offered and is obviously relevant to the query. There are some excellent organizations, which are listed below. Equally, there are some useful books that parents may find helpful.

For parents who are already home-educating their child, much of this book will prove useful for providing resources, lesson plans, ideas, information and worksheets. The only question is – which subject and for what age group?

Home tutors

These are tutors or teachers who teach in your home – or the pupil can go to theirs. Lessons are usually for one hour and are charged for.

First Tutors
www.letts-educational.com

Select Home Tutors from the top menu. Search by entering postcode, then subject, age group or level.

Where to look

Dowty, T. and Cowlishaw, K. (eds) (2001) *Home educating Our Autistic Spectrum Children: paths are made by walking*, Jessica Kingsley Publishers

Wilton, D. (2000) *The Kitchen Table Classroom: how to make your home a school*, Detselig Enterprises

This should be on every parent's bookshelf. Packed with practical ideas and activities for learning together within the home environment.

Websites and organizations

Education Otherwise

PO Box 3761

Swindon SN2 9GT

Helpline: 0845 4786345

www.education-otherwise.net

For those considering home education, this is the place to consult. It has an excellent section on home education and the law, covering Scotland and Northern Ireland too. It is a membership site if you want to use the forums etc., but there is lots of information accessible for non-members.

Free Range Education

http://free-range-education.org.uk

Click on Resources, then Practical. There is useful information on legal requirements and questions on home education. There are links to useful organizations.

HEdNI (Home Education in Northern Ireland)

www.hedni.org

The Home Education Network UK (THEN UK)

www.thenuk.com

Legal information on home education in England, Scotland, Northern Ireland and Wales.

Home School Education
www.myhomeschooleducation.com
Provides support for families that home-school. There are some free, downloadable worksheets and activities, but to be honest, this is not a patch on using many of the excellent resources listed under individual subjects in this book. The main reason for including it is the Geography worksheets, which are blank map templates, and the letter worksheets for the alphabet – both listed under Free Stuff, then Free Printables.

Schoolhouse Home Education Association
PO Box 18044
Glenrothes
Fife KY7 9AD
Tel: 01307 463120
www.schoolhouse.org.uk
Supports home education in Scotland.

What is Home Education?
www.bbc.co.uk/schools/parents/home-education
A basic guide to home education.

Tips and pitfalls

Home tutors can be hard to find and often rely on word of mouth. If you do have a local list available or if you are using the Yellow Pages, it is best to provide the contact details but not to recommend, leaving that decision firmly in the hands of the parent.

HOMEWORK

Typical questions

- How much homework should my son have?
- Can you tell me where to get information for my homework?
- What are the guidelines on homework?

Considerations

Many libraries these days offer out-of-hours online resources, available to library members via their library tickets. Essex Libraries (see below) offers dedicated online homework help, as well as access to its impressive online resources. Bradford Libraries offers an equally impressive collection with Enquire, a live question-and-answer service available 24 hours, every day. Titles that would be useful to pupils and are available via that service include Encyclopaedia Britannica Resource; Oxford English Dictionary; INFOTRAC; Oxford Art Online; Oxford Music Online and Oxford Reference Online. It is worth checking what your library has on offer by looking under Libraries on the council's web pages. Many of these online sources are useful for searching homework topics, in addition to offering specialized resources. Homework clubs run in local libraries are becoming popular, enabling out-of-school-hours access to books and the internet, and are often run by professionals from partnership organizations. If your library doesn't have such a service it is worth checking to see if there are any running in your area and, if so, to keep contact details handy and up to date.

Homework guidelines

www.direct.gov.uk/en/Parents
Select Schools, Learning and Development, School Life then Homework: what parents need to know.

Home–school agreements

www.education.gov.uk/schools/pupilsupport/parents/involvement/hsa
Home–school agreements cover, amongst other things, the school's and the parent's respective responsibilities for homework.

Homework support

Getting into Homework, **March 2010**
This provides ideas, solutions and encouragement, specifically around homework support, to enable parents to proactively support their child's learning in the home. Available from **www.education.gov.uk/publications**. Select Children and Families, then Parents, carers and families.

Where to look

Children's Illustrated Encyclopaedia, **Dorling Kindersley, 2010**
With 1000+ links to safe, homework-helpful websites.

Homework Encyclopaedia 5–7 years, **Dorling Kindersley, 2011**

Homework Encyclopaedia 9–11 years, **Dorling Kindersley, 2011**
Linked to the national curriculum, excellent for both homework and school projects.

Seed, A. (2006) *The Best Websites for Homework: recommended websites for key stage 3*, **Hodder Children's Books**
A pocket-book of websites, arranged by subject.

Websites

Essex Homework Helper
www.homework-helper.info
Pupils fill in an online form with their homework question and select CHAT. They are answered online and afterwards a full transcript of their chat session will be delivered to their email address. If the question is too complicated to do straight away, the Homework Helper will get back later. For the times when the Homework Helper service is closed the Online Reference Library is available for use by Essex Libraries members with a library ticket. It has a very impressive menu, including Credo Reference, World Book, Encyclopaedia Britannica, Gale Virtual Reference, Oxford Language Dictionaries and Issues Online, and lots more. These are all available online and are perfect for homework.

Fact Monster
www.factmonster.com
Select Homework Centre, then select from Subjects. It covers History, Geography, Maths, Science and language skills. Remember to bear in mind that this is an American site.

Grid Club
www.gridclub.com
This has over 500 activities linked to the curriculum for children aged 5 to 12. The activities support Maths, Literacy, Science, History, Geography, MFL, the Arts and Health. It is available for school, library and home use. There is an annual subscription fee; however, Tesco Clubcard points are accepted for payment of online subscriptions. Well, every little helps!

Homework Elephant
www.homeworkelephant.co.uk
Offers 5000 selected internet resources to help with homework. Also deals with homework worries.

Homework High
www.channel4learning.com/apps/homeworkhigh
Select from English, Maths, Science, Geography, Languages and History. Suitable for 11- to 16-year-olds either to browse the subjects and previously asked questions and answers or to ask a specific question.

Mrs Mad
www.mrsmad.com
Click on links, then select Homework for further links to some selected homework sites.

Topmarks
www.topmarks.co.uk
Search for sites by subject and/or age groups. There is a parents' area for advice.

Woodlands Homework Help for Primary Kids
www.woodlands-junior.kent.sch.uk/Homework

Presentation

To enhance homework presentation you may want to use some of the graphics and images from these websites.

Discovery Education Clip Art
http://schooldiscovery.com/clipart/index.html
This has over 3000 clip-art images which are organized into categories. It also has information on how to use clip art in documents.

Dorling Kindersley Clip Art
www.clipart.dk.co.uk
Provides thousands of images from the DK picture library. It enables you to browse by A–Z images or by school subject. It also provides help on how to use clip art in school projects. Excellent.

Freefoto
www.freefoto.com/index.jsp
If you need a photo to enhance a piece of school work or anything else that

is non-commercial, then this collection of 132,000 free photos is for you. The photos are organized into over 3600 categories. Very useful.

Tips and pitfalls

Just about everything in this book will help to answer homework questions! Try to think laterally as well as diving for the obvious – so many subjects and topics are intertwined. Also try to encourage children to think beyond giving the facts, to include newspaper information (current news), case studies and real stories, images, diagrams, quotes and statistics. See your role as being to make information fun and interesting. Children are curious creatures, and this is an ideal way to nurture their curiosity.

RELATIONSHIPS, SEX, SEXUAL HEALTH AND PUBERTY

Typical questions

- What is a sexually transmitted disease?
- What age is it legal to have sex?
- Where do babies come from?

Considerations

It is unlikely that you will be asked any of the above questions directly by a child or teenager, but they are certainly the types of question that the PSHE curriculum at school will cover or that children will want to find out about for themselves. For this reason, have a selection of books on your library shelves that deal with the whole range of topics connected with growing up. It is also one of those topics about which parents may ask for books or information to share with their child.

Where to look

Sex, sexual health and puberty

*Harris, R. H. and Emberley, M. (2010) *Let's Talk About Sex***, Walker Books**
Covers changing bodies, growing up, sex and sexual health, all with complementary cartoons to illustrate exactly the fact. Fantastic.

*Talking to Your Teenager about Sex and Relationships***, June 2009**
This leaflet provides advice and information to parents of teenagers to encourage them to talk to their children about sex and relationships. Available to download from **www.education.gov.uk/publications**. Select Youth and Adolescence, then Teenage Pregnancy and Sexual Health.

Sheen, B. (2009) *The Real Deal: adolescence***, Heinemann**
Looks at physical and emotional changes during adolescence.

Firth, A. and Leschnikoff, N. (2006) *What's Happening To Me?* **(boys edition), Usbourne**

Meredith, S. and Leschnikoff, N. (2006) *What's Happening To Me?* **(girls edition), Usbourne**
Deals with puberty for both boys and girls and their parents, tackling both physical and emotional changes. Suitable for KS2 and KS3.

Also worth looking at is:

Good Books for Tough Times: books for children aged 9–12 (2011) **Partnership for Children.**
This is an excellent publication with a foreword from Michael Morpurgo, who suggests during difficult times that 'reading is probably the best therapy there is, other than talking to mum or dad'. This gives suggestions of young fiction to read covering different situations, including coming of age and family issues. I would suggest many of the titles are suitable beyond age 12. Highly recommended. Available from **www.partnershipforchildren.org.uk.**

Websites

Avert
www.avert.org/teens.htm
Avert is an international HIV and Aids charity based in the UK. It has excellent information for teens on sex and relationships, puberty, birth control and safer sex, and more. Suitable for upper KS3 and KS4. There is lots of text, with some diagrams.

Childline
Helpline: 0800 1111
www.childline.org.uk
This service is provided by NSPCC, Weston House, 42 Curtain Road, London, EC2A 3NH. The helpline service provides confidential advice and someone to talk to. The website covers sex.

Like it is
www.likeitis.org/indexuk.html
A very flash site aimed at teenagers and covering puberty, sexuality, contraception, teenage pregnancy, periods and more. The information is concise and clear. Well worth a visit.

Radio 1 Advice
www.bbc.co.uk/radio1/advice
Provides advice on a wide range of issues and concerns including sex and relationships. For each there are further sub-headings of information and contacts for further help. However, a word of caution: the strong content of some of the material on some issues means that it is suitable for KS4 children – and for younger children only with adult guidance.

Relationships

Divorce

Edwards, N. (2005) *Talking about Divorce*, Chrysalis Children's Books

Websites

Separation and divorce

www.partnershipforchildren.org.uk/resources.html

Select Separation and Divorce for information, advice and links.

Domestic violence

Edwards, N. (2005) *Talking about Domestic Violence*, Chrysalis Children's Books

Websites

The Hide Out

www.thehideout.org.uk/default.aspa

Created by Women's Aid to help children and young people understand domestic abuse.

Young Carers

The Princess Royal Trust for Carers

www.youngcarers.net

Tips and pitfalls

Many of the subjects above are serious and emotive; deal with them sensibly, without asking too many awkward questions.

SCHOOL ATTENDANCE AND BEHAVIOUR

See also: **Part 3 – Home Education (includes home tutors)**

Typical questions

- What is exclusion?
- Is it compulsory to attend school?
- What is a pupil referral unit?

Considerations

Once your child is registered at a school, parents are legally responsible for making sure they attend regularly. A child becomes of compulsory school age when they reach the age of five and, where a parent has elected to register their child at school, they must start in the term following their fifth birthday. A child continues to be of compulsory school age until the last Friday in June in the school year that they reach the age of 16.

(School Attendance and Absence,
www.direct.gov.uk/en/Parents/Schoolslearninganddevelopment/
YourChildsWelfareAtSchool/DG_4016117)

Difficulties associated with school attendance can be an emotive issue. Exclusion from school, whether temporary or permanent, is never pleasant for those involved. If you are faced with queries related to exclusion and attendance, the best you can do is provide the information. Such cases are often complicated and should be dealt with by the relevant organizations.

Where to look

Behaviour and the Role of the Home–school Agreement, **March 2010**
Available from **www.education.gov.uk/publications**. Select Schools.

Advisory Centre for Education
www.ace-ed.org.uk
Advice Line for Exclusion – tel: 0808 800 0327
General Advice – tel: 0808 800 5793
Attendance – www.ace-ed.org.uk/advice-about-education-for-parents/School_Attendance

Behaviour and Attendance
www.education.gov.uk/schools/pupilsupport/behaviour

Discipline

http://familylives.org.uk/free-resources/get-leaflets

Select Discipline for a free downloadable leaflet from Family Lives, a national charity offering support and help to families.

School Discipline and Exclusions

www.direct.gov.uk/en/Parents/Schoolslearninganddevelopment/YourChildsWelfareAtSchool/DG_4016112

School Exclusion

www.education.gov.uk/schools/pupilsupport/behaviour/exclusion

School Exclusion

www.ace-ed.org.uk/advice-about-education-for-parents/exclusion_from_school

This has excellent information and provides access to downloadable guides, including:

Improving Behaviour and Attendance: guidance on exclusion from schools and pupil referral units, **Department for Education**

Permanent Exclusion 2011: a practical guide to parents' legal rights, **Advisory Centre for Education**

Fixed Period Exclusion 2011: a practical guide to parents' legal rights, **Advisory Centre for Education**

For Year 10 and Year 11

Having a Say: a young person's guide to exclusion

For Wales

Guidance on Exclusion from Schools and Pupil Referral Units, **Welsh Assembly**

SCHOOL TRAVEL

Typical questions

- How do I get a young person's bus pass?
- What time are the buses to . . . ?
- Does my school offer free school buses?
- Do you know if there is a 'walking bus'?

Considerations

Travelling to school is more involved than many of us realize. When children are at primary school they tend to live close to their school and often the mode of transport is dictated by parents. When children move to secondary school, travelling gets infinitely more complicated because secondary schools often serve wider catchment areas. Free school travel varies from region to region. In many cases free school travel is available to low-income families, but attending a school for religious reasons can also mean that you are eligible. Free school travel may mean having a special school bus or using the public transport with a pass. Parents need to check with their local council to see what is available and to make sure that they apply early, as pupils often need a boarding card or pass. Use your local council website for details of which department to contact. If the query involves another authority you could use the *Municipal Yearbook*, **Hemming Information Services, Annual** to find contact details.

For others not so fortunate to have a special school bus, the main option, other than car travel, is public transport. For bus timetables you can use the suggestion below, or it would be sensible to bookmark selected local bus timetables. Alternatively, your local bus station should have a good range of printed timetables to keep. The main thing is to remember to keep the information up to date, which means checking on a regular basis. You should also contact the local council for information on cycle routes and on 'walking buses' in operation, usually at primary schools – or contact the school direct.

Where to look

School Transport
  www.direct.gov.uk/en/Parents/Schoolslearninganddevelopment/
  index.htm
  Select School Transport.

Buses

Traveline

http://traveline.info

National link to local bus timetables. Select region, then timetable info, then type in the bus number, or select the journey planner if you don't know. Very impressive.

Trains

National Rail Enquiries

www.nationalrail.co.uk

Cycling

Bikeability

www.dft.gov.uk/bikeability.training

The National Standard for Cycling, i.e. cycling proficiency tests. You can find out if there is a scheme near you or how to get one. Packed with information.

Cycling to School

www.direct.gov.uk/en/Parents/Schoolslearninganddevelopment/
index.htm

Select Cycling to School.

Cycling Touring Club (CTC)

www.ctc.org.uk

National cyclists' organization.

National Cycle Network – Sustrans

www.sustrans.org.uk

Click on What we Do from the top menu. Then select National Cycle Network. For more information on cycling and schools' involvement click on Safe Routes for Schools.

Walking

Tales of the Road

http://talesoftheroad.direct.gov.uk

This site deals with road safety and is aimed at 6- to 11-year-olds. The animated videos are very powerful – even I as an adult sat up and took note. Excellent for information, animated films and free resources. Click on Grown Ups for lots of resources.

Walk to School Campaign
www.walktoschool.org.uk
Scheme available for primary and secondary schools.

Walking to School
www.direct.gov.uk/en/Parents/Schoolslearninganddevelopment/
index.htm
Select Walking to School.

SPECIAL EDUCATIONAL NEEDS (SEN) AND DISABILITY

See also: **Part 1, Section 1 – Schools and Education**

Typical questions

- Where can I go to have my child assessed for dyslexia?
- Are there any resources available for partially sighted children?
- Who can help me with 'statementing'?
- Are there any schools for children with special educational needs in ...?

Considerations

There is currently a review of special educational needs by the government. The consultation document *Support and Aspiration: a new approach to special educational needs and disability* is available at **www.education.gov.uk/ publications/standard/publicationDetail/Page1/CM%208027**.

For more general information and advice look at **www.direct.gov.uk/en/Parents/ Schoolslearninganddevelopment/SpecialEducationalNeeds/index.htm**.

The websites below offer some resources for parents and schools to use with children with special educational needs, and details of where to get further help, resources and advice. The list is by no means comprehensive but offers a good starting-point. Libraries too can offer resources such as audio-books and books by **Barrington Stoke, www.barringtonstoke.co.uk**, which publishes age-appropriate books for children with dyslexia and for reluctant and under-confident readers. The website is aimed at teachers and parents and features extracts from all Barrington Stoke's children's titles, as well as interviews with authors. There is also **Bag Books, www.bagbooks.co.uk**, which is a UK charity supporting the learning and development of children (and adults) with the most severe learning disabilities. It produces multi-sensory stories for people with profound learning disabilities. These are tactile and prop-based cards that are scripted for the story-teller. They are available to purchase for use in schools, libraries and at home. Visit the Bag Books website for more information. Some libraries may already have story times for children with special needs. For queries related to finding out about schools for special educational needs children, refer to Part **1, Section 1 – Schools and Education**.

Where to look

Like You, Like Me series from Evans Publishing focuses on a particular disability or medical condition through the eyes of a young person with the condition or disability. Suitable for primary school level. Titles include:

Powell, J. (2006) *Thomas Has Autism*, Evans Publishing

Muter, V. and Likierman, H. (2008) *Dyslexia: a parents' guide to dyslexia, dyspraxia and other learning difficulties*, Vermilion

Finding books to read

Barrington Stoke

www.barringtonstoke.co.uk

A specialist publisher that offers a range of books specially written for children with dyslexia or who are struggling readers. All the books are printed on buff paper and double spaced to aid reading. A full list of titles is available on the website. Also available are some excellent leaflets *Won't Read ... Could Read: information on reading for parents of teenagers*, *Is Reading a Challenge or a Mission Impossible? Why your child is reluctant or struggling to read and what you can do about it* (for parents of 9–12 year olds), *Onwards and Upwards: making the transition to secondary school*. Available from tel: 0131 225 4113. There is also a wealth of information on dyslexia. Well worth a visit.

Waterstone's Guide to Books for Young Dyslexic Readers, produced in association with Dyslexia Action

Reports

Department for Children, Schools and Families (March 2010) *Breaking the Link between Special Educational Needs and Low Attainment – Everyone's business*. Available from **www.education.gov.uk/publications**. Select Schools then Special Educational Needs
This report shares the good work of many schools and local authorities that already ensure high aspirations, progress and attainment for children with SEN. Its purpose is to raise awareness and influence the attitudes of school head teachers, senior leadership teams and heads of school improvement.

Department for Children, Schools and Families, *Information for Parents – Learning Difficulties*. Available from **www.education.gov.uk/publications**. Select Children and Families, then Early Support.
This is a guide for parents with young children who have a learning disability, describing the support that is available and answering the questions that many parents may have.

Websites

ACE (Advisory Centre for Education)

www.ace-ed.org.uk

A national charity that provides independent advice for parents and carers of children aged 5–16 years in state-funded education. It includes special educational needs.

Independent Parental Special Education Advice

www.ipsea.org.uk

Provides free legally based advice to families who have children with special educational needs.

National Parent Partnerships Network (NPPN)

8 Wakley St

London EC1V 7QE

Tel: 0207 843 6058

www.parentpartnership.org.uk

NPPN provides support and information to parent partnership services. Parent Partnership Services (PPS) are statutory services offering advice and support to parents and carers of children and young people with special educational needs (SEN). PPS are also able to put parents in touch with other local and national organisations.

Autism

National Autistic Society

www.autism.org.uk/living-with-autism/education.aspx

Covers information and advice on statementing (in England and Wales), transition issues when moving school, home educating, extra help at school and more.

Disability

Whizz-Kidz

www.whizz-kidz.org.uk/newsandresources

Select downloads for some excellent KS1–KS3 lesson plans on looking at disability. Select School Packs.

Hearing loss

Action on Hearing Loss (formerly RNID)

www.actiononhearingloss.org.uk

Learning difficulties

British Dyslexia Association (BDA)

www.bdadyslexia.org.uk/information-and-activities/teachers-and-schools.html

If, as a parent, you are concerned that your child may be dyslexic, or you are a teacher dealing with a dyslexic child, the *Dyslexia Friendly School Pack* from the BDA is worth looking at for identifying dyslexia and for lesson ideas.

British Institute of Learning Disabilities

www.bild.org.uk

Dyslexia Action

www.dyslexiaaction.org.uk

Provides information, contact details for local centres and advice.

Dyspraxia Foundation

www.dyspraxiafoundation.org.uk

Mencap – Learning Disability

www.mencap.org.uk

Click on Families for resources and support.

nasen (formerly National Association of Special Educational Needs)

nasen House
4/5 Amber Business Village
Amber Close
Armington
Tamworth
Staffordshire B77 4RP
Tel: 01827 311500

www.nasen.org.uk

Provides up-to-date information on SEN and disability issues. It promotes the education, training and development of all those with special and additional support needs.

Netbuddy

www.netbuddy.org.uk

This is an award-winning site for swapping practical tips and information on all aspects of supporting people with learning disabilities.

Special Needs Kids

www.special-needs-kids.co.uk

Blindness and partial sight

RNIB

www.rnib.org.uk

Select Teacher from Who Are You, then select School Based Learning for a wealth of information, including teaching the national curriculum subjects in mainstream education with partially sighted children. It also has information on children with complex needs. There is an area for parents too.

Tips and pitfalls

My experience is that parents with children who have special educational needs are very positive and well informed. They appreciate receiving positive help and information without being over-indulged with sympathy.

WORK EXPERIENCE

Typical questions

- How do I organize my work experience?
- Who offers work experience?
- Can I do volunteering?

Considerations

At some time during Year 9 or Year 10 pupils are given the opportunity to experience work through a work placement, usually for two weeks. Pupils usually obtain the placement for themselves. This can be the tricky part, and the first question is 'how?' The main route to securing a place is by contacting potential employers via letter or phone. There are lots of directories that give names and addresses of companies, organizations, universities and councils. Some of the main ones are listed below. Check to see what directories your library has and use those that are more child friendly. Take a few minutes to show them how the directory works. If your library does not have business information there are a number of free online directories available – try **http://gb.kompass.com**. If pupils have a specific type of work they would like to try there are a number of specialized directories. However, bear in mind that it is only for two weeks and, in the main, pupils opt for local work experience. Try directories such as *Optical Yearbook*, **Reed Business Information, Annual**. Try also the **Yellow Pages, www.yell.com**, which will list local companies, shops, beauty salons, dentists and so on, alphabetically by subject. Most libraries will have at least the Local Yellow Pages, as will many homes. Using local newspapers can also be useful to find out about smaller companies that may not be listed in the Yellow Pages. Once pupils have a list of potential contacts, the next stage is the letter writing. This is their chance to make an impression. Try to advise them not to rush into writing, to think carefully about the content, to be clear about when the work placement starts and finishes and to sound enthusiastic about the business, whatever it is. I would also suggest that they ring before sending their letter and ask for a named contact to send the letter to – many organizations have a specific person or department that deals with such schemes.

Letter writing

Chappell, C. (2006) *How To Write Better Letters*, **Penguin, Penguin Writers Guides series**

Of course, you can ask family and friends if they have any contacts for potential work placements and there is no harm in calling in at local shops, salons or schools and asking if they take work experience pupils. If you give the right impression this can be an excellent way to market yourself.

Where to look

Company details

Dun and Bradstreet Business Registers, 38 volumes, Dun and Bradstreet, **Annual**

This has a set of 30-plus regional directories. The listing includes businesses with five or more employees.

Kompass, 3 vols, **Reed Business Information**
www.reedbusiness.com

This has company details, including contacts.

Local authorities

Municipal Yearbook, **Hemming Information Services**

This provides an A–Z listing of all local authorities in the UK and covers every aspect of local government. It is now only available online **www.localgov.co.uk**. Enter your search term in Directory.

Academic institutions

You can use one of the many directories aimed at potential students choosing university courses. All of them will give contacts details, such as the suggestion below.

Boehm, K. and Spalding, J. L. *Daily Telegraph Guide to UK Universities: the one stop guide to UK universities*, **Annual**

This would be useful for university addresses, telephone numbers, e-mail and web addresses. This particular directory also lists the subjects each university offers, which would be useful if you wanted work experience in a particular field, for instance a science lab.

Schools

Schoolswebdirectory
www.schoolswebdirectory.co.uk

This lists 33,000 UK schools and colleges, with 20,000 websites, and allows searching by country, local education authority, name of school or postcode. It also includes independent schools. Excellent.

Information about work experience

Work Experience

> www.direct.gov.uk/en/EducationAndLearning/14to19/Years10and11/
> DG_10013569
>
> Explains work experience, how to organize a work placement and getting the most from it.

***Safeguarding Young People on Work-related Learning Including Work Experience*, March 2010**

> Available from **www.education.gov.uk/publications**. Select Children and Families, then Safeguarding.

Volunteering

Volunteering offers work experience and training from a variety of disciplines. It is certainly worth considering. Most volunteering is available from 16 years, which is just at the top of the age range that this book covers. Nevertheless, many Year 11 students during their GCSE year will start thinking about what they will be doing with their extended summer or how to get started in the world of work, for these reasons I have included it here.

Information about volunteering

www.direct.gov.uk/en/YoungPeople/Workandcareers/
> **Workexperienceandvolunteering/DG_066181**
> Explains volunteering.

Volunteering opportunities

BCTV (British Trust for Conservation Volunteers)
www2.bctv.org.uk
> An environmental charity offering volunteering and work experience opportunities for young people interested in environmental work. Click on Under 25 on the home page.

Community Service Volunteers (CSV)
www.csv.org.uk/volunteering/youth
> Young people aged 16–25 years can search for volunteering opportunities, including full-time volunteering projects where you can spend four months to a year away from home.

Girlguiding UK
www.girlguiding.org.uk/home.aspx
> Includes volunteering.

National Trust

www.nationaltrust.org.uk

Click on Get Involved, then Volunteering, then Youth Involvement. Lots of information on how to get involved, as well as work experience opportunities.

'V'

www.vinspired.com

A site from the V charity, which helps young people aged from 16 to 25 years to do voluntary work. The site allows searching for volunteering opportunities by interest.

Youth Action Network

www.youthactionnetwork.org.uk

Part 4

Hobbies, Leisure and Sport

Section 1 Hobbies and Leisure

ACTING AND PERFORMING

See also: **Part 2 – Drama and Theatre Studies; Part 4, Section 1 – Cinema, Film and Television**

Typical questions
- Do you know where I could do drama lessons?
- Are there any local stage schools?
- How can I find out about auditions?

Considerations
In the main, queries about acting as a hobby are concerned with finding local classes or courses appropriate for children, improving acting skills or finding out about auditions. Stage schools offer young people the chance to cover all the elements of performance: drama, singing and dance. There are a lot of resources suggested in the sections referred to under 'See also', above. Remember to keep contacts for local drama organizations accessible and up to date. There are also some suggestions below for improving acting skills and for finding auditions.

Where to look
Contacts and auditions
Actors' Yearbook: essential contacts for stage, screen and radio, **A&C Black, Annual**
Everything you'll need to know and what to do as an actor.

Contacts, **Spotlight Publications, Annual**
Provides lists of drama schools, contact details and names of agents. You can obtain a copy from **www.spotlight.com**.

Acting skills
Belli, M. L. and Lenney, D. (2006) *Acting for Young Actors: ultimate teen guide*, **Back Stage Books**

Henry, M. L. and Rogers, L. (2007) *How To Be a Working Actor*, 5th edition, Back Stage Books

Howl, J. (2008) *100 Exercises To Get You into Drama School: improve your acting and audition skills*, A&C Black

Levy, F. (2009) *Acting in Young Hollywood: a career guide for kids, teens and adults who play young too*, Random House

Mayfield, K. (2007) *Acting A–Z*, 2nd edition, Back Stage Books
This is the one book every aspiring child actor needs, covering auditions, casting, how to find work, headshots and more.

Morrison, H. (2003) *Acting Skills*, A&C Black

Paterson, L. and O'Connor, D. (2006) *Kids Take the Stage*, Back Stage Books
A practical guide to helping children from 8 to 18 years old get a show up and running.

Puppets

Baric, M. and Louhi, K. *Puppet Theatre*, Hawthorn Press
Offers 12 detailed, illustrated projects with all the techniques to set up a simple puppet show or full theatrical performance. It includes how to make puppets from just about anything, including twigs, create costumes, scenery, lighting and sound effects.

Journals

The Stage
The Stage Newspaper publisher
Tel: 020 7403 1818
Weekly
www.thestage.co.uk

Theatre Voice
www.theatrevoice.com

Young Performer Magazine
www.stagecoach.co.uk/stagecoach/html/subscribe.php

Websites

English National Ballet
www.ballet.org.uk
Click on Learning, then Resources for access to downloadable story sheets

of some of the major ballets. There are also resource packs available, suitable for KS3 and KS4.

Equity
www.equity.org.uk
The UK trade union that covers the rights of performers. Lots of information, especially links and where to get advice for younger performers.

National Youth Music Theatre
www.nymt.org.uk
Packed with information. Well worth a visit.

National Youth Theatre
www.nyt.org.uk

The Stage: Advice
www.thestage.co.uk
Select Advice, then How to guides. There is an excellent set of guides covering a wide range of subjects for theatre, including *How To Get into Drama School, How To Pass Auditions, How To Be an Extra.* Well worth a visit.

Stagecoach Theatre Art Schools
www.stagecoach.co.uk
This has 600 schools in the UK. To find the nearest one in your area use the postcode search. There is also lots of information on courses and opportunities.

ANIMATION, CARTOONS, COMICS AND MANGA

See also: **Part 4, Section 1 – Reading; Part 4, Section 1 – Drawing and Painting**

Typical questions

- How do I draw a cartoon character?
- What is manga?
- How do I draw like the graphic novel characters?

Considerations

In my experience, drawing and the creation of cartoons and characters are entwined with animation and comics in all their various forms, including graphic, manga and online. I have tried to offer suggestions by category, but as you will see, it is difficult to really segregate each into individual bits. As well as using the library's children's non-fiction section, head for your general non-fiction collection because this is a very popular subject, usually well catered for.

Where to look

Animation

Chatrain, C. and Paganelli, G. (eds) (2010) *Manga Impact: the world of Japanese animation*, Phaidon

Spillsbury, R. (2007) *Cartoons and Animation*, Heinemann, Art off the Wall series
Looks at the different stages in developing an animation project and animation techniques.

Williams, R. (2009) *The Animator's Survival Kit*, Faber and Faber
The standard work on animation.

Websites

Anim8ed
www.anim8ed.org.uk
An online resource from the National Media Museum on how to get started with animation.

Animation World Network
www.awn.com

One-Stop Animation
www.cleo.net.uk/resources/index.php?ks=2andcur=4
How to make one-stop animation.

Cartoons and comics

Byrne, J. (2001) *Collins Learn To Draw Comics*, Harper Collins

Hissey, I. and Tappenden, C. (2009) *The Practical Encyclopaedia of Cartooning*, Lorenz Books

For a step-by-step guide to drawing cartoons try:

Fairrington, B. (2009) *Drawing Cartoons and Comics for Dummies*, Wiley

or

Mostyn, D. (2010) *The Art of Cartooning: a complete guide to creating successful cartoons*, Arcturus Publishing

Robins, D. *Cartooning*, QED Publishing
Suitable for ages 7–11 years.

Rowson, M. How To Get Ahead in Cartooning. In *Writers' and Artists' Yearbook*, A&C Black, Annual

For creating online comics try:

Withrow, S. and Barber, J. (2005) *Webcomics Tools and Techniques for Digital Cartooning*, Ilex Press

For a list of magazines and newspapers that accept cartoons use *Writers and Artists' Yearbook*, A&C Black, Annual

Websites

Cartoons
www.toonopedia.com
Online encyclopedia of American cartoon characters and cartoonists.

Create a comic project
http://ccproject.comicgenesis.com/templates.html
Lots of templates, either blank or with pictures.

Tintin Cartoons
www.show.me.uk
Select Art and Design, then Tintin at Sea.

Manga and graphic novels

Amberlyn, J. C. (2009) *Drawing Manga, Animals, Chibis and Other Adorable Characters*, Watson Guptill Publishers

Chinn, M. and McLoughlin, C. (2007) *Create Your Own Graphic Novel*, Ilex

Coope, K. (2008) *How To Make Manga Characters*, Collins
A step-by-step guide to how to draw faces, dressing characters and making them move. Excellent.

Joso, E. (ed.) (2006) *Monster Book of Manga: draw like the experts*, Collins

Rough Guide to Manga, Rough Guides, 2009.

Spilsbury, R. (2007) *Comics and Graphic Novels*, Heinemann, Art off the Wall series

Website

Comic Master

www.comicmaster.org.uk
This allows children to create their own short graphic novel. They can choose characters and props as well as add dialogue, captions and special effects.

CHESS

Typical questions

- Are there any local chess clubs for children?
- Have you got any books on improving your chess playing?

Considerations

Chess is a very popular game and most regions will probably have some local chess clubs. It would be useful to find out from them which, if any, allow children to join. They will also be a useful source for information on chess tournaments and competitions. There are lots of books on improving your chess skills and you should check to see what your library has. There will also be books on chess in the general non-fiction section, so it is worth checking there too.

Where to look

Barnett, N. and Morkel, H. (2004) *Chess Makes Kids Smart,* Stanley Grundy Chess Foundation

Demonstrates via photos how each chess piece moves, and the associated strategies.

James, R. (2010) *Chess for Kids: how to play and win,* Right Way Books

Introduces children from age 7 to chess. It has 30 short lessons covering all the skills.

Jones, T. (2009) *How to Play Chess and Win!* Franklin Watts

Competitions

British Land UK Chess Challenge

www.ukchesschallenge.com/index.shtml

This is the largest chess tournament in the world, with 2000 schools taking part and 74,000 children from 5 to 18 years old. Any school can join.

Websites

ChessKIDSacademy

www.chesskids.com

Interactive chess lessons, learn about the chessboard and pieces, basic tactics and strategy, end-games and more.

ChessScotland

www.chessscotland.com

Gives a calendar of junior tournaments.

English Chess Federation
www.englishchess.org.uk
Click on ECF Junior. Lots of useful links and information.

Welsh Chess Union
www.welshchessunion.org.uk
Click on Junior for the Junior Chess pages.

World Chess Foundation
www.fide.com/index.php
For rules select FIDE, then Handbook.

CINEMA, FILM AND TELEVISION

Typical questions

- When was the first *Star Wars* film released?
- Which films has Robert Pattinson starred in?

Considerations

In my experience, young people love films and going to the cinema. Young people not only watch films but also produce their own short films. You have only to see that on YouTube. With this in mind, treat queries about cinema, film and television seriously. They are very much part of teen culture and lifestyle, as is demonstrated by young people's interest in the latest films, who plays who, what's on and how special effects are achieved. There is a place, next to good books, for good films. They stimulate conversation and debate as well as offering a harmless (mostly) leisure activity. However, the types of queries you could be asked are endless. Fortunately, there are lots of directories for cinema and films, many of which are very specific to films of a particular genre. There are some suggestions below, but your library may have others. For queries relating to cinema times and what's on, check the cinemas' websites. In addition, nearly all television channels have websites for TV programme updates, what's on and information.

Where to look

Cinema and films

Cinema history

Cinema Year by Year: the complete illustrated history of film, Dorling
 Kindersley, 2006
 Absolutely fascinating and highly addictive.

National Media Museum
 www.nationalmediamuseum.org.uk

Film recommendations

Pym, J. (ed.) (2011) *Time Out Film Guide*, 19th edition, Time Out
 This covers 19,000 films, from classic silent to Hollywood, Europe and
 Asia. Also lists 100 key film websites.

***Rough Guide to Cult Movies*, Rough Guides, 3rd edition, 2010**

Schneider, S. J. (ed.) (2010) *1001 Movies You Must See Before You Die*,
 Cassell

Film directors
Tasker, Y. (2011) *Fifty Contemporary Film Directors*, **2nd edition, Routledge**

Websites
BBC blast
 www.bbc.co.uk/blast/film

British Film Institute
 www.bfi.org.uk

BFI Future Film
 www.bfi.org.uk/futurefilm.html?q=futurefilm
 For 15- to 25-year-olds who love film.

Film Council
 www.ukfilmcouncil.org

Harry Potter
 www.harrypotter.com

National Media Museum
 www.nationalmediamuseum.org.uk

Screen Online
 www.screenonline.org.uk
 British Film Institute-sponsored encyclopedia of British cinema.

Cinemas
Cineworld
 www.cineworld.com
 To find the nearest Cineworld cinema, select Cinemas.

Odeon Cinemas
 www.odeon.co.uk
 To find the nearest Odeon cinema, select Cinemas.

Showcase
 www.showcasecinemas.co.uk
 To find the nearest Showcase cinema, select Cinemas.

UK Cinema Listings
 www.britinfo.net/cinema

Vue Cinemas
  http://new.myvue.com
  To find a Vue cinema, select Cinema.

Film making

BAFTA and Media Trust Youth Mentoring Programme
  www.bafta.org/access-all-areas/videos/youth-mentoring,855,BA.html

BBC Film Network
  www.bbc.co.uk/filmnetwork/filmmaking
  This is a film-making guide, starting at the scriptwriting and going through
  to post-production. It also has *How To* guides, including titles such as *How
  To Make a Horror Movie: blood.*

Boldface Productions
  www.boldfaceproductions.co.uk
  Provides young people with training to develop technical, creative and
  personal skills through film making.

The Co-operative British Youth Film Academy
  http://britishyouthfilmacademy.com
  Students have an opportunity to work with professional film makers on a
  real film set to produce a full-length feature film.

Guide to Film-making
  www.makingthefilm.com/guide.html
  Although the web pages haven't been updated for a while, the information
  is still relevant.

Television

Evans, J. (2011) *Penguin TV Companion,* **Penguin Books**
  Covers more than 2200 programmes, full cast lists, transmission dates and
  synopses.

Websites

BBC
  www.bbc.co.uk

BBC TV Guide
  www.bbc.co.uk/tv/guide

ITV
www.itv.com

ITV Player
www.itv.com/itvplayer

ITV TV Guide
www.itv.com/tvguide

Channel 4
www.channel4.com

Channel 4 TV Guide
www.channel4.com/tv-listings

S4C TV Guide
www.s4c.co.uk/e_listings.shtml

S4Croeso
www.s4c.co.uk

ScottishTV
www.stv.tv

SkyTV
http://tv.sky.com

Sky TV Guide
http://tv.sky.com/tvlistings

STV TV Guide
http://tvguide.stv.tv

COLLECTING THINGS

Typical questions

- How do I date this stamp?
- Where can I find old coins?
- Does anybody else collect . . . ?

Considerations

Children love collecting things and they can be very inventive as to what they collect. There are traditional items to collect such as coins and stamps; unusual items such as buttons; or new collectables often associated with a 'craze' that is hugely popular for a while but short lived. Whichever of the above you find yourself dealing with, this is an area where you are dealing with enthusiasts and it is a great opportunity to encourage them to use a wide variety of information sources. Take time to show them how to use well known reference books on their collections as well as using books for children. If you can emphasize how useful these books are to their hobby you will encourage return visits and use, as well as develop information skills. A number of collectables are mentioned below as suggestions for the types of collections you may be asked about, but this is by no means exhaustive. Many collectables have websites and some of the more suitable ones are mentioned. This is an area where a bit of lateral thinking comes in handy.

Where to look

KidsCollecting
    www.smithsonianeducation.org/students/smithsonian_kids_collecting/
    main.html

Coins

See also: **Part 1, Section 3 – Money.**

Mackay, J. (2007) *The World Encyclopaedia of Coins and Coin Collecting: the definitive illustrated reference to the world's greatest coins and a professional guide to building a spectacular collection featuring 300 colour images*, Lorenz Books

Mussell, J. W. and Mussell, P. (2010) *Coin Collecting Yearbook*, Token Publishing, Annual

Websites

Bank of England
www.bankofengland.co.uk/banknotes/index.htm
History of banknotes and how they are made today.

British Numismatic Society
www.britnumsoc.org
Junior membership is available.

Royal Mint
www.royalmint.gov.uk
Find out how British coins are made.

Fantasy figures and worlds

Games Workshop
www.games-workshop.com
For those interested in the world of fantasy battle.

Stamps (philately)

Collect British Stamps, 62nd edition, Stanley Gibbons, 2011

Mackay, J. *The World Encyclopaedia of Stamps and Stamp Collecting*, **Lorenz Books**
This mentions over 3000 of the world's best stamps, arranged by country. The first chapter is a guide to collecting stamps.

Stanley Gibbons Concise Stamp Catalogue, **Stanley Gibbons, 2011**

Websites

The British Postal Museum
http://postalheritage.org.uk/page/stamps
Select History and Learning, then Collections, then Stamps and Philately. Lots of interesting and useful information about collecting stamps. Also has links.

Planet Stamp
www.planetstamp.co.uk
The UK site for kids who collect stamps.

Stamp Magazine
www.stampmagazine.co.uk
Great for finding out the latest stamps available from the Post Office.

Shells (conchology)

Dance, P. (1990) *The Collector's Encyclopaedia of Seashells*, Zachany Kwintner

Saunders, G. (2006) *Usborne Spotter's Guides: shells*, Usborne

Wye, K. R. (1991) *The Encyclopaedia of Shells*, Facts on File Inc.

Website
British Shell Collectors' Club
www.britishshellclub.org
Includes a map of where to collect shells in the UK and lots of pictures of shells.

Autographs (philography)

Collect Autographs: an illustrated guide to collecting and investing in autographs, Stanley Gibbons, 3rd revised edition, 2009

Rawlins, R. (1997) *Guinness Book of World Autographs*, Guinness Books

Star Wars

Vitas, B. (2009) *The Complete Star Wars Encyclopaedia*, 3 vols, Titan Books
Thirty years of *Star Wars* information.

Website
Star Wars: Official Site
www.starwars.com

Dr Who

Corry, N. et al. (2010) *Dr Who Visual Dictionary*, Dorling Kindersley

Dr Who Encyclopaedia, Random House, 2011

Tribe, S. and Goss, J. (2011) *Dr Who: the Dalek handbook*, BBC Books

Magazine
Dr Who **magazine**
Panini
13 issues per year
Tel: 01892 500100

Website
Dr Who Official Site
www.bbc.co.uk/doctorwho/dw

Badges
Badge Collectors Circle
www.badgecollectorscircle.co.uk

Buttons
British Button Society
www.britishbuttonsociety.org

COMPUTER GAMES (FOR FUN)

Typical questions

- I want to play . . .
- Are there any games suitable for 5-year-olds?
- What's the website for dressing Barbie?
- Where's the pony-colouring site?

Considerations

Throughout this book I have marked websites with a $ to denote sites that I feel offer, in addition to learning, games that are fun and challenging. As well as these, listed below are some further sites for games. They are not necessarily linked to learning; fun is allowed (sometimes!).

Where to look

Websites

Astronomy Kids
www.kidsastronomy.com/fun/index.htm

CBBC games
www.bbc.co.uk/cbbc/games
Lots of games to play with many familiar BBC children's characters.

Funbrain Educational Games
www.funbrain.com
Great fun and very addictive, but with learning at heart.

Grepolis
http://en.grepolis.com
This is a game set in ancient times. Players build cities, alliances and harness the power of the gods to conquer. Very popular with boys.

Jig Zone
www.jigzone.com
Online jigsaw puzzles.

Yahoo! Kids
http://kids.yahoo.com/games

For younger children

Disney Junior
www.disney.co.uk/disney-junior/content/games.jsp

Fisher Price Online Games
www.fisher-price.com
Select Games and Activities, then Online Games.

COOKING AND BAKING

See also: **Part 1, Section 3 – Weights and Measures; Part 2 – Design and Technology**

Typical questions
- Have you got any cookery books for kids?
- How do I bake biscuits?
- What's the difference between self-raising flour and plain?
- How do I measure treacle?

Considerations

Anyone who knows me will know that for me, cooking and baking with children is almost as essential as breathing. In fact I would advocate baking for any parent. As an activity it offers quality time together, with a tasty product to share at the end. It also offers a host of learning experiences that children enjoy without realizing that they are using measurements, following instructions, reading, creating and designing, observing safety rules and working as a team – not to mention equipping them with a practical life skill.

Queries about cooking or baking tend to centre on finding recipes, for cooking at home, for pleasure or at school, especially when adapting recipes as part of the GCSE Food Technology syllabus. There are hundreds of cookery books published and any library will have a wide selection on offer. There has been a proliferation of cookery and baking books produced for children in recent years and a few recommendations are mentioned below. The better ones for beginners tend to have step-by-step instructions with bold, colourful pictures, while the more confident cook may find basic recipes in adult cookbooks suitable to follow. For parents, don't rule out using cookery books you may already have such as the ***Be-ro Flour Home Recipes*, 41st edition**. This includes a section on children's cooking. It is great for step-by-step instructions on the basics. However, the syrup pudding page is constantly peeled open by my son so he can whisk up his favourite, so I wouldn't limit children to the children's section. You can also use **www.be-ro.com** for baking basics and recipe remedies. Always useful!

Where to look

Blake, S. *Make and Eat Sandwiches and Snacks*, Wayland
   Aimed at younger children.

Cohen, W. L. *Baking Bread for Children*, Hawthorn Press

Techniques and recipes to use with children, together with stories, songs and poems to share along the way.

How to Cook, **Dorling Kindersley, 2011**
A step-by-step guide to creative cooking.

Star Cooks: cookbook for kids (2009) **Dorling Kindersley**
Easy-to-follow recipes with brightly coloured text and photographs from 24 celebrity chefs.

Stern, S. (2005) *Cooking Up a Storm: the teen survival cookbook*, **Walker Books**

Stern, S. (2006) *Real Food, Real Fast*, **Walker Books**

Stern, S. (2007) *Get Cooking*, **Walker Books**
These are a must for teenage boys. They are written and presented by Sam Stern, himself a 15-year-old boy, who makes cooking attractive, cool and fun for teenage boys. They are fantastic books with lots of pictures of young people enjoying socially what they have cooked, with the emphasis on quick, easy and nutritious food with, of course, delicious treats for afters. Inspirational for boys (and girls too!).

Vickers, R. (2009) *Confident Cooking*, **Life Skills series, Heinemann**
Looks at the basics, including kitchen safety, measuring, basic recipes and cooking methods. Aimed at teenagers. Excellent.

Some practical cookery/baking books to look out for include:

The Australian Women's Weekly Big Book of Kids' Cooking, **ACP Books, 2009**
This lists equipment to have, how to do some cooking basics and a glossary. The recipes cover breakfast, snacks, lunches and main meals, some basic baking and party food. Excellent.

Lewis, S. (2007) *Children's Book of Baking: 60 delicious recipes for children to make*, **Bounty Books**
Out of print but worth looking for on Amazon, as it is one of the best baking books for children I have come across.

There are also cookery/baking books linked to children's book characters, which can be encouraging. There are a few examples below that I have used, but there are a lot more available. The recipes are not always the best, but they can be a lot of fun.

Holabird, K. (2005) *Angelina Ballerina: my first cookbook*, Dorling Kindersley

Roald Dahl's Revolting Recipes, 1997, Red Fox

Roald Dahl's Even More Revolting Recipes, 2001, Jonathan Cape
Every recipe is taken from a food mentioned in one of Roald Dahl's children books. The recipe names are certainly original and inspirational for children who just can't resist recipes for 'A plate of soil with engine oil', amongst others.

For younger children:

Garland, S. (2006) *Eddie's Kitchen and how To Make Good Things To Eat*, Frances Lincoln

Supermarkets

As well as using cookery books you can also use recipe cards that are available free from supermarkets such as Sainsbury's, or store magazines, also free, such as the one produced by Morrisons. This has a great regular kids' cooking feature. You can also view this online at **www.morrisons.co.uk/magazine**. Looking out for new recipes in this way can be part of the fun.

Websites
Food: a fact of life
www.foodafactoflife.org.uk
Click on Other, then select Cook Club for a range of recipes designed for primary and secondary school lessons, all of which are suitable to use at home.

Great Grub Club
www.GreatGrubClub.com/cook-it
Provides healthy snack recipes for children, with step-by-step instructions. Excellent.

Cookery schools
There are lots of cookery courses and clubs for children these days. Try to find what's available locally and keep contacts and details available. A few are mentioned below by way of example of the different types available.

Let's Get Cooking
www.letsgetcooking.org.uk

A national network of cooking clubs with schools for children, using Big Lottery funding to set up 5000 clubs. There is a search facility to locate local clubs.

Jamie's Ministry of Food

www.jamie.oliver.com/jamies-ministry-of-food

The Ministry of Food promotes and provides lessons on cooking skills. There are centres in several locations in the UK offering hands-on cookery sessions.

Organic Cookery School

http://organiccookeryschool.org/current-projects

Offers family cookery activities to schools, children's centres and more. Also set to introduce the Duke of Edinburgh's Award cookery course. It is situated and works mainly in the South of England.

Prue Leith's Cookery School

www.leiths.com/enthusiasts-courses/one-day-classes/childrens-classes

If you want to spend some serious money, Prue Leith's Cookery School offers courses for children.

CRAFTS

Typical questions

- Have you got a book with how to start knitting?
- How do you make paper?
- What can I make from egg boxes?

Considerations

Many crafts are traditional skills, such as knitting and sewing, and in recent years these have been making a comeback, as cool things to do. However, crafts can be anything from gluing to cutting, making things out of recycled materials or painting plant pots. Some of the books in the library's general non-fiction collection will be useful, especially those offering step-by-step instructions. However, crafts are also about imagination, so art books, pictures, books on design, cars, science experiments and cooking are all great for ideas. There are a few suggestions below – but these are just the tip of the iceberg.

Where to look

Dickinson, G. (2006) *Crafts for Kids*, Hamlyn

Dickinson, G. and Owen, C. (2009) *Creative Crafts for Kids: over 100 fun projects for two to ten year olds*, Hamlyn

Martin, L. C. (2004) *The Art of Recycling: sock puppets, cardboard castles, bottle bugs and 37 more earth-friendly projects and activities you can create*, Storey Books

Watts, F. *365 Things To Do with Paper and Cardboard*, Usborne

Watts, F. et al. *The Usborne Big Book of Fairy Things To Make and Do*, Usborne

Try also:

Usborne Activities series. Titles include:

Watts, F. (2009) *Animal Things To Make and Do*, Usborne

Watts, F. (2010) *Christmas Things To Make and Do*, Usborne

Watts, F. (2008) *Cowboy Things To Make and Do*, Usborne

Needlecrafts

Hardy, E. (2010) *Sewing for Children*, **Cico Books**
Gives clear step-by-step instructions with easy sewing projects to do, with colourful pictures.

Montgomerie, C. (2010) *Knitting for Children: 35 simple knits kids will love to make*, **Cico Books**
Covers all the basic stitches and fantastic easy things to make in colourful, bold pictures.

Papercrafts

Ono, M. and Ono, R. (2010) *Origami for Children*, **Cico Books**

Watts, F. *365 Things To Do with Paper and Cardboard*, **Usborne**

Woram, C. (2010) *Paper Scissors Glue*, **Cico Books**
Instructions for 45 paper projects for children aged 3 to 10 years.

Magazines

Easy Peazy
Signature Publishing
Monthly
Tel: 01428 601020
Projects to make and bake for 5- to 9-year-olds.

Websites

Children Art and Craft Books: for teachers, parents and children
www.childrenscraftbooks.com
A series of books written by Mirian O'Donoghue covering a multitude of crafts.

Crafts
www.enchantedlearning.com/crafts
Provides instructions for hundreds of crafts. Select craft by using the alphabetical list. The great thing about this site is that most of the crafts don't need lots of resources and use mainly household items, such as food boxes. Very useful for a rainy day.

Things2Make
www.things2make.com/default.htm
Hundreds of things to make, arranged alphabetically or by project category. Excellent.

DRAWING AND PAINTING

See also: **Part 2 – Art; Design and Technology; Part 4, Section 1 – Animation, Cartoons, Comics and Manga**

Typical questions

- How do I draw faces?
- Have you got a book on painting trees?
- What is the difference between oil paints and acrylic?

Considerations

In the main, queries will be concerned with how to draw or paint a particular item. Most libraries will have lots of books on drawing, so try to select carefully, providing age appropriate titles. Younger children require step-by-step instructions to create simple pictures. Also remember to use the general non-fiction collection. For children who want to share their work with others some online art galleries are suggested below.

Where to look

Drawing

Robins, D. (2009) *Drawing and Sketching*, QED Publishing

For very young children:

Gibson, R. (2000) *I Can Crayon*, Usborne Playtime

Gibson, R. (1997) *I Can Draw Animals*, Usborne Playtime

Gibson, R. (1999) *I Can Draw People*, Usborne Playtime
These are great with younger children. Sadly they are out of print, but are available on Amazon.

or try:

How to Draw Animals, How to Draw Dinosaurs, How to Draw Trucks and Tractors, from Usborne.

For specific drawings:

Beaumont, S. (Illus.) (2011) *Drawing Dragons*, Drawing Legendary Monsters series, Franklin Watts

Try also from the same series: *Drawing Griffins, Drawing Werewolves, Drawing Unicorns, Drawing the Kraken, Drawing the Minotaur.*

Keck, G. (2009) *Draw Sci-fi*, Search Press

Keck, G. (2009) *Draw Gothic*, Search Press

Lovell, H. (2011) *Drawing Fashion*, Arcturus Publishing

Painting

Nicholson, S. *Painting*, QED Publishing
Learn all the basic skills and techniques of painting. Suitable for ages 7–11 years.

Specific genres:

Davies, P. B. et al. (2010) *Fantasy Art in Watercolour: painting fairies, dragons, unicorns and angels*, Search Press

Magazines

Art Attack
Panini
13 issues per year
Tel: 01372 802800

Cbeebies Art
BBC magazines
13 issues per year
Tel: 020 8422 2000
Art for 4- to 6-year-olds.

Websites

Art Attack
www.hitentertainment.com/artattack
This has dozens of factsheets giving step-by-step instructions on how to do every creative technique you'll ever think of. Very child friendly.

Artist's Toolkit
www.artsconnected.org/toolkit/index.html
This enables art students and teachers to explore how visual elements and principles of line, colour, shape and space can be used to create works of art. There is a facility to create your own art using the above principles.

The Campaign for Drawing
www.campaignfordrawing.org/home/index.aspx

International Children's Art Gallery
www.paintbrushdiplomacy.org/galleries
A wonderful collection of children's artwork.

Picture Gallery @ Natural History Museum
www.nhm.ac.uk/kids-only/picture-gallery
Allows children to send artwork and have it shown online.

Rainbows Fridge
www.girlguiding.org.uk/rainbows/fridge/fridge.html
Rainbows can send in their artwork.

Stone Soup
www.stonesoup.com
The art archive of the magazine *Stone Soup* by young writers and artists is inspirational, covering a collection of children's art collected by the magazine since the 1970s. It has 1300 works by children from 36 different countries.

Stories from the Web
www.storiesfromtheweb.org
This is a subscription-based online reader-development site managed by Birmingham Libraries on behalf of participating authorities. It is for children via libraries, schools or by family subscription. It encourages children to read, write and draw and to share their work via the online Gallery. There are three age groups 0–7 years, 7–11 years and 11+ years. It is a great way to show your work off to a national audience.

Winsor & Newton
www.winsornewton.com
This is very useful for information on materials and painting techniques. It also has an Artists' Glossary.

DUKE OF EDINBURGH'S AWARD

See also: **Part 3 – Work Experience; Part 4, Section 1 – Uniformed Organizations**

Typical questions
- Where can I do the Duke of Edinburgh's Award?
- What is the Duke of Edinburgh's Award?
- Whom do I contact about volunteering?

Considerations

This is fairly straightforward, as the main contact point is given below. For those already in the process of working towards their Duke of Edinburgh's Award and looking for volunteering work, voluntary organizations who accept young people are listed in **Part 3 – Work Experience**. For those looking for organizations that offer the Duke of Edinburgh's Award scheme, look at **Part 4, Section 1 – Uniformed Organizations**.

Where to look

Duke of Edinburgh's Award
Gulliver House
Madeira Walk
Windsor
Berkshire SL4 1EU
Tel: 01753 727400
www.dofe.org
There are lots of regional offices which you can contact via the website. There is lots of information for Duke of Edinburgh's Award candidates, parents and leaders.

Magazine

Award Journal
The Award Scheme
3 issues per year (January, April and September)
Tel: 01753 727400
www.theaward.org
The magazine of the Duke of Edinburgh's Award.

FAMILY HISTORY

Typical questions

- How do I trace my family history?
- Do you have any books on family history?
- Have you got the Census 1911?

Considerations

Family history or tracing family ancestors has become a hugely popular activity. Whereas in the past discovering your family tree was left to eccentric uncles (eccentric uncles please don't write in!), TV programmes such as *Who Do You Think You Are?* have ignited interest in discovering our past amongst both young and old. It is not an easy activity for young people to undertake but it can be immensely rewarding. It is our role to highlight to young people that, firstly, family trees are difficult and time consuming to create; secondly, they may not find all the information they want from one source, or indeed one library; thirdly, they can cost money. Young people require guidance to get started, and that can be time consuming; however, they are usually computer literate, so using online resources is not an issue and requires minimal training. Interpreting the data – well, that is another ball game. So, provided that we have managed to negotiate all the potential hurdles listed above, where does a young person start? Below are a number of resources that should get them started.

Where to look

Adolph, A. (2009) *Who Am I? The family tree explorer*, Quercus

Annal, D. (2005) *Easy Family History: stress free guide to starting your research*, The National Archives
A highly readable pocket-size book.

Barnett, N. (2006) *Who Do You Think You Are? Encyclopaedia of genealogy: a definitive guide to tracing your family history*, Harper Collins Publishing
Excellent and not beyond a child's use, with adult support.

Blake, P. and Loughran, M. (2006) *Discover Your Roots: 52 brilliant ideas for exploring your family and local history*, Infinite Ideas

Family Tree Kit, Dorling Kindersley, 2007
This has an interactive album, family tree poster and CD-ROM.

★Jolly, E. (2008) *Family History for Kids*, Pymer Quantrill Publishing

Looks at the basics of genealogy and shows children how to begin to investigate their family tree and how to discover how their ancestors lived. Also takes into account the diverse and multi-cultural range of backgrounds of today's children. It is linked to the English and Welsh national curriculum. Excellent.

Waddell, D. (2010) *Who Do You Think You Are? Be a family tree detective,* **Walker Books**
This is a great little book to get started with family history. It has ten easy-to-follow spreads to get any child started on finding out about their ancestors' lives.

Beginner's online guides
Family History
www.bbc.co.uk/history/familyhistory
An excellent site for beginners.

Family History for Kids
www.genealogic.co.uk
Select Kids Family History.

Who do you think you are?
www.bbcwhodoyouthinkyouaremagazine.com

Getting started online guides with access to national records
Ancestry
www.ancestry.co.uk

National Archives
www.nationalarchives.gov.uk

Scotland People
www.scotlandspeople.gov.uk

Census
The UK national census started in 1801 and has been taken every tenth year, with the exception of 1941. It provides details of every person living at a specific address. The Census is confidential for 100 years and the latest available is 1911.

Ancestry Library
www.ancestrylibrary.com

This is a subscription service often provided free by public libraries, with access to all censuses.

Find My Past
>**www.findmypast.co.uk**
>This is a subscription service but some libraries offer free access. Includes an excellent getting-started guide.

Lumas, S. (2002) *Making Use of the Census*, **Public Record Office**
>A useful guide to the census, but requires adult guidance to use it successfully.

Blank templates

There are lots of family history sites offering free templates for research recording. Those suggested below are, in my opinion, more accessible by children.

Family research forms
>**www.genealogysearch.org/free/forms.html**

Family tree blank templates
>**www.familytreemagazine.com/info/basicforms**

Family tree charts
>**www.ancestry.co.uk/trees/charts/ancchart.aspx**

Storing family trees

You may want to consider storing your research online.
Try **http://tribalpages.com** for free storage or try
www.legacyfamilytreestore.com for free software.

Magazine

Family Tree Kids
>**www.familytreemagazine.com/kids**

Tips and pitfalls

Family history is complicated and time consuming. There is a need here to keep a balance between getting young people started and doing the research for them. Resist the temptation to take over complicated searches; instead, offer information bit by bit to avoid overwhelming their research. This is an area where developing their skills first is essential and the research will follow.

FISHING

Typical questions

- How do I do an angler's knot?
- Where is a safe place to fish?
- What equipment do I need to go fishing?
- Do I need a fishing licence?

Considerations

In the main, the types of query are fairly straightforward: either how to improve fishing techniques or how to find a place to fish legally in the local area. In order to fish, you need a valid Environment Agency rod licence if you are aged 12 or over and fish for salmon, trout, freshwater fish, smelt or eel in England (except the River Tweet), Wales and the Border Esk and its tributaries in Scotland. There are junior (12–16) concessions, and for children under 12 years the licence is free. These are available online at **www2.postoffice.co.uk/counter-services/licences-vehicle-tax/rod-fishing-licence/buy-licence** or from selected Post Office branches. There are a number of websites below, including the Environment Agency, that provide information on where you can fish.

Where to look

Befus, T. (2006) *A Kid's Guide to Flyfishing: it's more than catching fish*, Johnson Books

Ellison, G. et al. (2011) *Teach Me Fishing! The best way to learn to fish for kids ages 3 to 13*, Wonderdads
Highly recommended.

Ford, M. (2009) *Fishing*, Wayland, Master This series

Seeberg, T. (2004) *Freshwater Fishing*, Child's World Inc, Kids guides series

Sims, L. and Edon, H. (2004) *Starting Fishing*, Usborne, Usborne First Skills series

Websites

Angling Trust
    www.anglingtrust.net
    This has a Find a Club and Find a Coach facility. Search by postcode or town. Junior members (17 and under) have free membership and get all the

benefits of adult membership. Also includes lists of competitions such as the National Championships.

Fishing

www.environment-agency.gov.uk/homeandleisure/recreation/fishing/default.aspx

This is packed with information on fishing and includes where to go fishing; fishing events; information on river levels; fish species; rod fishing byelaws and how to get your rod licence.

Fishing.com

http://fishing.com/

Information on all types of fishing and the equipment to use for each.

Fishing in the UK

www.fishing.co.uk

Includes where to fish in England, Wales and Scotland.

GAMES – INDOOR AND OUTDOOR

See also: **Part 4, Section 1 – Chess; Part 4, Section 2 – Sports**

Typical questions

- How do you play hopscotch?
- Do you know any games to play on a train?
- What are the rules of rounders?

Considerations

Games can include traditional, e.g. hopscotch, outdoor, e.g. rounders, and indoor, e.g. charades. Often both children and adults forget the rules of a particular game, especially traditional games, which over the years can change or evolve. Modern-day rounders is an example of this. Games are fantastic for developing children: there are so many to help with coordination, e.g. crazy golf; with fitness, e.g. skipping; with numeracy, e.g. bingo; with literacy, e.g. Scrabble. But most of all they are fun, help build friendships and develop many of the qualities taught on the Citizenship syllabus. Many board games have a place in children's libraries and to have some available for rainy afternoons would not be unreasonable. Make sure that you have a good games rule book handy.

Where to look

Morehead, A. H. et al. (2001) *Hoyle's Rules of Games: the essential family guide to card games, board games, parlor games, new poker variations and more plus a new section on computer games*, 3rd revised edition, Signet

Try also:

Arnold, P. (2009) *Chambers Card Games for Families*, Chambers Harrap
Find out how to play over 50 card games suitable for families with children from 6 years. Includes a list of games by the number of players and a list of games by the age of the children. All instructions are easy to follow.

Curran, J. (2009) *Organised fun*, Pan Macmillan
A compendium of how to play games.

Official Scrabble Player's Dictionary, Merriam-Webster, 2005

Regan, L. (2010) *Games on the Move*, QED Publishing

Regan, L. (2011) *Indoor Games*, QED Publishing

Regan, L. (2010) *Outdoor Games*, QED Publishing

Toseland, M. and Toseland, S. (2010) *365 Everyday Games and Pastimes: something fun for everyone*, Square Peg
Has party, word, ball, memory and card games; marbles, magic; games for the beach, park, car and kitchen.

Websites

Games Cabinet
www.centralconnector.com/GAMES/GameCab.html
This provides instructions for many well known board games, including Monopoly, Jenga and Mastermind.

Kids Games
www.gameskidsplay.net
This has an extensive list of games and how to play, including some traditional games such as marbles and hopscotch.

Marble games and rules
www.centralconnector.com/GAMES/marbles.html

GROWING FRUIT, VEGETABLES AND FLOWERS

Typical questions

* How do I grow pumpkins?
* How do I make compost?
* Which flowers are easy to grow?

Considerations

Many queries will be to do with actually growing vegetables or flowers. For most of these, check what you have on the library shelves. Don't limit children to children's books on growing: use also some of the simpler step-by-step books that can be found in the general non-fiction. Sometimes you may get asked for flower or vegetable shows that accept children's entries. Many local shows will probably have children's categories, so try to keep details of show organizers and whom to contact, as there are often entry deadlines.

Where to look

Buczacki, S. and Buczacki, B. (2009) *Young Gardener*, Frances Lincoln

Dannenmaier, M. (2008) *A Child's Garden*, Timber Press
Special gardens for children to enjoy.

Every School a Food-growing School 2011
This report highlights the benefits of food-growing activities in schools. It is produced by a coalition of gardening and education charities. A copy of the report is available to freely download at: **www.sustainweb.org/ childrensfoodcampaign/food_growing_in_schools**.

Hendy, J. (2010) *The Ultimate Step by Step Kids First Gardening Book*, Lorenz Books
120 projects to do, step by step.

Johnson, S. and Evans, C. (2003) *Usborne Starting Gardening*, Usborne

Lockie, B. (2007) *Gardening with Young Children*, Hawthorn Press
Includes growing in limited spaces, such as window sills.

McCorquodale, E. (2010) *Kids in the Garden*, Black Dog Publishers
Gardening for children and parents.

Royal Horticultural Society (2010) *Ready Steady Grow*, Dorling Kindersley

Royal Horticultural Society (2011) *How Does My Garden Grow*, Dorling
Kindersley

For younger children
Garland, S. (2006) *Eddie's Garden and how To Make Thing Grow*, Frances
Lincoln

Garland, S. (2007) *Doing the Garden*, Frances Lincoln

Websites
BBC Gardening with Children
www.bbc.co.uk/gardening/gardening_with_children

Campaign for School Gardening
http://apps.rhs.org.uk/schoolgardening/default.aspa
Aims to encourage and support schools to create and actively use a school
garden. Lots of information on how to get started, and fantastic resources.

Royal Horticultural Society
www.rhs.org.uk/children
Loads of information for children to encourage them to grow plants.

MAGIC AND MAGIC TRICKS

Typical questions

- How do I make a coin disappear?
- What is plate spinning?
- Is there a magic club I can join?

Considerations

In the main, queries will be fairly straightforward, relating to how to do various tricks. Most libraries will have some books on magic tricks, so check what is available on your library shelves.

Where to look

Fullman, J. *The Great Big Book of Magic Tricks*, QED Publishing
Step-by-step instructions of performing magic tricks. Suitable for ages 7–11 years.

Szwast, U. (2005) *Magic*, Get Going! Hobbies series, Heinemann

Websites

British Magical Society
www.britishmagicalsociety.co.uk

$Magic Tricks Online
www.kidzone.ws/magic/index.htm
Instructions for lots of magic tricks.

Young Magicians Club
www.youngmagiciansclub.co.uk
A youth initiative from the Magic Circle for 10 to 18-year-olds.

MUSIC – ENJOYING AND PLAYING MUSICAL INSTRUMENTS

See also: **Part 2 – Music**

Typical questions

- How can I play in a band?
- Where do I learn to play drums?
- Have you got the music for . . . ?
- Are there any choirs for children?

Considerations

There are so many different styles of music that it is essential to clarify queries about music or playing a musical instrument before rushing off to the music books. Outside of studying for GCSE music or an instrument exam, young people are often interested in playing in bands or orchestras, singing in choirs, learning well known songs or going to see bands. The resources listed below should point you in the right direction.

Where to look

Musicians and Songwriters' Yearbook, **A&C Black, Annual**

Playing Musical Instruments

Burrows, T. (2010) *First Guitar Tutor: learn to be a real guitar hero*, **Carlton Books**

Maran Illustrated Piano, **MaranGraphics, 2005**

The *Should I Play* **series by Harcourt Education, 2007** introduces children to a number of different musical instruments and allows them to see major features of each one, enabling them to decide what they might like to learn to play. Titles include: *Should I Play the Clarinet?*, *Should I Play the Drums?*, *Should I Play the Guitar?*, *Should I Play the Piano?*, *Should I Play the Trumpet?*, *Should I Play the Violin?*

Scott, J. (2009) *Learn to Play Drums: a beginner's guide to playing drums,* **Apple**

Websites

How to find out how the acoustic guitar works
www.entertainment.howstuffworks.com/guitar.htm
Click on Guitar Images Gallery while you're here to see some great photos of famous guitar players.

How to find out how the electric guitar works
www.entertainment.howstuffworks.com/electric-guitar.htm

Bands

International Showcase Music Business Guide, **Showcase, Annual**
www.showcase-music.com
Useful for finding studios and recording studios.

How band equipment works
http://entertainment.howstuffworks.com/band-equipment.htm
Great for those new to playing gigs with their band.

Websites

British Youth Band
www.byba.org.uk

Rock School
www.rockschool.com
Offers courses for teenagers (aged 10 to 16) to experience performing in a band, as well as writing their own material.

Gigs and festivals

Use the magazines listed below as well.

Clickmusic
www.clickmusic.co.uk
Gives details of bands, gigs and groups.

Federation of Festivals
www.federationoffestivals.org.uk
Click on affiliated festivals.

Choirs

Choir Schools Association
www.choirschools.org.uk

National Youth Choir of Scotland
www.nycos.co.uk

Youth Choir UK
www.youthchoiruk.com/l.html
For young people 14 to 22 years old. For auditions click on Auditions.

Orchestras

European Union Youth Orchestra
www.euyo.org.uk
If you are 14 to 24 years old you can apply for the European Union youth orchestra. However, you must be at least conservatoire standard.

National Youth Orchestra of Great Britain
www.nyo.org.uk
This is a youth orchestra of teenagers from across Britain. To apply for an audition either as an instrumental player or as young composer, see the website.

National Youth Orchestra of Scotland
www.nyos.co.uk/orchestras-youth.html

National Youth Orchestra of Wales
www.nyaw.co.uk/e_nyow.html

Songs, singing and tab

For song writing try:

Cahn, S. (2009) *The Songwriter's Rhyming Dictionary*, Souvenir Press

Rooksby, R. (2004) *Melody: how to write great tunes*, Backbeat Books

For songs try:

Pollock, B. (2005) *Rock Song Index*, Routledge
This has 7500 entries covering classic rock, heavy metal, punk, rap, disco and British invasion.

Rock Guitar Songs for Dummies, Herriges, 2007

Websites

BBC 2 Radio 2's Great British Songbook
www.bbc.co.uk/radio2/music/great-british-songbook/songs

How to play 4 guitar riffs
http://entertainment.howstuffworks.com/4-guitar-licks.htm

Lyrics
www.songlyrics.com
Probably all you need, covers every music genre, with an extensive artists list.

Lyrics A–Z Universe
www.azlyrics.com
Browse by artist/band name or search by artist, album or song.

Musical Exercises in Tab Style
www.houlston.freeserve.co.uk
Tab for mainly traditional songs and nursery rhymes.

Magazines

Kerrang
Bauer Consumer Media
Weekly
Tel: 020 7182 8000
www.kerrang.com
Gives news, gig guides and reviews of rock, metal and punk.

New Musical Express (NME)
IPC ignite!
Weekly
Tel: 020 3148 5000
www.nme.com

NATURE

See also: **Part 2 – Geography**

Typical questions

- Where is the nearest nature reserve?
- What do sparrows look like?
- How many different animals are there?
- Do all ladybirds have the same number of spots?
- Have you got a book about different trees with leaf pictures?

Considerations

Nature is a vast subject, but very popular in its different forms with children. At some time or other children will dig a hole in your flowerbed, looking for worms, collect a box of woodlice, collect shells or crabs and maybe even watch a butterfly land on a flower. This is called exploring nature. There are lots of books on the subject, either to identify species or to suggest activities to discover nature. There are some suggestions below but this is not exhaustive; your library may have other titles. Some queries may be about joining a nature club. Many local conservation or environmental groups offer children's groups; it is worth finding out details and keeping contact information available. Try contacting some of the national organizations listed below to see what they offer locally.

Where to look

Burnie, D. et al. (2010) *Nature Explorer*, **Dorling Kindersley**
    Covers bird watching, bug hunter, stargazing, rock and fossil hunter, nature ranger, i.e. finding animal footprints, looking at leaves, seeds, rock pools and weather watcher. It gives practical activities to do, equipment and what to look for. Excellent.

Dalby, E. (2003) *Usborne Internet-linked Mysteries and Marvels of Nature*, **Usborne**

Nature Encyclopaedia, **Dorling Kindersley, 2008**
    This covers forests, rainforests, grasslands, deserts, mountains, oceans, towns and cities.

Websites
BBC Nature
    www.bbc.co.uk/nature/uk
    The home of Springwatch and Autumnwatch.

iSpot

www.ispot.org.uk

This is the place to identify what you see with other nature enthusiasts.

Natural History Museum

www.nhm.ac.uk

Select Kids Only for lots of information, activities and the naturecams.

Nature Detectives

www.naturedetectives.org.uk

This has over 1000 free activities, games and downloads for families and schools. Excellent.

Nature Reserves

www.rspb.org.uk/reserves

Enables searching by postcode or place name. Does only give RSPB nature reserves. It also has a Things To Do facility that provides details of events happening at RSPB nature reserves.

UK Safari

www.uksafari.com

Covers the wildlife of the UK. It has a search facility packed with information and an Idenitfy It facility.

Wildlife Trusts

www.wildlifetrusts.org

There are more than 2000 nature reserves in the UK cared for by the Wildlife Trust. To find the nearest one to you select Reserves and search by postcode, town or county.

Young People's Trust for the Environment

www.ypte.org.uk

This aims to encourage young people's understanding of the environment. Lots of animal and environment factsheets. Excellent.

Magazine

National Geographic Kids

Attic Media Network

Monthly

Tel: 020 7014 3777

The children's magazine covering wildlife, science and technology, world events and the environment.

Animals

Goodman, P. (2007) *Animal Classification: a guide to vertebrates*, Wayland

*National Geographic Encyclopaedia of Animals, National Geographic, 2006
Covers mammals, birds, reptiles, amphibians, fish and invertebrates.

Parker, S. (2004) *Large as Life: 100 animals actual size*, Miles Kelly
Publishing
This has life-like, life-size artworks, such as the actual size of a rhinoceros's
eye. Fascinating.

Web, B. (2010) *Animal Disguises*, Kingfisher
Animal camouflage and changing colours.

Websites

Animal Corner
www.animalcorner.co.uk
This has a huge quantity of information and pictures.

BBC Nature
www.bbc.co.uk/nature/animals
Packed with information and video clips of hundreds of animals.

The Mammal Society
www.mammal.org.uk
This has a good set of factsheets available. Select About British Mammals.

WWF
www.panda.org
Select Teachers, then select Games with a message under Teacher
Resources. Games include issues such as endangered species.

Young Batworkers' Club
www.bats.org.uk/pages/batsforkids.html
This is for children, from the Bat Conservation Trust.

Birds

Chandler, D. (2005) *RSPB Children's Guide to Bird Watching*, A&C Black

Websites

Birds
www.enchantedlearning.com/subjects/birds
Learn all about birds.

Hawk and Owl Trust
www.hawkandowl.org

Royal Society for the Protection of Birds (RSPB)
www.rspb.org.uk
Lots of information on birds and wildlife. It has an A–Z guide to bird names; an A–Z of birds by family and a bird identifier.

Wetland and Wildlife Trust
www.wwt.org.uk/learn
Learn about the world's wetlands and their wildlife. For teachers there are lesson plans for KS1, KS2 and KS3. For children there is Kids Zone.

Insects

*Chinery, M. (2009) *Collins Complete Guide to British Insects: a photographic guide to every common species*, Collins

Martineau, S. (2007) *Bugs in the Garden*, b small publishing

*Tolman, T. and Lewington, R. (2009) *Collins Butterfly Guide: the most complete guide to the butterflies of Britain and Europe*, Harper Collins

Websites

Buglife – the Invertebrate Conservation Trust
www.buglife.org.uk/discoverbugs

Butterflies
www.enchantedlearning.com/subjects/butterfly
A fantastic amount of information on butterflies and moths, with an illustrated butterfly dictionary and printouts to label. Excellent.

Butterfly Conservation
www.butterfly-conservation.org

Plants

Goodman, P. (2007) *Plant Classification*, Wayland

*Sterry, P. (2008) *Collins Complete Guide to British Trees: a photographic guide to every common species*, Collins

*Streeter, D. et al. (2010) *Collins Flower Guide*, Collins

Voake, C. (2009) *The Little Guide to Trees*, Eden Project Books

Voake, C. (2009) *The Little Guide to Wild Flowers*, Eden Project Books

Websites

Plants
www.enchantedlearning.com/subjects/plants
This includes an illustrated plant dictionary and lots of other printouts and information.

Science and Plants for Schools
www.saps.org.uk
Click on Beyond the Classroom for activities with plants to do at home.

PETS

See also: **Part 4, Section 2 – Horse and Pony Riding**

Typical questions

- What does a hamster eat?
- Do I have to take my dog for a walk?
- I want a snake – what do I need?
- Is there a local dog show?

Considerations

There are lots of books and a number of series available on keeping pets, and most of them will be suitable for the types of questions asked. A few suggestions of titles and series are given below, but these are by no means the only ones to consider. In the main, children will want information on how to look after a pet such as a hamster or dog, but sometimes it could be a lizard, snake or rat, so try to have a range available. Try also some of the websites below. Sometimes children may want to know about local pet shows, so keep local contacts and details available, especially as there is often an entry deadline.

Where to look

Know Your Pet series from QED Publishing. Includes the following titles:

Miller, M. (2007) *Dogs and Puppies*

Miller, M. (2008) *Rabbits*

Head, H. (2008) *Cats and Kittens*

Head, H. (2007) *Horses and Ponies*

Try also: **You and Your Pet** series, also from QED Publishing.
Titles include *Guinea Pig, Hamster and Gerbil, Mouse, Rabbit and Rat.*

For unusual pets try: **Extreme Pets** series from Franklin Watts Publishers.
Titles include: *Lizard, Piranha, Rat, Salamander, Snake, Spider.*

Magazine

Animals and You Magazine
DC Thompson
Monthly
Tel: 020 74001030
www.dcthompson.co.uk

Websites

Blue Cross

www.bluecross.org.uk/1741/Looking-afteryourpet.html

Blue Cross is the charity for sick and unwanted pets. It has a range of animal factsheets available to download covering health, behaviour and safety. The list of animals includes cat, dog, horse, rabbit, hamster, gerbil, rat, chinchilla, guinea pig, mouse and degu. There are also factsheets on finding the right pet, animals and fireworks, and pets and floods. In addition, there is a Blue Cross Kids site with information and games especially for younger children. Excellent.

RSPCA

www.rspca.org.uk

Click on All About Animals, then select Our Pets. This gives advice on how to keep pets healthy. For horses click on Our Horses. This gives information on how to keep horses and ponies healthy.

Cats

Cats for Kids

www.cats.org.uk/cats-for-kids

All about cats and more, especially for children, from the organization Cats Protection.

Dogs

Dogs Trust

www.dogstrust.org.uk/az/factsheetsanddownloads/default.aspx

Lots of factsheets, from getting a dog to training.

Young Kennel Club

www.ykc.org.uk

For young dog fans from aged 6 to 24 years. It has special sections for kids and teens. It also gives details of shows.

Fish

Federation of British Aquatic Societies
www.fbas.co.uk

First Fish Tank Guide
www.firsttankguide.net

Pet shows

London Pet Show
www.londonpetshow.co.uk
For dogs, cats, small furries, exotics and aquatics.

Horses

British Horse Society
www.bhs.org.uk/Horse_Care/Horse_Care_Advice/Publications/
Download.aspx
Provides horse-care advice.

PLACES TO VISIT AND THINGS TO DO

Typical questions

- Is there anything on for children this summer?
- Where is the nearest museum?
- Have you any children's activities at the library?
- What are the opening times for the swimming pool?

Considerations

There is simply nothing that offers more fun than having a day trip with the children, whether it is to the seaside, the art gallery or the local park with a picnic. Queries about places to go with children tend to come along more often during school holidays, and for this reason it is sensible to have relevant leaflets on what is happening in your local area easily accessible. In the current climate, activities and places to go for little cost will probably be popular! As well as the local museums, parks and art galleries, your own library may have summer or half-term events. Many of the details of local council events can be found on their website, as will those of local galleries and museums; however, printed programmes are worth collecting and having to hand. If you have somewhere to display these, make sure that you also keep a reference copy. Day trips are not just about the destination but also about how to get there. Make sure that you can answer such queries fully by offering bus and train travel information, opening times of museums, libraries and art galleries etc., and don't forget to mention websites like **Martin's Money** for handy, money-off vouchers, **www.moneysavingexpert.com/deals/cheap-days-out**; and of course it's always useful to check the weather, **www.bbc.co.uk/weather**.

Buses

Traveline
> **http://traveline.info**
> National link to local bus timetables. Select region, then timetable info, then type in the bus number, or select journey planner if you don't know. Very impressive.

Trains

National Rail Enquiries
> **www.nationalrail.co.uk**
> Select journey planner.

Cars and walkers

Most libraries will have local street maps and many will have a selection of regional and national road and street maps.

Alternatively try:

www.streetmap.co.uk

or

AA Route Planner
www.theaa.com

Where to look

As to ideas for entertaining the children, these are littered throughout this book and I have highlighted with a $ those websites that I feel are useful for games or activities when all else fails. There are books available that provide hundreds of ideas for keeping children occupied and a selection are mentioned below. Most libraries will offer similar titles.

Places to visit

500 free days out, **AA Publishing, 2010**

★1001 Great Family days out, **AA Publishing, 2010**
From museums to zoos, arranged by county.

Calder, J. and Bruce, A. (2005) *The Oldest: in celebration of Britain's living history*, **Cassell Illustrated**
This covers the oldest things not found in museums, such as the oldest bank, chemist, hedgerows, lead statue and hundreds more. This could make for some interesting day trips.

'Time Out' London for Children 2011: the essential guide for parents, **Time Out, 2010**

Websites

DaysOut
www.daysout.co.uk
This is the official website of *Days Out* magazine. It is a very useful starting-point for finding somewhere to go. You can search by postcode and within a certain radius, or search by region, or by attraction.

Days Out UK

www.daysoutuk.com

Enables you to find out about discounted days out in the UK.

Days Out with the Kids

www.dayoutwiththekids.co.uk

Choose a region, the type of activity, either indoor or outdoor and the children's age range. Provides a list of family days out, places to go, with full details. Excellent.

Discover Northern Ireland

www.discovernorthernireland.com

Enjoy Britain

www.enjoybritain.com

A very accessible directory of places to visit and things to do.

Enjoy England

www.enjoyengland.com

Official website for tourism in England.

Freedom Days

www.freedom-days.co.uk

Visit Scotland

www.visitscotland.com

Official site of Scotland's tourism.

Visit Wales

www.visitwales.com

Farms

Farms to Visit

www.ukagriculture.com/farms_to_visit/farms_to_visit.cfm

A really useful site to find farms in your local area that allow visits by families and schools. Provides detailed description, facilities and activities available, contact, location and web addresses of individual farms.

Houses and historical sites

Hudson's Historic Houses and Gardens, Castles and Heritage Sites (2011), **Hudson**

Websites
CADW
www.cadw.wales.gov.uk
The official guardian to the built heritage of Wales. Click on Places to Visit.

English Heritage
www.english-heritage.org.uk

Historic Scotland
www.historic-scotland.gov.uk
Responsible for safeguarding Scotland's historic environment. Click on Places to Visit.

Hudson's Heritage
www.hudsonsheritage.com
Type in where you're planning to visit to find a list of historic attractions.

National Trust
www.nationaltrust.org.uk
Click on Find a Place to Visit.

Libraries

Libraries and Information Services in the United Kingdom and the Republic of Ireland, **Facet Publishing, Annual**
This lists nearly 3000 libraries. However, individual branch libraries within local authorities are not always listed, only main library service contacts.

For individual branch libraries use the local council's website, where details of all its libraries should be given, including opening times and locations. In addition, details of regular story times and special activities, such as the Summer Reading Challenge activities, should also be available. Try also:

UK Public Libraries List
http://dspace.dial.pipex.com/town/square/ac940/weblibs.html
Excellent.

Museums and galleries

Museums and Galleries Yearbook, **Museums Association, Annual**
A directory of museums in the UK giving full details for each museum. Excellent.

Culture 24

www.24hourmuseum.org.uk

This is a gateway to over 3000 UK museums, galleries and heritage attractions.

Nature Reserves

Nature Reserves

www.rspb.org.uk/reserves

Enables searching by postcode or place name. Does only give RSPB nature reserves. Also has a Things To Do facility which provides details of events happening at RSPB nature reserves.

Wildlife Trusts

www.wildlifetrusts.org

There are more than 2000 nature reserves in the UK cared for by the Wildlife Trust. To find the nearest to you, select Reserves and search by postcode, town or county.

Parks, gardens and picnics

Lambert, K. and Gatti, A. (2010) *The Good Gardens Guide 2010–2011: the essential independent guide to the 1200 best gardens, parks and green spaces in Britain, Ireland and the Channel Islands,* **Reader's Digest**

The Yellow Book, **National Garden Scheme, Annual**

Detailed listings of thousands of gardens open for visiting.

For individual parks use local council websites, where local parks should be listed, including details of facilities and any special events.

Websites

Nature Detectives Picnic Kit

www.naturedetectives.org.uk/packs/picnic_pack.htm

The Woodland Trust has a free picnic kit, which includes an activity booklet, recipes, leaf doilies, picnic spotter sheet, adventure booklet and more.

National Garden Scheme

www.ngs.org.uk

Gardens open to the public for charity. You can do a garden search by postcode, town, county or garden name.

Picnics

www.netmums.com/food/Picnics.1258

Handy for the picnic checklist and picnic recipes.

Swimming pools

For individual swimming pools use the local council's website, where details of all its pools should be given, including opening times, facilities, location and details of any special activities.

Zoos

Zoos UK

www.zoosuk.zookeepers.co.uk

Alphabetical and regional listing of all UK zoos. Also includes sealife and aquaria, bird gardens, safari parks, butterfly and insect houses and city farms.

Lo-cost or no-cost

Beaches Blue Flag Award

www.keepbritaintidy.org/Programmes/Beaches/
OurAward-winningBeaches/Default.aspx

Good Beach Guide

www.goodbeachguide.co.uk

Devised by the Marine Conservation Society. Select a region to find a recommended beach.

Heritage Open Days

www.heritageopendays.org.uk

These are held in one weekend in September when there is free access to properties that are usually closed to the public or normally charge admission. Includes synagogues, churches, town halls, castles, shops, clock towers and more.

Things to do

Bailey, E. (2011) *The Girls' Rainy Day Book*, Buster Books

Bailey, E. (2011) *The Boys' Rainy Day Book*, Buster Books

Brooks, H. (ed.) (2009) *Rainy Day Book*, Guardian Books

Simple and inexpensive ideas for science and craft activities.

Time Out 1000 Things for Kids To Do in the Holidays, **Ebury Press, 2009**
Sights, excursions and events in Britain, as well as activities at home, under various categories from toddler to teens.

Website

Things To Do: activities run by the BBC and partners
www.bbc.co.uk/thingstodo
Find activities by searching by town, city or postcode. It provides lists of activities in date order. Click on chosen activity for more details, which include cost, location and who's running the activity. Very useful.

READING

See also: **Part 4, Section 1 – Animation, Cartoons, Comics and Manga**

Typical questions

- What books would you suggest for my 9-year-old son?
- Do you know of any novels for teenagers that deal with bullying?
- Are there any children's reading groups in my area?
- What picture books would you recommend for 4-year-olds?

Considerations

Reading for enjoyment is very personal for all of us, and that is true for children's reading too. When it comes to children, reading is not simply about books but also about comics, manga, graphic novels and magazines; and it's not just about fiction but also non-fiction (information books), poetry and jokes. It is difficult to recommend titles for children because so many other considerations have to be taken into account. Not all children read at the same level at the same age, and individual likes, dislikes and experiences influence choice. However, you can point to the many websites offering reviews, recommendations (some by children themselves) and book lists, some of which are given below. Of course, there is nothing wrong in offering your own suggestions, so long as you are not too disappointed if the child doesn't agree with you. There is an increasing interest in reading groups for children and teenagers; however, it is often difficult to track these down. The shadowing site for the **Carnegie Medal, www.carnegiegreenaway.org.uk** is worth looking at because it provides an alphabetical list of children's reading groups that have taken part, many of which, especially those organized through libraries, have contact details. The added feature of listing other groups in the vicinity is very useful too.

Where to look

Book reviews and recommendations

There are many guides available to buy that list recommended books and children's books that should be read. The choice is endless and most reference collections should at least have one. However, there are free resources available and there are two suggestions below which in my opinion are excellent.

Best Books for Kids: a guide to Egmont books for toddlers to teenagers, **Egmont, 2010**
> An excellent guide to classic and popular Egmont children's titles. There is lots of good quality advice, and tips for enjoying reading with children. This guide is available free from **www.egmont.co.uk**.

***Puffin Handbook: the perfect little guide to the 70 best books for children,*
Puffin, 2010**
This was produced to celebrate Puffin's 70th birthday and is a very useful guide to children's books from baby to teen. Far from covering Puffin's complete catalogue it selects its classic children's titles and gives tips and expert advice on reading. Well worth having on your bookshelves. Copies are available free from **www.puffin.co.uk**.

The following titles to buy are great too.

Eccleshare, J. *1001 Children's Books You Must Read before You Grow Up,*
Guardian Books
Introduces the wealth of children's books to parents and children, from picture books to classics. It includes author biographies and over 800 illustrations.

Hahn, D. and Flynn, L. (2010) *The Ultimate Book Guide: over 600 great*
books for 8–12s, **A&C Black**

Hahn, D. et al. (eds) (2010) *The Ultimate Teen Book Guide,* **A&C Black**
Over 750 books listed with the basic plot, and suggestions for what to read next.

Websites

Accelerated Reader Book Finder
www.arbookfind.co.uk
This is a free online tool from Renaissance Learning which allows age- and grade-appropriate searching for book titles by pupils, parents, teachers and librarians.

Barrington Stoke
www.barringtonstoke.co.uk
Publishes age-appropriate books for children with dyslexia and for reluctant and under-confident readers. The site is aimed at teachers and parents and features extracts from all its children's titles as well as interviews with authors. It also gives advice about helping reluctant readers aged 8 to 16.

Bookbox
www.channel4learning.com/sites/bookbox
See and hear 30 well known children's authors talk about writing and their work.

Booktrust
www.booktrustchildrensbooks.org.uk
Lots of recommended books, competitions and advice. Excellent.

Cool Reads
www.cool-reads.co.uk

Lovereading 4 Kids
www.lovereading4kids.co.uk
This has a range of reviews and suggestions, with a facility to download extracts. Provides titles listed in age groups and special features such as Books for Boys. Some features require registration.

Mrs Mad's Book-a-Rama
www.mrsmad.com
This offers hundreds of reviews of books for children and teenagers and allows them to upload their own reviews. It has lists of reviews by themes, age groups and authors. Well worth a visit by children, parents, librarians and teachers alike. Lots of useful links too.

Seven Stories: the Centre for Children's Books
www.sevenstories.org.uk

Stories from the Web
www.storiesfromtheweb.org
This is a subscription-based online reader-development site managed by Birmingham Libraries on behalf of participating authorities. It is for children via libraries and schools or by family subscription. It encourages children to read, write and draw and to share their work via the online Gallery. There are three age groups 0–7 years, 7–11 years and 11+ years. It is a great way to show your work off to a national audience.

The Word Pool
www.wordpool.co.uk
Has an excellent range of books and a fantastic list of author profiles, sadly, no longer updated, but worth looking at for well known names.

Authors

To find specific author websites you can use one of the familiar search engines such as **www.google.com** – they will usually offer good results. The secret is to make sure that you spell the name correctly. If you find that you have repeated requests for authors it may be useful to bookmark a few. Alternatively, many of the review sites mentioned above have author-information sections and links. There are also books published on some of the better known authors, such as **Senker, C. (2010)** *J. K. Rowling: creator of Harry Potter,* **Wayland**

Roald Dahl
   www.roalddahl.com
   Fabulous for fans and schools everywhere.

ContactAnAuthor
   www.contactanauthor.co.uk
   Useful for librarians and schools wanting to book author visits.

Book awards

Blue Peter Awards
   www.booktrust.org.uk
   Click on Prizes and Awards. Select Blue Peter Book Awards. Established in 2000, books are shortlisted by adult judges, then a group of young Blue Peter viewers judge the three categories: Books I Couldn't Put Down; Best Book with Facts; Most Fun Story with Pictures.

Carnegie and Kate Greenaway Medals
   www.carnegiegreenaway.org.uk
   The Carnegie Medal is awarded by children's librarians for an outstanding book for children or young people. The Kate Greenaway Medal is awarded for the illustration of a children's book. The site lists all previous winning titles and has reviews from hundreds of children's reading groups.

Other prizes

Roald Dahl Funny Prize

Booktrust Teenage Prize

Booktrust Early Years Awards

For all use **www.booktrust.org.uk**. Click on Prizes and Awards.

Book events

National Children's Book Week
   www.booktrustchildrensbooks.org.uk
   This is an annual celebration of reading for enjoyment for children. Select Children's Book Week.

National Literacy Trust
   www.literacytrust.org.uk/events

This provides an extensive list of book-related events, arranged by month.

Summer Reading Challenge
www.readingagency.org.uk

Select Summer Reading Challenge. This is the national annual reading challenge that takes place in libraries during the school summer holidays.

World Book Day
www.worldbookday.com

World Book Day (WBD) was designated by UNESCO as a worldwide celebration of books and reading and is marked by over 100 countries. The main aim of World Book Day is to encourage children to explore the enjoyment of books and reading by providing them with the opportunity to have a book of their own. Children are entitled to receive a WBD £1 book token to exchange for a specially published book.

Book sequels

Look no further than:

Children's Book Sequels ... what comes next?
www.childrensbooksequels.co.uk

Absolutely wonderful, providing the right order for just about every known series of children's books – and it's kept up to date too. It has an A–Z sequence by author and series. It also has a search facility. Not only does it give the titles in series order but also provides the link to the related website. Highly recommended, and one to bookmark.

Comics

See: **Part 4, Section 1 – Animation, Cartoons, Comics and Manga**

Reading isn't only about books; it's whatever reading matter a child enjoys. I have long been an advocate of comics, graphic novels and magazines. Comics, according to Elaine Feinstein in *Ted Hughes: the life of a poet*, were his first introduction to literature. I rest my case.

List of comic titles and details

Willings Press Guide, Cison, Annual

For a listing of children's comics and magazines, look under Section 2 UK Periodicals by Classification – Children and Youth. Then for full details of each title look under Section 4 Consumer Magazines. Titles are arranged alphabetically within this section.

Reading groups and how to set up

Reading groups for children and teenagers are becoming increasingly popular, which is wonderfully reassuring in this computer-driven age. However, many people believe they don't know where to start. Believe it or not it isn't that difficult. If you are considering it as a library or school, the main considerations are where, when and who will facilitate the group. Decide 'the who' first, and their availability and work location may dictate 'the where and when'. Of course, you want the group to be suitable for children and their parents, who will be doing the dropping off and picking up, but it is a common mistake to try to get all of this right at the beginning. Start with what you can do, and change as and when you need to, within the limitations of the library/school. This way you actually do get started. Second, you need to find a group of like-minded children. Advertise in the library/school, the local paper or local authority free paper or school magazine if you have one. Put posters up anywhere and everywhere that you feel is appropriate and sensible. Make sure that you have a contact number on the poster. Or you may already have children who visit the library regularly who want to join or make a group. Don't wait to have loads of interested children – just get started, even if you have one or two children. Their experience on that first meeting will be your best advertisement, and if they enjoy themselves they'll bring their friends along next time. This approach does work; my teen group grew from two teens to over 20 and has met monthly for the last four years.

For parents who want to set up a group, the above applies too. However, the group may be a group of friends or members of the same class. Libraries/schools and parents need to work together to encourage reading groups, and this includes helping to obtain books and passing on interesting competitions etc. that would be useful for the group. Also, enlist the help of group members and be prepared to empower them to start their own groups independently.

Book-it! reading clubs
www.continyou.org/school/files/book-it_resource

ContinYou helps schools to set up reading groups and has produced an excellent guide for sustainability.

Tips and pitfalls

In order to offer quality information with regard to book choice and recommendations for children try, firstly, to keep up to date with books that are published. Secondly, make sure that some of the above review sites are bookmarked and viewed regularly, and to try to read a selection of the books. That way you can talk to both parent and child knowledgeably and offer genuine suggestions. Thirdly, don't forget that reading is about more than books, and find out about comics, manga, magazines and graphic novels. Finally, have enthusiasm – it's very contagious!

UNIFORMED ORGANIZATIONS

Typical questions

- At what age can my son start Beavers?
- Are there any local Brownies?
- Where can I buy an Explorer shirt from?

Considerations

Queries are usually for the contact details or information on the Scouting Association or Girlguiding UK, both of which can be found below. However, there are other uniformed organizations which include, amongst others, the Army and Sea Cadets; the Boys' Brigade and the Girls' Air Cadets – all of which have excellent websites.

Where to look

Bailey, J. (2010) *Complete Guide to Scouting Skills*, Doubleday

Websites and organizations

Scouting and Guiding movement

Rainbows
www.girlguiding.org.uk/rainbows

Brownies
www.girlguiding.org.uk/brownies

Guides
GirlGuiding UK
Commonwealth HQ
17-19 Buckingham Palace Rd
London SW1W 0PT
Tel: 020 7834 6242
www.girlguiding.org.uk/home.aspx

Beavers
http://scouts.org.uk/beavers
Beaver scouts are the youngest in the scouting family, aged 6 to 8 years. You can join Beaver scouts in the three months leading up to your 6th birthday.

Cubs
http://scouts.org.uk/cubs
Has a search facility to find your nearest cub pack.

Scouts
Scouts Association
Scout Information Centre
Gilwell Park
Chingford
London E4 7QW
Tel: 0845 300 1818
http://scouts.org.uk

Explorers
http://scouts.org.uk/explorers

Magazines
Guiding Magazine
Girl Guiding UK
Monthly
Tel: 020 7834 6242

Scouting
The Scout Association
6 issues per year
Tel: 020 8433 7100

Other uniformed organizations for young people
Army Cadet Force: Cadets
www.armycadets.com/home
For 12- to 18-year-olds who want action and adventure.

Boys' Brigade
www.boys-brigade.org.uk

Church Lads' and Church Girls' Brigade
www.clcgb.org.uk
Anglican uniformed youth organization for 5- to 21-year-olds.

Girls' Venture Corps Air Cadets
www.gvcac.org.uk

Jewish Lads' and Girls' Brigade
www3.jlgb.org
For 8- to 18-year-olds.

Royal Air Force Air Cadets
www.raf.mod.uk/aircadets
For 13- to 17-year-olds. Select Cadets.

Sea Cadets
www.sea-cadets.org

St John Ambulance Cadets
www.sja.org.uk/sja/young-people/cadets.aspx
For 10- to 16-year-olds.

WRITING

See also: **Part 2 – English (Literacy) and English Literature**

Typical questions

- How do I become a writer?
- My daughter's teachers say that she is a gifted writer – who would be able to help get her work published?
- I'd like to join a creative writing club.
- How do I write poetry?

Considerations

This can be quite varied because you may find parents who are asking, on behalf of their children, either about how to improve their child's writing skills or how to find out if they have a budding Jacqueline Wilson in the family. Queries relating to writing skills will probably be fairly straightforward to answer, using material you have in the library. Some suggestions for good printed sources are listed below. Queries relating to finding publishers interested in children's work can be difficult, but hopefully the websites given below will offer some help. I am also a great advocate of entering creative writing competitions, as they are often linked to publication prizes and can offer the break-through many seek. Some of the books listed below on how to write for publication are not directed at writers who are children, but the information in them is exactly what all budding writers need to consider. Hopefully, writers over the age of 11 should be able to cope with much of the information offered in these books. For younger children, parents and teachers need to offer guidance.

Where to look

Brodie, A. (2009) *Brilliant ideas To Get Boys Writing 7–9*, A&C Black

Children's Writers' and Artists' Yearbook, A&C Black, Annual
> Excellent articles about writing for children, from editors, agents and writers, as well as all the advice you need on agents and publishers.

Try also:

Children's Writer's Handbook, Macmillan, Annual

Cleaver, P. (2010) *Writing for Children*, 4th edition, Howtobooks
> Not only does this cover planning and how to write, doing research and finding a publisher, but it has a very useful section called 'Useful

Information for Writing Children's Books', which is a collection of oddments and trivia, such as lists of ways to describe colours.

Farrell. T (2010) *Be a Creative Writer,* **Tick Tock Books**
This is produced specially for children and covers writing styles, creating characters and plots and how to get started. Highly recommended.

Jordan, L. (2010) *How to Write for Children and Get Published,* **Piatkus Books**
Packed with information on how to write and how to get published.

Mace, L. and Vincent-Northam, M. (2010) *The Writer's ABC Checklist,* **Accent Press**
An A–Z of how to write to get published.

Warren, C. (2007) *How to Write Stories,* **QED Publishing**
Written for children.

Websites

Kids on the Net
www.kidsonthenet.org.uk
This is for children interested in writing. It provides advice on how to write stories and poetry. It includes stories written by children to read online. There is also a teachers' section providing downloadable resources for creative writing.

Stories from the Web
www.storiesfromtheweb.org
This is a subscription-based online reader-development site managed by Birmingham Libraries on behalf of participating authorities. It is for children via libraries and schools or by family subscription. It encourages children to read, write and draw and to share their work via the online Gallery. There are three age groups 0–7 years, 7–11 years and 11+ years. It is a great way to show your work off to a national audience.

Why Write?
www.bl.uk/learning/artimages/why/whywrite.html
This looks at writing and ways of writing. It includes lots of activities centred around the alphabet.

Writers' Toolkit
www.channel4learning.com/sites/bookbox/writerstoolkit/home1.htm
This is excellent for young writers. It has advice on beginnings, endings, characters, locations, words, dialogue, the plot, and more general support, all from well known writers. Well worth a visit.

Writing Mysteries
http://kids.MysteryNet.com
An interesting site for those interested in developing mystery-writing skills.

Writing with Writers
http://teacher.scholastic.com/writewit/index.htm
Help with various forms of writing; news writing, book reviews, descriptive writing, scientific and more.

History of writing

French, V. and Collins, R. (1999) *Write around the World: the story of how and why we learnt to write,* **Zero to Ten Ltd**
The history of writing told in a humorous way for children.

Tips and pitfalls

For those working in libraries, avoid commenting on the merits of writing created by children. Parents need to seek advice from would-be publishers and children require guidance from teachers and parents. This does not mean that you cannot read and encourage children to write, especially if you are running reading groups. Also don't forget to look at the suggestions for improving writing skills in **Part 2 – English (Literacy) and English Literature.**

Section 2 Sports

AN OVERVIEW OF SPORTS

See also: **Part 1, Section 3 – Olympics; Part 2 – P.E. (Physical Education)**

Typical questions

- What are the rules of tennis?
- Are there any junior football teams in the area?
- Have you got any books on ballet?
- I'm doing a project on famous cricketers, have you got …?
- Who won the World Cup in 1998?

Considerations

There are a variety of sport enquiries. They can be related to improving skills, looking for sport rules, local clubs or sport personalities. The more in-depth queries relating to sport development, fitness and nutrition are covered in **Part 2 – P.E.** Many of the books on your library shelves will help with rules, how to improve and well known sport personalities. However, queries about local sports will depend very much on the sport itself: some, such as football, are easier to find out about than others. Increasingly, even local amateur groups are putting information on the internet, so it is worth doing some research and bookmarking some of the more popular local groups. This is also an area where the local telephone directory is useful for contact numbers for the local leisure centres; however, the local council's website should have all this information on its web pages. On occasion, children ask about sports personalities – usually in relation to projects such as those that celebrate Black History Month – and I would predict that projects on the Olympics will become increasingly popular. The sources below should help with the more general sport-related queries, including information for projects, and the sections that follow may help with individual sports. However, the list is by no means exhaustive. For sports not covered here use the ***Directory of British Associations and Associations in Ireland,*** **CBD Research**. This covers over 7000 national associations, societies and institutes. There is a subject index that lists relevant groups. It is worth checking to see if your sport has an organization dedicated to it.

Where to look

The Official Countdown to the London 2012 Games, **Carlton Books, 2010**
> Covers the sports; the sports stars; records; puzzles and games. Very well presented and probably well worth having over the next year.

The Sports Rules Book: essential rules, terms and procedures for 54 sports, **Human Kinetics with Thomas Hanlon, 3rd edition, 2009**

Websites and organizations

$BBC Sport Academy

http://news.bbc.co.uk/sport1/hi/academy/default.stm
This is excellent for finding out tips and techniques via short video clips from some of the best known sportsmen and women from a variety of sports. Once you have clicked on your chosen clip it allows you to also have access to a wealth of information on that particular sport, including skills. Well worth a visit.

BBC Sports Village

www.bbc.co.uk/cbbc/sportsvillage
Information about athletes and some games mainly for younger children.

Fact Monster

www.factmonster.com
Click on Sports, select specific sports – but do bear in mind that this is an American site.

Sainsbury's UK School Games

www.ukschoolgames.com
An annual event for school-age children who excel in their sport.

Sport England
> 3rd floor
> Victoria House
> Bloomsbury Square
> London WC1B 4SE
> Tel: 08458 508508
> **www.sportengland.org**

Sport Northern Ireland
> House of Sport
> 2a Upper Malone Road
> Belfast BT9 5LA
> Tel: 028 9038 1222
> **www.sportni.net**

Sport Scotland
> Doges
> Templeton on the Green
> Templeton St
> Glasgow G40 1DA
> Tel: 0141 534 6500
> **www.sportsscotland.org.uk**

Sport Wales
> Sophia Gardens
> Cardiff CF11 9SW
> Tel: 0845 045 0904
> **www.sportwales.org.uk**

Sports
> **http://sports.yahoo.com**
> Has all the latest news, fixtures and more on all sports, including some of the more contemporary such as skateboarding. It is worth bearing in mind that this site is not designed for children.

Youth Sport Trust
> **www.youthsporttrust.org**
> Excellent for knowing what is or could be happening in schools.

Sport and disability

Disabled Sports
> **www.paralympics.org.uk**

Disability Sport Wales
> **www.disabilitysportwales.org**

Disability Sports Northern Ireland
> **www.dsni.co.uk/cms**

English Federation of Disability Sport
> **www.efds.co.uk**

National Association of Swimming Clubs for People with Disabilities
www.nasch.org.uk

Scottish Disability Sport
www.scottishdisabilitysport.com

UK Sports Association for People with Learning Disabilities
www.uksportsassociation.org

Wheelpower
www.wheelpower.org.uk
British wheelchair sport.

Tips and pitfalls

This is an area where it is useful to know if colleagues are involved in or have an interest in any particular sport; this is true whether you work in libraries or schools. Many will be only too happy to share their knowledge with an enthusiastic child or may point you in the right direction for local clubs or teams.

ATHLETICS AND FIELD ATHLETICS

See also: **Part 1, Section 3 – Olympics**

Typical questions
- Who holds the world record for 100m?
- What are the rules for hurdles?
- Are there any junior running clubs?

Considerations

Athletics can be field or track. Track athletics are very popular amongst children and there are loads of books on the sport. There are some suggestions below, but don't limit yourself to children's books only. Teenagers especially would benefit from using books on athletics skills and techniques that are more detailed. With this in mind, don't be afraid to show them the sports books in the general non-fiction shelves. There are a number of popular sports personalities in athletics and they are often selected for topics on famous people or as positive role models for Citizenship. As well as books, try using some of the suggested websites below. For queries for local clubs use **UK Athletics, www.ukathletics.net.**

Where to look

Field Athletics: the Olympic sports, **Tick Tock Books, Clever Clogs series, 2008**

Gifford, C. (2008) *Running*, **Tell Me About Sport series, Evans Publishing**

Gifford, C. (2010) *Field Athletics*, **Tell Me About Sport series, Evans Publishing**

Hunter, R. (2009) *Starting Sport: athletics*, **Franklin Watts**
Explains rules, tactics and how to run. Contains lots of clear text and complementary photographs.

Track Athletics: the Olympic sports, **Tick Tock Books, Clever Clogs series, 2008**

Websites
Athletics
www.olympic.org
Within the official site of the Olympic movement, select Sports from the top menu, then Athletics. There is a huge amount of information,

including equipment, history and techniques. The detail given about the sport is excellent and will help anyone enjoy watching the athletics at the Olympics.

Athletics Northern Ireland
www.niathletics.org

England Athletics
www.englandathletics.org/schools
This is useful for everything to encourage young people in schools to try and to enjoy athletics. Lots of links given.

Scottish Athletics
www.scottishathletics.org.uk
Select Get Involved, then Development and Schools.

UK Athletics
www.ukathletics.net
To find athletics clubs, select Grassroots, then Club search. It also has an excellent athletics hall of fame. Not only fascinating for athletics fans but useful for topics on famous people.

Welsh Athletics
www.welshathletics.org
Click on Schools for how to get involved.

Triathlon

British Triathlon
www.britishtriathlon.org

Triathlon England
www.triathlonengland.org
Click on Children, Young People and Schools. Here there are lots of developments planned to encourage young people to compete and train for triathlon.

Triathlon Scotland
www.triathlonscotland.org
Click on Youth.

Welsh Triathlon
www.welshtriathlon.org

BOXING

Typical questions

- Where can I learn to box?
- Are there any boxing clubs for juniors?

Considerations

In the main, queries will relate to where to join a club or how to improve skills. For queries on local classes use the **Amateur Boxing Association**, **www.abae.co.uk/aba**. Select Clubs, then Club Finder. Search by postcode, town or county. You may find using books in the general non-fiction section useful. There are a few suggestions below.

Where to look

Amateur Boxing Association and Hickey, K. (2006) *Boxing*, Amateur Boxing Association, Know the Game series

Blower, G. (2007) *Boxing: training, skills and techniques*, The Crowood Press

Mullan, H. (2010) *The Ultimate Encyclopaedia of Boxing*, Carlton Books

Websites

Amateur Boxing Association
www.abae.co.uk/aba
Select Clubs, then Club Finder. Search by postcode, town or county.

Amateur Boxing Scotland
www.amateurboxingscotland.co.uk

British Boxing Board of Control
www.bbbofc.com
This is for professional boxing. It is useful for results and schedules.

Welsh Amateur Boxing Association
http://welshboxingassociation.org
Select Clubs to find contact details of local clubs.

CRICKET

Typical questions
- Who plays for Pakistan?
- What are the rules of one-day cricket?

Considerations
There are lots of books on cricket, so with any luck most of the queries will be answered by looking at what you have on your library shelves. Don't be afraid to use the general non-fiction library as well as children's books. For scores, fixtures and results some websites are suggested below. It is probably worth bearing in mind that many cricket websites, including the ones below, are not designed especially for children and therefore should be used with adult guidance. For queries regarding local cricket clubs use **www.cricketstix.com/home.php**.

Where to look
The Cricketers' Who's Who, **G2Entertainment, Annual**

de Lisle, T. and Booth, L. (2011) *Young Wisden: a new fan's guide to cricket*, **A&C Black**
Gives all the statistics, the stars, and explains the world of cricket from scorecards to Test Cricket. Excellent.

Gifford, C. (2009) *Cricket*, **Tell Me About Sport series, Evans Publishing**

Sellers, L. (2008) *Know the Game: cricket fielding and wicket keeping*, **A&C Black**
Provides techniques and training for young players.

Wisden Cricketers' Almanac, **A&C Black, Annual**
Useful for the full laws of cricket.

Magazine
Cricketer
The Cricketer Publishing in association with Wisden
Monthly
Tel: 0207 705 4911
www.wisdencricketer-magazine.co.uk

Websites

Cricket Commentary
http://sport.guardian.co.uk/cricket

Cricket Ireland
www.irishcricket.org
Covers Northern Ireland and youth cricket

Cricket News
http://news.bbc.co.uk/sport1/hi/cricket

CricketOnline
www.cricket.co.uk
Includes cricket news, fixtures, results and league tables.

Cricket Scores and Statistics
www.cricinfo.com
Not designed specifically for children, but packed with scores, fixtures, results and more.

Cricket Scotland
www.cricketscotland.com
Click on Youth.

England and Wales Cricket Board
www.ecb.co.uk/development

Lords
www.lords.org
The home of cricket.

Stix
www.cricketstix.com/home.php
A cricketing website for young people aged 12 to 16 years from the England and Wales Cricket Board. This has lots of information, including cricket news, how to improve your cricketing skills and your favourite cricket players. You can also search for local cricket clubs.

CYCLING

See also: **Part 3 – School Travel**

Typical questions
- Are there any junior cycling clubs?
- Do you know the local cycle paths?
- What is the Tour de France?

Considerations

Cycling is not only a serious sport but also a hobby and leisure activity enjoyed by many children and families. Queries regarding cycling mainly centre around cycling for enjoyment or as a mode of transport. Hence, having information on local cycle routes available is useful, but remember to keep it up to date. You may get queries regarding cycling proficiency, in which case try **Bikeability, www.dft.gov.uk/bikeability.training.** This covers the National Standard for Cycling, i.e. cycling proficiency tests. You can find out if there is a scheme near you or how to get one started.

Cycling has many guises in sport. It can be an 'extreme sport' when it is mountain biking, and it is part of triathlon (swimming, running, cycling) or duathlon (running, cycling), as well as an entity in itself. As with many sports, as well as using the books within the children's library, also use the general non-fiction collection.

Where to look

Gifford, C. (2010) *Cycling*, **Tell Me About Sport series, Evans Publishing**

Know the Game: cycling, **A&C Black in association with British Cycling, 2008**
Looks at equipment, rules and techniques.

Mason, P. (2011) *Know Your Sport: cycling*, **Franklin Watts**

Websites
Bike Hub
  www.bikehub.co.uk
  Packed with information for everyone who owns a bicycle. Includes teaching your child to ride a bike; cycle commuting; how to buy bikes; cycling and the law, and much more. Also has a cycle route finder. Excellent.

British Cycling Federation
www.britishcycling.org.uk
Provides information on all types of cycling, and you can search for local clubs.

Cycling Ireland
www.cyclingireland.ie
Use for Northern Ireland.

Scottish Cycling
www.britishcycling.org.uk/scotland

Sustrans
www.sustrans.org.uk
Excellent for safe cycle routes to school and cycling maps for leisure. It has information for schools, parents and young people on how to enjoy cycling more and how to partake in national cycling initiatives.

Welsh Cycling
www.welshcycling.co.uk

Competitions and events

Sky Ride
www.goskyride.com
Sky Ride city events are a nationwide series of summer events to encourage people to get back on their bikes. Cyclists of all ages and abilities are given the freedom to ride traffic-free streets as the Sky Ride takes over city centres. The website also lists other cycling activities to take part in.

Tour de France
www.letour.fr/indexus.html
Gives the tour routes stage by stage and lots more.

Tour de France Information
www.goskyride.com
Provides a beginner's guide to understanding the Tour de France. Click on Get into Cycling.

Union Cycliste Internationale
www.uci.ch
Information on world competition events.

Triathlon

British Triathlon
www.britishtriathlon.org

Triathlon England
www.triathlonengland.org
Click on Children, Young People and Schools. There are lots of developments planned to encourage young people to compete and train for triathlon.

Triathlon Scotland
www.triathlonscotland.org
Click on Youth.

Welsh Triathlon
www.welshtriathlon.org

DANCE

See also: **Part 4, Section 1 – Acting and Performing**

Typical questions
- What is the story of *Swan Lake*?
- Have you got any books on modern dancing?
- Are there any local dance classes?

Considerations
There are so many different styles of dancing that, in reality, the queries are endless. However, the main queries are usually regarding where to find specific dance classes. For queries regarding improving techniques many of the books on your library shelves may be sufficient. The problem can be that with so many styles it is hard to cater for all at any one time. As with all sports, don't be afraid to venture out of the children's library and to use the general non-fiction collection. There are some suggestions below.

Where to look
General
Ashley, L. (2008) *Essential Guide to Dance*, Hodder Education

Ctaine, D. (2010) *Oxford Dictionary of Dance*, Oxford University Press

Grau, A. (2005) *Dance*, Dorling Kindersley, Eyewitness series
   Covers the different types of dance, costumes, choreography, famous dancers and dance crazes.

Specific dances
Gogerly, L. (2011) *Street Dance*, Wayland

Hackett, J. (2008) *Ballerina: a step-by-step guide to ballet*, Dorling Kindersley

Hodge, S. (2008) *Latin and Ballroom*, Heinemann, Dance series

Minden, E. G. (2006) *The Ballet Companion: a dancer guide to the techniques, traditions and joys of ballet*, Simon and Schuster

Solway, A. (2009) *Country and Folk Dance*, Heinemann, Dance series

Storey, R. (2005) *Irish Dancing and Other National Dances*, Franklin Watts, Get dancing series
Other titles in the series: *Street Jazz and Modern Dance, Rock 'n' Roll and Other Dance Crazes, Line Dancing and Other Folk Dances.*

Storey, R. (2010) *Samba and Salsa*, Franklin Watts, Simply Dance series
Other titles in the series: *Tango and Paso Doble, Jive and Street Dance, Waltz and Quick Step.*

Magazine

Dancing Times
  Dancing Times Ltd
  Monthly
  Tel: 020 7250 3006
  www.dancing-times.co.uk

Websites

Ballet.co
  www.ballet.co.uk
  Great for finding out about ballet legends.

Council for Dance
  www.cdet.org.uk

English National Ballet
  www.ballet.org.uk
  Click on Learning, then Resources to download story sheets of some of the major ballets. There are also resource packs available that are suitable for KS3 and KS4 and a ballet glossary under the section Ballet Explored.

Indian Classical Dance
  www.tarang-classical-indian-music.com

Royal Academy of Dance
  www.rad.org.uk

Royal Ballet School
  www.royal-ballet-school.org.uk

Young Dancers
  www.young-dancers.org
  A teen site covering all aspects of dancing.

Youth Dance England
    www.yde.org.uk
    Packed with information, including guidance sheets covering, for instance, the use of recorded music in dance performances.

Dance schools

Dance Schools and Places to Dance in the UK
    www.dancesport.uk.com/studios/index.htm
    Select county from menu for a list of dance schools in the region. It covers ballroom, Latin, salsa, tango and other forms of partner dancing.

Strictly Come Dancing
    www.bbc.co.uk/strictlycomedancing
    Includes dances classes in Britain.

FOOTBALL

Typical questions
- Who won the last World Cup?
- What was the score for the match . . . ?
- Have you any books on football skills?
- What does 4-4-2 mean?

Considerations
There are lots of books on football, so with any luck most of the queries will be answered by looking at what you have on your library shelves. Don't be afraid to use the general non-fiction library as well as children's books. For scores and league tables the BBC has excellent coverage and the website is mentioned below. It is probably worth bearing in mind that many football websites, including the ones listed, are not designed especially for children and therefore should be used with adult guidance.

Where to look

Cook, M. (2009) *101 Youth Football Drills Age 12–16*, **3rd edition, A&C Black**
   Designed especially for young players, it contains a wide range of practice drills, all illustrated, including essential technical skills.

Try also:

Football Focus series, Wayland, 2009
   Titles include: *The Business of Football, Players and Skills, Rules of the Game, Teamwork and Tactics.*

Gifford, C. (2008) *Football*, **Tell Me About Sport series, Evans Publishing**

Welsh, A. (2004) *The Soccer Goalkeeping Handbook: the essential guide for players and coaches*, **2nd edition, A&C Black**
   Covers techniques and skills for goalkeepers.

Magazines
Four Four Two
   Haymarket Consumer Media
   Monthly
   Tel: 020 8267 5000
   www.fourfourtwo.com
   Has player profiles and interviews.

Match of the day
 BBC
 Weekly
 www.motmag.com

Websites

English Football Association
 www.thefa.com

Football Association of Wales
 www.faw.org.uk

Football League Tables
 http://news.bbc.co.uk/sport1/hi/football/tables/default.stm

Footy4kids
 www.footy4kids.co.uk
 Loads of coaching, practice, skills and tactic tips.

Irish Football Association (Northern Ireland)
 www.irishfa.com

Scottish Football Association
 www.scottishfa.co.uk

Welsh Football Trust
 www.welshfootballtrust.org.uk

World Cup
 www.fifa.com/worldcup/index.html

GOLF

Typical questions
- How do I play golf?
- What is a birdie?
- Where can I learn to play golf?

Considerations

As with most sports, don't be afraid to use the sports books within the general non-fiction as well as those in the children's library. Golf is becoming increasingly popular with young children and, as a result, there are a number of books around. Find out what local golf facilities are available for younger players and keep contact details to hand as well as up to date. You can use **Golf Club UK**, **www.theinternetgolfclub.com/clubsearch.asp**. This allows you to search by town, club name (if known), postcode or county. It provides full details of clubs, including whether junior players are welcome, and fees. Excellent, and one to bookmark.

Where to look

Gifford, C. (2009) *Master This! Golf*, Wayland

Gifford, C. (2010) *Golf: from tee to green – the essential guide for young golfers*, Kingfisher

Websites

Get into Golf
www.getintogolf.org
Includes a search facility to locate clubs that has Golfmark, the accreditation scheme that identifies junior and beginner friendly facilities.

The Golf Foundation
www.golf-foundation.org
The Golf Foundation offers the Golf Roots national initiative, which introduces children to golf and teaches them 'skills for life' at the same time. Select a Find a Golf Roots Centre.

Tournaments

Golf Empire
www.golfempire.co.uk
Provides information on amateur open golf tournaments. Search by region

or by category. The category search includes Junior for players under 18. Well worth a visit.

Open Championships
www.opengolf.com

GYMNASTICS

Typical questions
* Where can I learn gymnastics?
* Have you any books on gymnastics?

Considerations
The main queries are usually about how to improve techniques and where gymnastics classes are offered. Local leisure centres should have gymnastics classes and you can use the local council's web pages to find out where these are offered. However, some of the websites below have Find a Club facility that offers more scope for venues and includes accredited clubs.

Where to look
Bray-Moffat, N. (2007) *I love gymnastics: learn how to be a gymnast at a real-life gymnastics school*, Dorling Kindersley

Brown, H. (2009) *How To Improve Gymnastics*, Tick Tock Books

Gifford, C. (2010) *Gymnastics*, Tell Me About Sport series, Evans Publishing

Mason, P. (2008) *Gymnastics*, Franklin Watts, Know Your Sports series

Websites
BBC Gymnastics
http://news.bbc.co.uk/sport1/hi/other_sports/gymnastics/default.htm
This has some video clips of gymnastics demonstrations.

British Gymnastics
www.british-gymnastics.org
The website of the UK national governing body for gymnastics. It is useful for current information on what is happening in gymnastics. It also has a Find a Venue search facility, which enables you to find a British Gymnastics registered club, school or leisure centre near you. In addition it has an events calendar – select Events and Travel, then Calendar, which is useful for knowing which competitions are taking place and where.

European Union of Gymnastics
www.ueg-gymnastics.com
Lots of information, including statistics. This gives comprehensive results from the various competitions, including the Olympics since 1996.

Fédération Internationale de Gymnastique
www.fig-gymnastics.com
The International Gymnastics Federation is the official governing body for gymnastics in the world. Includes the rules and calendar of events.

Gymnastics
www.olympic.org
Within the official site of the Olympic movement, select Sports from the top menu, then Gymnastics and then either trampoline gymnast, artistic gymnastics or rhythmic gymnastics. For each there is a huge amount of information, including equipment, history and techniques. The detail given about the sport is excellent and will help anyone enjoy watching the gymnastics at the Olympics.

Gymnastics
http://tinyurl.com/ysul2s
This has animated tutorials of basic gymnastics techniques, together with advice for improving.

Gymnastics England
www.gymnasticsengland.org
This has a facility for finding an accredited club in your area with the GymMark. The GymMark is British Gymnastics' endorsement of a quality-run gymnastics club.

Gymnastics Northern Ireland
www.northernirelandgymnastics.org
Select Membership from top menu, then Find a Club.

Gymnastics Revolution
www.gymnasticsrevolution.com/GymInteractive-Index.htm
This has photos, diagrams and information on all the gymnastic moves, from handstands to a wolf jump. Excellent.

Scottish Gymnastics
www.scottishgymnastics.com

Welsh Gymnastics
www.welshgymnastics.org
Include Find a Club and competitions.

HOCKEY

Typical questions

* What are the rules of hockey?
* Do boys play hockey?
* Are there any hockey clubs in the area?

Considerations

Hockey has become increasing popular over the years, especially with boys, and has moved on from the image of muddy pitches mercilessly hacked at by screaming teenage girls. As a result, there are now some excellent books for skill development and techniques written for children. As with all sports, don't be afraid to use the general non-fiction as well. There are also numerous websites.

Where to look

Gifford, C. (2010) *Know Your Sport: hockey*, Franklin Watts

Hay, D. and Dempster, S. (2009) *101 Youth Hockey Drills*, A & C Black

Hockey, 4th edition, Hockey England, 2008, Know the Game series

Powell, J. (2009) *Hockey: skills, techniques, tactics*, The Crowood Press, Crowood Sports Guides

Websites

England Hockey
> www.englandhockey.co.uk
> This includes the indoor and outdoor hockey rules available to download. Also has a section for schools. Click on Take Part. Packed with information on how to be involved and what's available to young people. Excellent.

European Hockey
> www.eurohockey.org

International Hockey Federation (FIH)
> www.fih.ch/en/home
> As well as news and events from the world of hockey this also has a very useful section on the rules of the game. Select Sport from the top menu, click on Rules.

Irish Hockey
> www.hockey.ie

Includes information for young people with downloads on how to play.

Planet Field Hockey
www.planetfieldhockey.com
Not a great-looking site but good for coaching and skill techniques.

Quicksticks
www.playquicksticks.co.uk
Quicksticks is the England Hockey board's introductory game, designed specifically for primary schools and 7- to 11-year-olds.

Scottish Hockey Union
www.scottish-hockey.org.uk
Useful for youth participation and how to find a club.

Welsh Hockey Union
www.welsh-hockey.co.uk
Packed with information for young people, schools and parents, with a host of documents to download.

HORSE AND PONY RIDING

Typical questions

- Are there any stables in the local area?
- Where can I get riding lessons?
- Do you know where I can find information about pony riding competitions?

Considerations

In the main, queries are usually concerned with where to find stables and where to have riding lessons. For both, use **British Riding Schools, www.abrs-info.org**.

Where to look

Bird, J. (2008) *Better Riding: young rider's handbook*, **Interpret Publishing**

Draper, J. (2006) *My First Pony Show: from practice and plaits to gymkhanas and jumping*, **Kingfisher**

Sims, L. (2003) *Starting Riding*, **Usborne**
Introduces younger children to riding.

Usborne Riding School, **Usborne, 2011**
An equestrian guide that includes grooming, stable management, how to train for shows and competitions and choosing and caring for a pony.

Magazine

Pony Magazine
Signature Publishing
4-weekly
Tel: 0844 4991767
www.ponymag.com
Includes the Pony Directory for equestrian products, services and contacts.

Websites and organizations

Association of British Riding Schools
www.abrs-info.org
Has a search facility to locate a riding centre. Also gives exam materials for equestrian courses.

Horse of the Year Show
www.hoys.co.uk/index.php

United Kingdom Pony Club
www.pcuk.org

ICE SKATING

Typical questions
- Where can I learn to ice skate?
- Where is the nearest ice rink?

Considerations
Most of the queries will be fairly straightforward, concerned mainly with finding ice-skating venues or ice-skating lessons. Both of these can be answered using the **National Ice Skating Association of Great Britain and N.I. (NISA)**, www.iceskating.org.uk.

Where to look
Preston, D. (2004) *A World-class Ice Skater*, Heinemann, The Making of a Champion series

Schulman, C. (2001) *The Complete Book of Figure Skating*, Human Kinetics Europe Ltd

Websites
Frogs on Ice
www.frogsonice.com
A guide to ice-skating positions, demonstrated by frogs.

Golden Skate
www.goldenskate.com
This is a resource for figure skating and includes a directory of Figure Skating Clubs and Ice Rinks in the United Kingdom.

Ice Dance
www.ice-dance.com

National Ice Skating Association of Great Britain and N.I. (NISA)
www.iceskating.org.uk
As well as news, information and details of events, this has an excellent learn-to-skate rink and club finder. Click on your region of the UK on the map provided and a list and contact details are given.

MARTIAL ARTS

Typical questions

- Are there any aikido classes in the area?
- Have you any books on judo?
- What do the different colour belts mean in karate?

Considerations

In the main, queries will relate to where to join a club or how to improve skills. For queries on local classes use **Martial Arts Clubs UK, www.martialartsclubs.co.uk.** Search by town, county or style. This provides full details of clubs, including websites and age groups catered for. Well worth bookmarking. There are hundreds of books on martial arts covering judo, karate, kickboxing, taekwondo, ju jitsu and aikido. Within these there are also different styles, depending on their origin. With this in mind, queries, for example about a specific karate, may be hard to answer using only books in the children's library and it is worth looking at the general non-fiction sport books. For children interested in developing skills and techniques, some of the books listed below or similar ones may be useful.

Where to look

Bjorklund, R. (2011) *Aikido,* **Marshall Cavendish Children's Books, Marshall Arts in Action series**

Gifford, C. (2008) *Kickboxing,* **Franklin Watts**

Gifford, C. (2009) *Martial Arts,* **Tell Me About Sport series, Evans Publishing**

Martial Arts series, David West Children's Books (2003)

Titles include:

Judo, Karate, Kickboxing and *Tae Kwon Do*
These include history as well as moves and techniques.

Walker, D. (2008) *Jiu Jitsu for All: yellow belt to green belt,* **A&C Black**

Walker, D. (2008) *Jiu Jitsu for All: purple belt to dark blue belt,* **A&C Black**

Walker, D. (2008) *Jiu Jitsu for All: brown belt to black belt,* **A&C Black**

Websites

British Aikido Federation
www.bafonline.org.uk

British Judo Association
www.britishjudo.org.uk
Has a Find a Club facility.

British Karate Association
www.thebka.co.uk

British Taekwondo Control Board
www.britishtaekwondo.org.uk
This has a Find a Club facility. Search by postcode or county.

English Karate Federation
www.englishkaratefederation.com/clubs/index.php

World Kickboxing Association
www.wka.co.uk

NETBALL

Typical questions

- What are the rules of netball?
- Are there any local netball clubs?

Considerations

In the main, queries will be concerned with improving techniques, the rules of the games and where to play or take lessons. To find out the rules of netball look no further than **Netball Rules, www.internationalnetball.com/netball_rules.htm**.

Where to look

Gifford, C. (2010) *Netball*, **Wayland, Sporting Skills series**
  Gives detailed instructions on techniques and skills.

Websites

England Netball
  www.englandnetball.co.uk
  To find clubs select In My Region, then the relevant county. This provides regional contacts and includes the regional websites.

International Netball
  www.internationalnetball.com/index.html

International Netball Federation
  www.netball.org
  Includes world rankings.

Netball Northern Ireland
  www.netballni.org
  Select Clubs from the menu.

Netball Resource
  www.ucl.ac.uk/~uczcw11/baseres.htm
  Now slightly dated, it still provides some useful links to lots of netball websites.

Netball Rules
  www.internationalnetball.com/netball_rules.html

Netball Scotland
  www.netballscotland.com

This has an excellent guide to netball called 'What is Netball?' It includes diagrams of netball players' positions.

Netball Skills
www.bbc.co.uk/schools/gcsebitesize/pe/video/netball
Videos of netball skills, including shooting, blocking, catching, landing and pivoting.

Welsh Netball
www.welshnetball.co.uk

RUGBY

Typical questions

- What are the rules of rugby union?
- Are there any junior rugby clubs?
- What is a conversion?

Considerations

Queries looking for rugby clubs or where to play can be directed to **Rugby Clubs and Rugby Associations in the UK, www.rugbyclubs.info/rugbylinks.shtml**. This lists rugby union clubs, rugby league clubs and school rugby clubs in the UK. This is probably all you need. As with all sports, don't restrict yourself to using only the books in the children's library – try also the books in the general non-fiction collection.

Where to look

Gifford, C. (2009) *Tell Me about Sport: rugby,* **Evans Publishing**
Learn about the game of rugby and develop rugby skills. Clear text with complementary photographs.

IRB World Rugby Yearbook, **Vision Sports Publishing, Annual**
Includes results, statistics and records.

Morgan, P. (2008) *Rugby: a new fan's guide to the game, the teams and the players,* **A&C Black**
An introduction to rugby union, including the rules, the players and facts.

Websites

All Blacks
http://allblacks.com

International Rugby Board
www.irb.com
Useful to find out world rankings.

Irish Rugby
www.irishrugby.ie

Official Six Nations Rugby
www.rbs6nations.com/en/home.php

Planet Rugby
www.planetrugby.com

Rugby Football League
www.therfl.co.uk

Rugby Football Union
www.rfu.com

Scottish Rugby
www.scottishrugby.org

Scrum
www.espnscrum.com
The home of Rugby League.

Small Blacks
www.smallblacks.com
For those aspiring All Blacks (New Zealand) players, this site offers an interactive fun site with games and tips to improve skills.

Welsh Rugby Union
www.wru.co.uk

SKATEBOARDING AND SCOOTERING

Typical questions

- Where is the nearest skate park?
- What is street skating?
- What is an ollie?

Considerations

Skateboarding is hugely popular, with teems of young people skateboarding in local skate parks. The main question you'll encounter is about the location of the nearest skate park, in which case use the local council's website, where local parks should be listed, including details of facilities such as skate parks.

Where to look

Badillo, S. (2007) *Skateboarding Legendary Tricks*, Tracks Publications

D'arcy, S. and Marshal, P. (2010) *Freestyle Skateboarding Tricks*, A&C Black
An excellent little book giving step-by-step instructions on doing tricks for flat ground, rails, slides and grinds and transitions.

Gifford, C. (2010) *Skateboarding*, Tell Me About Sport series, Evans Publishing

Morgan, J. (2010) *Skateboarding*, Franklin Watts, No Limits series
An introduction to one of the popular extreme sports. There are other titles in the series.

Thomas, K. (2003) *Blades, Boards and Scooters*, Maple Tree Press, Popular Mechanics for Kids series
Although slightly dated for such a 'happening' sport, it does have excellent instructions on basic skills, as well as mentioning maintenance of equipment and safety rules for skate parks.

Websites

how2skate
www.how2skate.com
A great skateboarding resource with skateboard tricks, maintenance and techniques.

Transworld Skateboarding
www.skateboarding.com
Lots of information on skateboarding techniques.

United Kingdom Skateboarding Association
www.ukskate.org.uk

This includes an events calendar and details of two UK programmes that aim to embrace skateboarding and harness the enthusiasm of young people to take part in an action sport – Action Sports in Schools and Radworx.

SWIMMING

Typical questions

- Where is the nearest swimming pool?
- Are there any swimming lessons for pre-schoolers?

Considerations

Swimming is not only a sport, it is an essential skill. Many queries will be in connection with where to have swimming lessons. Most swimming pools offer lessons and the details of local swimming pools, such as contacts and opening times, can be found on local authority websites. The details of swimming lessons need to be discussed with individual leisure centres. You can also use **British Swimming**, **www.swimming.org** to Find My Pool, which includes swimming pools at universities and private health clubs as well as local authority leisure centres.

Where to look

Gifford, C. (2008) *Swimming*, Tell Me About Sport series, Evans Publishing

Mason, P. (2005) *How To Improve at Swimming*, Tick Tock Books
    A very well organized step-by-step guide to improving strokes, turns and starts, as well as race tactics.

McLeod, I. (2010) *Swimming Anatomy: your illustrated guide to swimming strength, speed and endurance*, Human Kinetics

Websites

BBC Swimming
    http://news.bbc.co.uk/sport1/hi/other_sports/swimming/default.stm
    This has audio and video clips of swimming highlights.

British Swimming
    www.swimming.org
    An excellent site for information and tips on learning to swim, with a section dedicated to parents. It also has a Find My Pool search facility.

British Swimming
    www.swimming.org/britishswimming
    Find out information about top performance swimming. It includes swimming, diving, synchronized swimming, water polo and disability swimming.

English Schools' Swimming Association
www.essa-schoolswimming.com
Gives a full programme of schools swimming events, both nationally and internationally.

Federation International de Natation Amateur
www.fina.org
The international governing body for swimming. For swimming records, look under Statistics.

Scottish Swimming
www.scottishswimming.com

Swimming
www.olympic.org
Within the official site of the Olympic movement select Sports from the top menu, then Aquatics and then Swimming or Synchronized swimming. For each there is a huge amount of information, including equipment, history and techniques. The detail given about the sport is excellent and will help anyone to enjoy watching the swimming at the Olympics.

Swimming.org
www.swimming.org

SwimWales
www.welshasa.co.uk

Triathlon

British Triathlon
www.britishtriathlon.org

Triathlon England
www.triathlonengland.org
Click on Children, Young People and Schools. There are lots of developments planned to encourage young people to compete and train for triathlon.

TENNIS

Typical questions
- What are the rules of tennis?
- Are there any local tennis clubs?
- How do I book the local tennis court?

Considerations
There can be a surge of interest in tennis during Wimbledon fortnight, and it is useful to be prepared with details of local tennis courts and clubs. Tennis courts provided by the local council should be listed on the council's web pages and you can also use the **Lawn Tennis Association, www.lta.org.uk** to find courts available through clubs. For books on improving skills, have a look at what you have in the children's library as well as using the general non-fiction.

Where to look
Gifford, C. (2008) *Tennis*, Tell Me About Sport series, Evans Publishing

Parsons, J. (2007) *The Ultimate Encyclopaedia of Tennis*, Carlton Books

Pearson, A. (2006) *SAQ Tennis: training and conditioning for tennis*, A&C Black
A step-by-step guide to skills; also includes a tennis programme.

Porter, D. (2003) *Winning Tennis for Girls*, Facts on File
An excellent all-round tennis book not only looking at skills but also at physical fitness for the game.

Websites
All England Lawn Tennis Club
www.wimbledon.org

Lawn Tennis Association
www.lta.org.uk
Useful for parents, teachers and children alike to find out about where to play, competitions, choosing equipment and finding a coach.

Lawn Tennis Association: Scotland
www.lta.org.uk/in-your-area/Scotland

Tennis Wales
www.tennis.wales.org

Index

Know it All, Find it Fast

An A-Z source guide for the enquiry desk

Third edition

Bob Duckett, Peter Walker and Christinea Donnelly

'Know It All, Find It Fast remains a book to be kept to hand, not on the reference shelf...The word "essential" is often over-used by reviewers, but it covers this book, just as it is essential that the compilers continue to keep it up to date with regular new editions.' REFERENCE REVIEWS

'...there is much to treasure in this new edition of KIAFIF and it is an essential source for anyone dealing with enquiries. Buy it if you have not already done so.' REFER

'This book should still be kept at hand by everyone providing an enquiry service.' LIBRARY & INFORMATION UPDATE

This award-winning sourcebook is an essential guide to where to look to find the answers quickly. It is designed as a first point of reference for LIS practitioners, to be depended upon if they are unfamiliar with the subject of an enquiry – or wish to find out more. It is arranged in an easily searchable, fully cross-referenced A-Z list of around 150 of the subject areas most frequently handled at enquiry desks.

Each subject entry lists the most important information sources and where to locate them, including printed and electronic sources, relevant websites and useful contacts for referral purposes. The authors use their extensive experience in reference work to offer useful tips, warn of potential pitfalls, and spotlight typical queries and how to tackle them. This new edition has been brought right up-to-date with all sources checked for currency and many new ones added, especially subscription websites. The searchability is enhanced by a comprehensive index to make those essential sources even easier to find – saving you valuable minutes!

2008; 496pp; paperback; 978-1-85604-652-7; £44.95

Know It All, Find it Fast for Academic Libraries

Heather Dawson

This is a comprehensive and easy-to-use version of the best-selling *Know it All Find It Fast* developed specifically for information professionals working in academic libraries. This will help you to tackle the questions most commonly asked by students, academics and researchers. A broad crossdisciplinary A-Z of themes including topics such as literature searching, plagiarism and using online resources are covered helping you to address any query confidently and quickly. Each topic is split into four sections to guide your responses:

• Typical questions: listing the common enquiries you'll encounter
• Considerations: exploring the issues and challenges that might arise
• Where to look: listing annotated resources in print and online
• Tips and pitfalls: outlining useful suggestions and common problems.

This will prove an indispensable day-to-day guide for anyone working with students, academics and researchers in an academic library

2011; 192pp; paperback; 978-1-85604-759-3; £44.95

There are three easy ways to order Facet Publishing titles

• Online www.facetpublishing.co.uk
• Phone +44 (0)1235 827702
• E-mail facet@bookpoint.co.uk

Get the latest information about Facet books and details of special offers delivered to your desktop each and every month by subscribing to our monthly **eBulletin**. Visit www.facetpublishing.co.uk to sign up. You can also keep up-to-date by following us on Twitter @facetpublishing.